# THE WAYS AND WONDERS OF

## SOUTH AFRICAN

# TREES

## WILLEM FROST

*Dedicated to the glory of God, Creator of all life.*

Published by Struik Nature
(an imprint of Penguin Random House South Africa (Pty) Ltd.)
Reg. No. 1953/000441/07
The Estuaries No. 4, Oxbow Crescent, Century Avenue, Century City, 7441
PO Box 1144, Cape Town, 8000 South Africa

Visit www.struiknature.co.za and join the Struik Nature Club for updates, news, events and special offers.

First published in 2024
1 3 5 7 9 10 8 6 4 2

Publisher: Pippa Parker
Managing editor: Roelien Theron
Editor: Heléne Booyens
Designer: Emily Vosloo, Sheryl Buckley
Picture researcher: Colette Stott
Proofreader: Tina Mössmer
Indexer: Emsie du Plessis

Reproduction by Studio Repro
Printed and bound in China by Golden Prosperity Printing & Packaging (Heyuan) Co., Ltd.

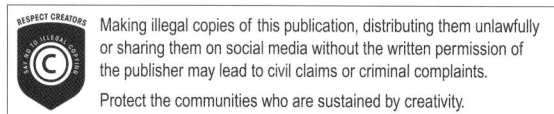

MIX
Paper | Supporting
responsible forestry
FSC
www.fsc.org
FSC® C178225

ISBN 978 1 77584 887 5 (Print)
ISBN 978 1 77584 888 2 (ePub)

Common names of trees used in this book are those recommended by
the Flora of the Southern Africa (FSA) Tree Species List.

# CONTENTS

*Trees are sanctuaries. Whoever knows how to speak to them, whoever knows how to listen to them, can learn the truth … That is home.*
Hermann Hesse

# FOREWORD

There is an extraordinary bond between trees and people. Willem Frost is living proof of this very special, almost mutualistic relationship with trees. He understands the language of trees and, in return, they give context to his existence. In his world, trees foster a sense of belonging and empower him with hope and joy.

Plants, including trees, are part of the cycle of life. Simply stated, they provide humans with oxygen and, in return, absorb the carbon dioxide that we produce. All of this is part of the ebb and flow of the life-giving energies that protect our planet.

Willem explores not only the taxonomy and visible aspects of trees, but also takes the reader on a voyage of discovery into the hidden world of underground trees, and investigates and celebrates the mythological, spiritual, medicinal, magical and cultural aspects of our indigenous tree heritage. He draws attention to South Africa's rich biodiversity, encouraging us all to appreciate our indigenous trees, to further our knowledge of the natural world, and to protect this diverse botanical heritage. Finally, he challenges *Homo studiosus* – 'the intelligent man' – to spend time studying the ways and wonders of South African trees.

New writings always capture our imagination and curiosity, and give impetus to our quest to expand our knowledge and experience. In this book, Willem succeeds in redrafting existing stories into something new and meaningful through his intimate knowledge of trees. He highlights the endurance, longevity and life-giving forces of trees. This brings to mind the chasm between nature and humankind's relentless pursuit to exploit land, often destroying the natural environment in the process. He recognises that the degradation of nature causes an imbalance. But instead of despairing, the reader is encouraged to engage with the wonder of trees and so appreciate what nature has to offer.

The book comes to life through the beautiful colour photographs that complement the text, grabbing our attention and stimulating our minds as we contemplate the majesty of the arboreal world. But it is our 'likeness' to trees that could be the most provocative idea of all. Not only do we stand upright, like trees, but we are reminded that we are as rooted and interconnected in communities as are trees in forests, in groves, in thickets or in small stands. And we are as dependent on trees as they are on our preservation of them.

I trust this book will encourage everybody to actively spend more time in the company of trees.

**NAAS GROVÉ**
PRESIDENT: Dendrological Society of South Africa

# PREFACE

Although I never studied biology or botany formally, except for the first three years in high school, I have been fascinated by the trees around us from a very young age. I can clearly recall how I marvelled at the big wild figs, marulas and milkwoods along the Magaliesberg, or the thorn trees of the western bushveld. So, I suppose it is no surprise that I attempted to put some information and thoughts together on the trees that I encountered.

> *And God said, 'Let the earth bring forth grass, the herb yielding seed, and the fruit tree yielding fruit after its kind, whose seed is in itself, upon the earth, and it was so. And the earth brought forth grass, and the herb yielding seed after his kind, and the tree yielding fruit, whose seed was in itself, after his kind: and God saw that it was good.'*   Genesis 1: 11–12

To be among trees is to come closer to the presence of God because trees seem to be able to remove obstacles between God and humanity. When one is in the veld among the tall trees at dawn and one hears the soft, sweet voice of the leaves whispering in the wind, one is humbled. At such times it is easy to believe that their lives are as sacred as the lives of humans. After all, they also know about good times and bad times, about joy and horror, and they also praise the Creator with arms outstretched to the heavens. If one has learned to listen to the trees, one will hear them telling us that life is not about hardship or prosperity or wealth or fear, but about discovering and living the purpose of one's life. And life is not about taking from this world, but rather about giving to this world. This reminds me of the words of a 19th-century Irish-American, Nelson Henderson, who once said: 'The true meaning of life is to plant trees, under whose shade you do not expect to sit.'

**WILLEM FROST**
Goedgedacht, Limpopo

Marula

Red-stinkwood

# ABOUT THIS BOOK

South Africa is home to a remarkable diversity of trees: from towering, lichen-covered forest species to stocky, hardy desert trees.

The purpose of this book is to draw attention to the rich diversity and beauty of the trees that surround us in this country; to help stimulate an interest in the study of trees; to encourage an appreciation for our indigenous trees; to provide a brief introduction to the remarkable physiology and behaviour of trees; and to promote the conservation of our floral heritage. This book is therefore not a field guide or scientific reference work. Nor is it meant to help the reader identify trees, although some of the photographs and descriptions may be useful in this regard.

PART ONE of the book deals largely with the behaviour and physiology of trees. In undertaking research for this book, I soon became aware of how little studied this topic was. Not surprisingly, a great deal more study of trees has been undertaken in the northern hemisphere. But such research can be very useful, nonetheless, because the findings can be extrapolated to our own species. The underlying assumption is that the various processes function in a similar way irrespective of species, which is usually (but not always) the case. So, the purpose of Part One is to lift the lid just a little on the fascinating ways in which trees work and thereby stimulate some interest in the reader.

PART TWO showcases a small selection of our indigenous species, and aims to illustrate the diversity, characteristics and beauty of South African trees. There are many other remarkable trees to be found in the country – the ones that made it into this book are simply those that made an impression on the author, variously for their beauty, or the extent to which they characterise the essence of Africa, or for their successful and remarkable adaptation to a specific habitat, or for some distinctive attribute such as the quality of the wood. Species accounts are organised by family and include the most popular common names used in various local languages, the abbreviations of which are explained on page 316.

# PART ONE
# THE WORLD OF TREES

*Baobab*

# WHAT IS A TREE?

There is no universally accepted scientific or precise definition of what a tree is. In South Africa, the National Forests Act No. 84 of 1998 defines a tree as 'a self-supporting woody plant with a stem diameter of larger than 10mm at breast height, which is higher than 3m if single-stemmed and higher than 5m if multi-stemmed'. The height refers to the typical height that a species commonly reaches. Most local tree identification books, however, tend to include non-woody species with tree-like shapes (morphology), such as baobabs. Some scholars include in their definition a reference to a defined crown and lateral branches at some distance off the ground.

Trees have vascular tissues called 'xylem' and 'phloem', which link all parts of the plant and transport water, minerals and nutrients from one part of the tree to another. Trees may be cone-bearing plants (gymnosperms), flowering plants (angiosperms) or ferns. All trees are perennial plants, meaning that they persist for several years. Trees tend to live longer than most other plant forms, some enduring for hundreds of years.

We did not even know how many tree species existed on Earth until a group of botanists published a comprehensive list of the world's tree species in the *Journal of Sustainable Forestry* in April 2017. They concluded that there are currently 60,065 species of tree known to science. The study also found that almost 58 percent of all tree species are single-country endemics. Brazil, Colombia and Indonesia have the largest number of endemic tree species.

Plants are not as diverse as animals (nothing beats beetles for diversity), but they nevertheless dominate life on Earth. Even though it is estimated that there are now almost 50 percent fewer trees than there were 12,000 years ago when agriculture emerged as a human survival strategy, plants still make up something like 99 percent of the Earth's biomass. The thought that all the planet's animals – including termites, pachyderms, whales and humans – make up only one percent is difficult to comprehend.

# THE IMPORTANCE OF TREES

Trees play a special role in nature: they not only provide the oxygen that all animals need to live, but also absorb the greenhouse gasses that human activities emit; and they provide fruit, shade, nesting sites for birds, fodder for animals, nectar for birds and insects, firewood, and wood for the production of furniture and other household goods, as well as for commercial items. Traditionally, trees have had many medicinal uses and are still being used in this respect.

Some ecologists regard the trees of the forests as pumps that generate rain and significantly impact the global water cycle. Through the process of transpiration, water taken up from the ground is released through the surface of a tree's leaves, thereby cooling the surrounding air. It is one of the major processes whereby water vapour is returned to the atmosphere to replenish the world's freshwater resources. Trees also block sunlight, helping to keep the ground cool. Trees drive many of the biophysical forces that make our planet habitable for humans and animals.

The conservation of plant life also has significant spin-offs for the well-being of humans and animals. The connection between humans and trees goes much deeper than survival. Trees are an inspiration to the philosophers, poets and artists among us. Trees seem to calm the mind, stimulate creative thinking, or even hasten the recovery of the sick. Research has shown that a walk in a forest can reduce stress, strengthen the immune system, lower blood pressure and reduce blood sugar levels.

## TREES UNDER THREAT

According to *National Geographic*, some 30 percent of the planet's land mass is covered by forest. However, humanity has invaded each and every habitat type on Earth and is responsible for deforestation and large-scale destruction of natural habitat, pollution and, some would argue, even climate change.

The International Union for Conservation of Nature (IUCN) and the Food and Agriculture Organization of the United Nations estimate that about half the world's tropical forests have been cleared for other land uses. Earth is still losing more than 7 million hectares of forest each year, with an estimated 15–17 percent of all greenhouse gas emissions resulting from deforestation. It is said that the destruction of the world's rainforests causes the release of more carbon dioxide in the atmosphere every year than all of the world's transportation combined. This is because the carbon locked up in their tissues is released into the atmosphere when trees die or are cut down, thereby contributing further to global warming. In addition, the affected forest's ability to absorb existing carbon dioxide is reduced.

### PROPOSED SOLUTIONS

While deforestation must be a major contributor to the greenhouse effect, the restoration of the world's forests and woodlands is probably our most effective weapon for combating climate change. International conventions dealing with climate change and biodiversity conservation have programmes and incentives that promote the reduction of deforestation linked to climate change.

LEFT *Woodland kingfishers breed in tree holes.*

RIGHT *Leopards use trees for resting and for storing their prey out of reach of other carnivores.*

One of these is carbon trading, whereby a polluting industry in Europe, for example, can offset its carbon emissions by investing in afforestation, such as spekboom planting in the Eastern Cape.

The United Nations initiated a programme known as Reducing Emissions from Deforestation and Forest Degradation (REDD+), which is a mechanism developed by countries, including South Africa, that ratified the Framework Convention on Climate Change. According to the United Nations, this 'creates a financial value for the carbon stored in forests by offering incentives for developing countries to reduce emissions from forested lands and invest in low-carbon paths to sustainable development'.

Southern Africa has very little indigenous forest habitat (in South Africa it is less than 0.5 percent of the total land surface) and deforestation would appear to be much less of an issue than in the Amazon basin, the Congo basin and Southeast Asia (especially Indonesia, Malaysia and Thailand). Our forests have in the past been reasonably well protected, but have, over the last few decades, come under increasing pressure.

According to research published in 2018, deforestation and degradation of our savannah woodlands (which cover about 80 times the surface area of our forests) is happening faster than previously thought – the loss of carbon into the atmosphere is three to six times more than previous estimates. The major driver behind this is land-use change. In southern Africa, there has been an alarming increase in the unsustainable harvesting of trees for the charcoal industry, and now also for timber that is exported.

Trees hold a major part of the answer to our quest to slow down – and even reverse – the rate of climate change, preserve wildlife and nature, and support the now more than 8 billion people on Earth by neutralising carbon dioxide emissions.

Two separate studies estimated that there are about 3 trillion trees currently on the planet. According to Dr Thomas Crowther at Crowther Lab, if another 1.2 trillion trees were planted on Earth, this would cancel out the last 10 years of carbon dioxide emissions. He has made a strong case for trees being our most powerful weapon in the fight against climate change, adding that if we could really plant that many trees, it would have a bigger impact on the environment than initiatives like switching to clean energy. The big question is whether it is possible to plant 1.2 trillion trees (which is highly unlikely); such reforestation would take decades. Fortunately, there are already several reforestation projects by governments and non-governmental organisations under way across the globe. More importantly, new technology, such as tree-planting drones distributing biodegradable seedpods, could turn such an ambitious dream into reality. These drones are already successfully operating in several countries, including Australia, Canada and Myanmar.

The World Economic Forum has launched a plan to promote the planting of one trillion trees globally. This plan, however, has met with severe criticism. Joseph Veldman, the lead author of a report by a team of scientists, argues that planting trees where they do not belong can actually harm ecosystems.

In South Africa, some scientists argue that the scope for tree planting should be limited to the rehabilitation of degraded woody habitats such as savannah and thicket, and that large-scale tree planting in other biomes such as grassland and fynbos must be avoided.

The focus in this country is more on urban greening, where trees play an important part in people's living conditions. In densely populated rural areas, the focus is on woodlots and fruit trees, involving exotic tree species. The annual Arbor month activities during September include the prestigious Arbor City awards for which municipalities compete through their urban greening schemes.

## What is dendrology?

The word dendrology is derived from the Ancient Greek words *dendron* ('tree') and *logos* ('study'). Dendrology thus refers to the study, characterisation, identification and classification of woody plants (trees, shrubs and lianas) and, specifically, their taxonomic classifications. Dendrology covers all woody plants, native and non-native, that occur in an area. It is a subcategory of botany, which is the study of all plants.

TOP RIGHT  The tropical Amazon rainforest is under pressure from deforestation.

BOTTOM RIGHT  For many animals, such as giraffes, the leaves and other parts of trees are essential for their survival.

The largest known living tree in the world, located in the Giant Forest of Sequoia National Park in California, USA, is a giant sequoia known as General Sherman.

# THE OLDEST, TALLEST AND LARGEST

Trees have been around on Earth for much, much longer than has *Homo sapiens*, the first trees having appeared almost 400 million years ago (mya). Earth is 4.5 billion years old, but plants, most likely mosses and liverworts without true roots, may only have emerged on land as recently as 470 mya. Vascular plants with tissues that conduct water and nutrients followed about 50 million years later, and for millions of years after that there were no plants taller than about one metre.

The earliest trees were found all over the planet and were especially abundant in wet areas. Temperatures were much warmer then and those early trees occupied a niche somewhat similar to today's mangrove habitat.

These early plant forms were followed by the first land-based animal life, some 425 mya. Plant and animal life were thus set up to co-exist in the terrestrial world that they had colonised.

From about 420 to 370 mya a mysterious genus, known as *Prototaxites*, flourished. It had a trunk up to one metre wide and about eight metres in height. Scientists have long debated whether these were ancient trees, but recently concluded that they were fungi, not plants.

The first known tree is from the genus *Mattieza,* identified from 385 million-year-old fossils found in what is now New York, where it formed the first known forests. The plants in this genus may have lacked leaves, instead growing frond-like branches with branchlets. Although not closely related to tree ferns, these plants shared their method of reproducing by spores, not seeds.

The first woody trees appeared about 375 mya. These were progymnosperms such as *Archaeopteris,* which is an important fossil marker in that it combines spore-releasing reproductive organs, similar to those of ferns, with an anatomy, particularly in its wood structure, that resembles that of present-day conifers. These trees were the first to form forests on a truly global scale. In South Africa, fossils of *Archaeopteris notosaria* were discovered in a road cutting on the Makhanda bypass.

Tree-like seed ferns, for example *Glossopteris* species, became the dominant trees of Gondwana about 270 mya and are the source of most of South Africa's coal. Fossilised tree trunks of *Dadoxylon* species, which thrived from 300 to 200 mya, can be seen around the Dutch Reformed church in the Free State town of Senekal.

*A fossilised* Dadoxylon *tree trunk, dating from 300 to 200 mya, was discovered in Senekal in the Free State.*

*This aerial photograph shows the oldest known forest on the planet, located outside Cairo, New York, USA.*

## ANCIENT WONDERS

Trees are the largest and tallest living organisms on our planet and are probably one of humans' oldest natural resources. In Europe, the oldest non-clonal tree – meaning that it is the original tree, and not a genetic duplicate of a parent tree – is a Heldreich's pine (*Pinus heldreichii*), also known as the Bosnian pine. This tree, which grows in Italy's Pollino National Park, has been dated scientifically to be 'only' 1,230 years old. There could, however, be older trees in Europe that have not yet been dated.

For a while, the oldest known non-clonal tree was a bristlecone pine (*Pinus longaeva*) in the White Mountains in eastern California, USA. Nicknamed Methuselah, it is estimated to be 4,852 years old. However, an even older specimen, proved to be 5,065 years old, was found in the same region in 2012, making it the oldest non-clonal tree in the world.

In Africa, we have a few baobabs estimated to be about 5,000 years old, although this seems unlikely. Unfortunately, the faint growth rings produced by the African baobab and the presence of large internal hollow parts pose problems for accurate dating. The oldest known tree in South Africa is a partially collapsed baobab on a farm near Hoedspruit, which was carbon-dated to be about 1,840 years old.

## WHAT DETERMINES AGE?

Trees growing in forests, where they can prosper in a healthy 'society', typically live much longer than isolated ones. The fact that a large part of southern Africa is typically savannah, with many species growing relatively isolated from one another, may at least partially explain the shorter lives of our trees. Trees age in different ways, and it is important to note that just because a tree is very large does not mean it is very old, and just because it is very old does not necessarily mean it is very large.

Those species with wood that is exceptionally hard and heavy (for example, leadwood, camel thorn, zebrawood and red bushwillow) must inevitably have a much longer lifespan than species with soft and light wood, such as sweet thorn. There is, however, always an exception to any rule: the baobab has soft fibrous tissue for wood, yet it survives to a very ripe old age.

Growing in a twisted, gnarled fashion, bristlecone pines
are the oldest living non-clonal trees in the world.
This extremely rare species is found in isolated
groves only in California, Nevada and Utah, USA.

Sadly, large old trees are on the decline globally, mainly owing to overharvesting and habitat loss. By keeping a record of trees of exceptional size and age we can be reminded on an ongoing basis of the maximum potential that a species can achieve. The wonder of walking among grand old trees should never be forfeited for short-term economic gain.

## LOCAL RECORD-BREAKERS

In terms of height (as opposed to trunk and crown width), the indigenous trees of southern Africa compare poorly with America's giant redwoods. If a tree on the savannah reaches 30m in height, it is generally regarded as being very tall.

The tallest specimen in a stand of exotic saligna gums (*Eucalyptus saligna*), planted in 1906 in Magoebaskloof in Limpopo, is 83.7m. This tree now holds two records: tallest tree ever measured in Africa, and tallest planted tree in the world. The gum trees in Magoebaskloof have been declared 'champion' trees in South Africa – a project of the Department of Environment, Forestry and Fisheries to list and protect trees of national conservation importance based on criteria such as outstanding size, historical significance and age.

The Dendrological Society of South Africa keeps a national register of South Africa's largest indigenous trees according to a customised index. The height, mean crown spread, circular crown cover, girth and trunk diameter at breast height are registered in a mathematical formula to arrive at an index value. The largest tree thus measured is a sycamore fig near the confluence of the Shashe and Limpopo rivers in Botswana.

The tallest indigenous tree in the register is a 600-year-old Outeniqua yellowwood (*Afrocarpus falcatus*). Currently 41m tall, it grows on a slope of the Blouberg in Limpopo. A red-stinkwood (*Prunus africana*) at Straalhoek in the Eastern Cape is close on the yellowwood's heels, at 40m.

Another Outeniqua yellowwood, near Amersfoort in Mpumalanga, is potentially South Africa's tallest indigenous tree. The tree was measured in 2015 by Hartwig von Dürckheim and Herman Pieters and found to be 44.2m high, with a trunk circumference of 7.5m at a height of 1.4m. Unfortunately, the tree grows on a rather steep mountain slope among dense brush, which makes it difficult to measure the height accurately with a clinometer. The height of this tree will have to be measured again, preferably by climbing it.

The well-known giant baobab (*Adansonia digitata*) at Sagole in Limpopo, is the second-thickest tree in the world, with a trunk diameter of 10.97m, a trunk circumference of 32.89m, a crown diameter of 38.20m and a height of 20.5m. Its age has been determined by carbon dating to be about 1,300 years. The world record for trunk thickness is currently held by a Montezuma cypress (*Taxodium mucronatum*) near the city of Oaxaca in southern Mexico: 11.6m at breast height.

In 2016, a German scientist, Adrian Hemp, claimed that he had found the tallest indigenous tree in Africa, a Tiama mahogany (*Entandrophragma excelsum*) growing in a remote valley on Kilimanjaro in Tanzania. Reaching a height of 81.5m, it is estimated to be about 600 years old. The measurement of a tall tree in thick and inaccessible forest, with only laser instruments and not the more exact measurement by tree climbers, however, casts some doubt on the claim.

## GLOBAL RECORD-BREAKERS

The largest known living tree in the world, by volume, is a giant sequoia (*Sequoiadendron giganteum*), located in the Giant Forest of Sequoia National Park in California, USA. Known as General Sherman after the American Civil War general, it has a height of 83.3m and a trunk diameter at breast height of 7.7m.

The tallest tree in the world is a coast redwood (*Sequoia sempervirens*), named Hyperion, in the Redwood National Park in California, USA. This tree measures 115.6m in height. Two other trees of almost the same height are a mountain ash (*Eucalyptus regnans*) in Tasmania, Australia, and a coast Douglas fir (*Pseudotsuga menziesii* var. *menziesii*) in Coos County, Oregon, USA, both just a few centimetres short of 100m.

The tallest tropical tree in the world, at over 100.8m, is a yellow meranti (*Shorea faguetiana*), discovered in a forest in Sabah, a Malaysian state on the island of Borneo in 2018. It was spotted from the air by a survey airplane, and then painstakingly measured by professional tree climbers.

**TOP RIGHT** *Europe's oldest non-clonal tree is a Bosnian pine, found in the Pollino National Park in Italy.*

**RIGHT** *South Africa's tallest indigenous tree is this 600-year-old Outeniqua yellowwood in Limpopo, which measures 41m.*

Savannah

Forest

Nama Karoo

# BIOMES

South Africa is considered to be one of the most biologically diverse countries in the world. The country's land surface is less than one percent of the world's total land surface, yet the country is home to about 10 percent of the world's plant, bird and fish species and over six percent of the world's mammal and reptile species.

The biosphere (that is, the life-supporting part of the Earth's surface) is made up of a number of biomes. Biomes are specific geographic areas notable for the species living there and the general structure of the landscape and vegetation. Scientifically speaking, a biome can be described as the largest geographic biotic unit (aquatic or terrestrial) that is home to a major community of animals and plants living under similar environmental conditions. It can span extensive and separate geographical regions, such as different continents, provided environmental conditions are the same. Climate is determined by average annual rainfall (precipitation) and temperature.

An ecosystem refers to the communities and interaction of biotic phenomena (mammals, reptiles, birds, fish, insects, micro-organisms, and so forth) and abiotic phenomena (such as minerals, soil, water, sunlight and climate)

Fynbos

Albany thicket

Succulent Karoo

in a specific environment. A biome comprises several ecosystems, which can range in size from very small (such as a tidal pool) to very large (such as a game reserve).

Biomes are not static zones, but evolve and adapt to long- and medium-term changes and fluctuations in the climate. For example, thousands of years ago, the Sahara Desert was a lush landscape traversed by rivers and lakes and featuring abundant trees and wildlife. As climate changed over time, the area dried out to become desert. The Karoo is a similar example. Biomes have, in fact, changed and moved many times during Earth's history.

Consequently, the plant and animal life within their ambit has undergone similar adaptations in order to adjust to the environment.

In recent times, human activities have accelerated this trend and altered the ecological balance in most of the Earth's biomes. Conservation is crucial to mitigating the effects of climate change and in protecting and preserving endangered plants and animals.

In South Africa, nine distinct biomes are recognised. Of these, three are dominated by trees: savannah, forest and Albany thicket.

## SAVANNAH

In South Africa, the savannah biome is also known as bushveld. It occurs in the more tropical regions of the country where temperatures are high, rainfall occurs in the summer months, and winters are dry. Savannah consists of low to medium trees – many of which provide good browse – scattered across grassland, which dominates the undergrowth. The tree density varies significantly, from near-forest to almost open grassland. Owing to regular fires during the dry winter season, the trees have evolved well-developed root systems that allow them to resprout quickly after having been burnt. Throughout undisturbed savannah, there is a delicate balance between the tree and grass components of the vegetation.

## NAMA KAROO

The Nama Karoo is an extremely arid biome with winter rainfall ranging from 50 to 300mm. It is characterised by dwarf shrubs and grasses; trees are not a feature of the vegetation.

## SUCCULENT KAROO

The succulent Karoo biome is recognised for its high degree of plant endemism. Succulent plants dominate and are able to survive dry seasons by using water stored in their leaves and stems. Trees are usually scattered, but may occur in dense stands along watercourses. In some areas, such as the mountains around Willowmore, the veld may resemble savannah.

## DESERT

The desert biome extends along the western coastal plain from just south of the Orange River northwards to Angola, and is characterised by plants that endure long periods without water and extreme temperature fluctuations. Most true desert in South Africa is found in the Springbokvlakte, in the lower Orange River valley. Desert vegetation includes annual grasses and succulents such as *Euphorbia* species. Plants not directly dependent on rainfall, such as camel thorn trees which grow along drainage lines or dry riverbeds, are not considered to be true desert plants.

Desert

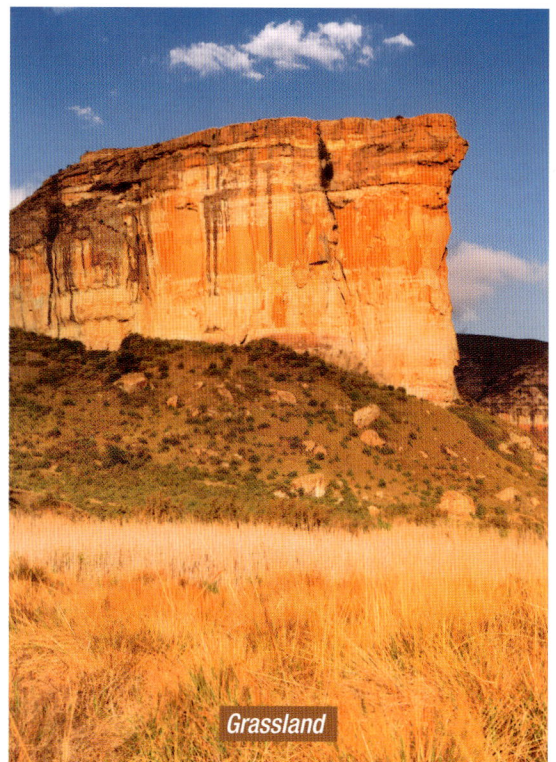

Grassland

## ALBANY THICKET

The vegetation of the Albany thicket biome consists mainly of short trees, low intertwining shrubs and vines, interspersed with large open spaces. The thickets are characterised by an abundance of succulent and spiny vegetation and can be impenetrable.

## FYNBOS

The fynbos biome mainly occupies the winter-rainfall region of the Western Cape and is characterised by extraordinary biodiversity, a high degree of endemism, and plants that do not lose their leaves. Medium to large-sized trees are relatively sparse, but very small trees or shrubs (including a variety of proteas and pincushion species) may be abundant.

## FOREST

The forest biome is dominated by trees, some of which are large, forming a more or less closed canopy. Forests occur in the high-rainfall areas and are characterised by vertical layering of vegetation. The forest floor has a relatively sparse layer of plants and decaying matter. Above that is an understorey of shrubby foliage. A layer of trees rises above that. These layers, comprising a relatively wide variety of tree and shrub species, provide complex habitats for the organisms living there. Most of the plants are evergreen and little light reaches the forest floor.

## GRASSLAND

In the grassland biome, the vegetation is dominated by grass, sometimes interspersed with patches of forest or clumps of bush (savannah-like tree pockets), especially on hills and along rivers. Grasslands occupy a large part of the higher-lying eastern regions of the country, particularly areas that are relatively cool, with summer rainfall in excess of 600mm.

## INDIAN OCEAN COASTAL BELT

The Indian Ocean coastal belt occupies a narrow strip along the coast, from the mouth of the Great Kei River to the Mozambique border. It is a high-level vegetation biome comprising mostly coastal dunes, with pockets of natural forest, savannah or thicket, interrupted by coastal grassland.

Indian Ocean coastal belt

# TAXONOMY

Taxonomy, as developed by the Swedish scientist Carl Linnaeus (1707–1778), is the science of naming and classifying organisms.

The ancient Greeks classified plants according to their general form: trees, shrubs, undershrubs and vines, and referred to them by vernacular (or common) names. This approach lasted for more than 1,700 years. However, as people discovered and described more and more living organisms, the use of common names led to much confusion – they can differ greatly from area to area, and the same common name may also be used for different species in different parts of the world. Common names still present problems today. In South Africa, for example, the species *Senegalia erubescens* is known as white thorn (*withaak*) in the Marico bushveld region, but east of this region it is called yellow thorn (*geelhaak*). The more accepted common name, however, is blue thorn (*blouhaak*)!

Linnaeus came to the rescue in 1753, when he introduced a naming system known as 'binomial nomenclature', which is still in use today. Living organisms are each given a two-part name, consisting of a genus and a species name. This unique binomial eliminates any possible confusion. To avoid having the nations of the world arguing over which language to use for naming organisms, Linnaeus used Latin, the international language of science at the time. Additionally, as a 'dead' language, Latin is unchanging.

## FROM DOMAIN TO SPECIES

Taxonomic classification is a hierarchical system with various levels: domain, kingdom, division (phylum), class, order, family, genus and species. All life on Earth can be classified into three domains: Archaea, Bacteria and Eukarya. Eukaryotes are organisms that have cells with a nucleus. Eukarya can be divided into the six kingdoms, namely Archaebacteria, Eubacteria, Protista, Fungi, Animalia and Plantae. Trees belong to the kingdom Plantae, sub-kingdom Tracheophytae, which are vascular plants.

The kingdom Plantae can be divided into four groups, namely green algae, bryophytes (mosses), pteridophytes (ferns) and spermatophytes (seed plants). Seed plants have historically been divided into two groups: gymnosperms and angiosperms.

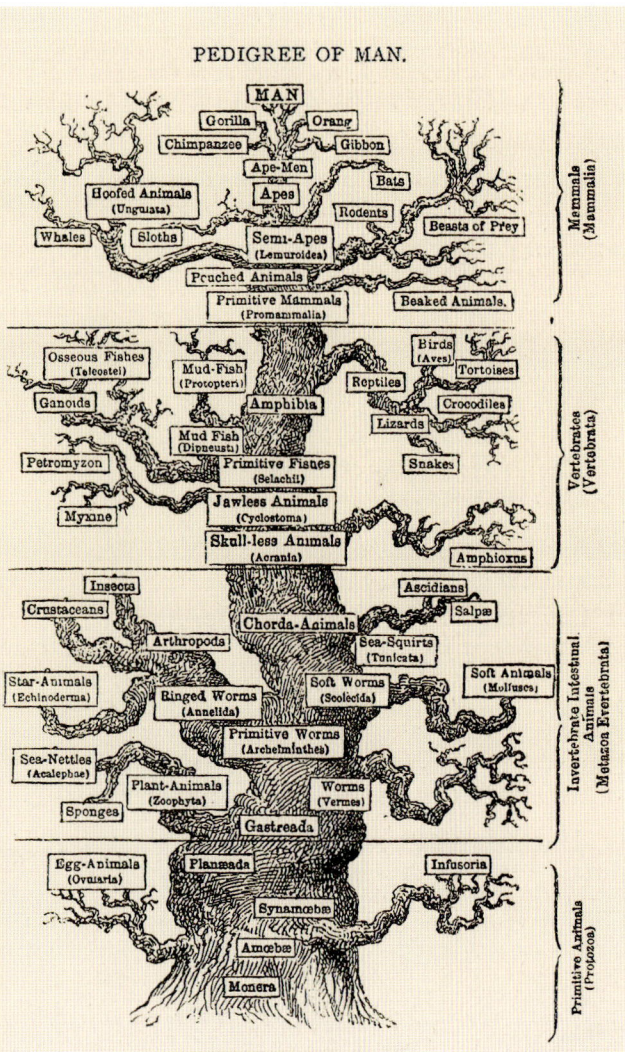

PEDIGREE OF MAN.

**LEFT** *German biologist Ernst Haeckel's Tree of Life illustrates common descent as understood in the 1800s.*

## GYMNOSPERMS

Gymnosperms, meaning 'naked seed', do not produce flowers or fruit, but have seeds that are borne in cones. Gymnosperms were particularly abundant during the Jurassic period, but today we have only a small remnant left of this class of plant. South African examples of gymnosperms are the cycad family (Zamiaceae) and the yellowwood family (Podocarpaceae).

## ANGIOSPERMS

All plants that produce flowers and bear their seed in fruits are angiosperms, meaning 'vessel seed'. Angiosperms represent the largest and most diverse group in the plant kingdom. Trees in this group evolved alongside insects, birds and mammals and often rely on them for pollination.

The angiosperms have historically been divided into two classes:

- **Liliopsids (monocotyledons)**: These plants have an embryo with a single cotyledon (that is, a seed leaf, the first leaf that emerges as the seed germinates) and parallel-veined leaves. They are mostly herbaceous plants and they do not have a taproot. Monocots include grass, maize, wheat, sugarcane, bananas, sisal, palms, aloes and orchids.
- **Magnoliopsids (dicotyledons)**: These plants have two cotyledons. Nearly all dicots have branching veins and flower parts in multiples of four or five. They also have a taproot.

Linnaeus was the first to apply the concept of **orders** to plants and animals, in an attempt to subdivide the classes into more comprehensible smaller groupings. Each order consists of one or more **families**, which in turn comprise genera that resemble each other in general appearance and technical characters.

Trees of a **genus** share the same basic flower structure and may look similar to other members of the genus in outward appearance. However, trees within a genus can still vary significantly in general form, bark colour, fruit and leaf shape.

A tree **species** shares common characteristics at the lowest taxonomic level. Trees of the same species have the same characteristics of general appearance, bark, leaf, flower and seed, and tend to grow together in geographic areas with similar climatic and soil conditions.

A **subspecies** is a subdivision of a species that has a distinct, though often inconspicuous, difference, and propagates true to that difference. The differences from the original type at subspecies level are insufficient to justify a new species and are usually the result of fairly permanent geographic isolation.

A **variety** is a taxonomic category that ranks below species or subspecies (where present). Its members differ from others of the same species or subspecies in minor but permanent or heritable characteristics. These differences are not necessarily distinctly separate nor are they geographically confined, yet they occur sufficiently frequently to warrant classification below the species or subspecies level. For example, bushveld gardenia (*Gardenia volkensii* subsp. *volkensii* var. *saundersiae*) from KwaZulu-Natal and southern Mozambique has large fruit covered with lenticels and flowers with large calyx lobes.

Traditionally, plant taxonomists have relied on the form of plants' reproductive structures to determine their evolutionary relationships. More recently, they have also used biochemical characteristics, DNA sequences and additional features. Occasionally, there are disagreements about the relationships of different plant species and we often see reclassification and renaming.

In identifying a tree, dendrologists do not always rely on reproductive structures because these are often available for only a brief time of the year. In practice, they typically use features of a tree's general shape and appearance, the leaves, the twigs, the bark, the wood and habitat as clues for identification. There are exceptions to the rule.

# THE ACACIA ARGUMENT

The genus *Acacia* has been synonymous with Africa since it was first described by Philip Miller in 1754. It is also widespread in Australia, Asia and the Americas. Scientific studies, however, showed that these species were not all closely related and should instead be divided into at least three separate genera. This was first suggested by Australian botanists in 2003.

In 2005, the unthinkable happened: the Nomenclature Section of the XVII International Botanical Congress held in Vienna reserved the genus name *Acacia* for the Australian wattles. Although traditional rules for plant names would have kept the name *Acacia* for the African species, this exception was made for the sake of stability: more than 950 of the 1,300 species are Australian, compared to the 140 or so African species.

Africa's *Acacia* were transferred to two distinct genera. The species with curved prickles now belong to the genus *Senegalia*, while those with straight spines are grouped in the genus *Vachellia*. Other differences, in the form and shape of the leaves and flowers, serve to differentiate between the two genera. *Vachellia* species usually have large, feathery compound leaves and round flowerheads, while *Senegalia* species generally have compound leaves with roundish leaflets and flowerheads in the form of spikes.

The decision made at the International Botanical Congress in 2005 was confirmed in 2011 after heated debate, despite the facts that: the word *Acacia* is derived from the Greek word *akis* and refers to the thorns of the trees (the Australian wattles have no thorns!); Africa's scented-pod was the first *Acacia* species to be scientifically named, having been described as early as 1753 as *Mimosa scorpioides*; and *Acacia* are commonly called 'acacias' in Africa, whereas the Australians call their trees 'wattles'.

Despite many South Africans' unhappiness about the decision, there are sufficient scientific grounds to justify the splitting of our *Acacia* species into two distinct genera. Additionally, 72 percent of *Acacia* species names remain unchanged. So, in this book the names *Senegalia* and *Vachellia* are used, but the index also lists the previous names.

Africa's iconic acacias have been split into two distinct genera: Senegalia and Vachellia.

# HOW TREES FUNCTION

## THE PARTS OF A TREE

### ROOTS

All trees have lateral **roots** that branch into smaller and smaller roots and, more often than not, extend horizontally beyond the diameter of the crown. The roots of a tree are multifunctional: they absorb water and nutrients from the soil; they store sugars and starches; and they serve to anchor the tree in the soil.

For the tree to access the available nutrients, its roots must penetrate large volumes of soil. Each root is covered with thousands of **root hairs** located just behind the hard, earth-probing root tips that burrow, elongate and expand in search of moisture. Millions of delicate, microscopic root hairs wrap themselves around individual grains of soil and are able to absorb moisture along with dissolved minerals necessary for growth. These nutrients are moved through the tree's tissues to other organs.

Gradually, the tiny roots reach out to so many particles of earth that the soil becomes a firm base for the tree. As a result, the soil is capable of resisting the erosion of wind and rain and provides a firm foundation for the tree itself.

Interestingly, root hairs have a very short life, so the root system is always in expansion mode, growing to provide sustained maximum root hair production. Most of the root system is located in the upper layers of soil because essential oxygen is most abundant there. It also means that the roots can take full advantage of available moisture.

### TRUNK

The trunk, or **stem**, supports the crown and is largely responsible for the shape and strength of the tree. **Bark** encloses the trunk, and also the branches, twigs and roots, and protects the tree from insects, disease and extreme temperatures. In some species, the outer bark, comprising a layer of dead corky cells, also protects the tree from fire.

Immediately beneath the outer bark, the **phloem** (inner bark) is found. It is a live, spongy layer that acts as a food-supply line by carrying sap (sugar and nutrients dissolved in water) from the leaves (the 'food producers') to the rest of the tree. Inner bark eventually grows out to form new outer bark. In fact, new bark is constantly being made on the inside and pushed out. Consequently, older trunks often have rough outer bark that sometimes peels or flakes away, while the bark of young trees is usually quite smooth.

On the inside of the phloem is the **cambium**, a very thin layer of growing tissue that produces new cells. These can become phloem – adding to the outer bark – or xylem, to

form the sapwood on the inside of the cambium. The cell division that occurs in the cambium gives rise to visual growth rings as the diameter of the tree increases.

The **xylem** brings water and nutrients up from the roots through tubes to the leaves and other parts of the tree. When a complete band of bark is removed from around a trunk, the living phloem and xylem cells that transport food and water are removed too, and the tree will starve to death. Removal of bark in this way is known as ringbarking.

As a tree grows, older xylem cells in the inner part of the trunk become inactive and die, forming the tree's **heartwood.** The main function of the heartwood is to support the tree. Since this is the site of stored sugar, resins and oils, the heartwood is usually darker than the sapwood.

## CROSS SECTION OF A TREE TRUNK

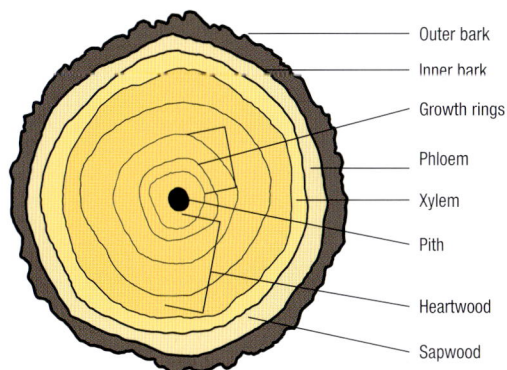

- Outer bark
- Inner bark
- Growth rings
- Phloem
- Xylem
- Pith
- Heartwood
- Sapwood

## CROWN

The **crown** consists of the tree's branches and leaves and can be regarded as its food factory. The leaves contain chlorophyll, a green pigment that absorbs sunlight and through the process of photosynthesis converts carbon dioxide to glucose. The shape of a tree crown varies considerably; it can be round, conical, upright, flat, sparse, dense, layered, drooping, oval, open, spreading or irregular. Crown size is a good indicator of a tree's health.

The **canopy** is the upper layer of mature tree crowns of a community of trees, or even of an individual tree. Canopies can cover vast areas and when seen from the air may appear to be a continuous mass. However, despite overlapping branches, forest canopy trees rarely touch each other, even in rainforests.

## LEAVES

The **leaves** are the primary food-producing parts of a plant, where photosynthesis takes place and hormones and other chemicals are produced. Leaves come in a variety of shapes and sizes, ranging from broad, flat leaves to long, thin needles. Trees can be evergreen (keep their leaves through the winter) or deciduous (lose their leaves in the winter), or semi-deciduous (lose some of their leaves).

TOP *Tsitsikamma's 'Big Tree', an ancient Outeniqua yellowwood, towers above the rest of the canopy.*

The leaves are usually the starting point in identifying tree species. The following leaf characteristics are important to note in this process:

- Whether the leaves are simple (consisting of a single blade) or compound (broken up into a number of leaflets)
- Leaf arrangement on the stem, for example, in whorls, or as opposite or alternate leaves
- The characteristics of the leaf margins
- The texture of the leaves above and below
- The veins on the leaf
- The colour differences between the upper and lower surfaces of the leaf
- The presence of secretory cavities in the leaf blade
- The presence of bacterial nodules on the leaf
- The features of the leaf stalk (petiole)
- The smell of the leaves

## PARTS OF A LEAF

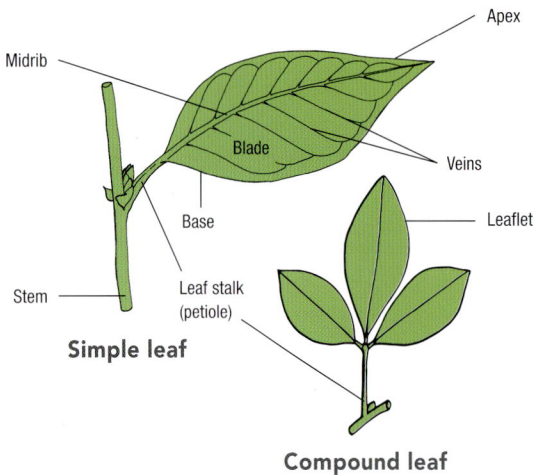

Apex

Midrib

Blade

Veins

Base

Leaflet

Stem

Leaf stalk (petiole)

**Simple leaf**

**Compound leaf**

## LEAF ARRANGEMENT

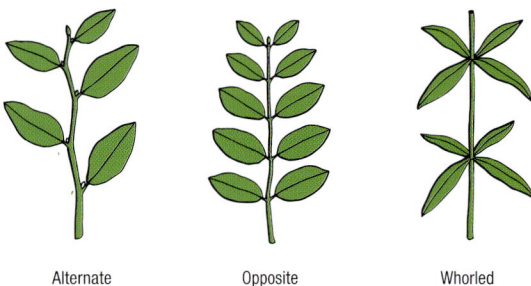

Alternate

Opposite

Whorled

*The leaves of the kuduberry have an alternate arrangement on the twigs.*

*The simple leaves of the red ivory are pale below and dark green above, with veins going straight to the margin.*

*Sicklebush flowers are long, fluffy, pendulous spikes borne in the leaf axils.*

## FLOWERS

Flowers are the organs for reproduction. Trees that produce flowers are known as **angiosperms**. Male and female parts of a flower can be in the same flower (bisexual) or in separate flowers (unisexual). Trees rely on a range of different strategies to attract pollinators, such as colour, scent, heat, nectar glands and edible pollen. Many species have developed flower parts that attract insects, which then spread the pollen from one flower to the next. Flowers of wind-pollinated trees have no need to be conspicuous or showy, and tend to lack petals or sepals; these trees typically produce large amounts of pollen and pollination often occurs early in the growing season, before leaves can interfere with the dispersal of the pollen.

## PARTS OF A FLOWER

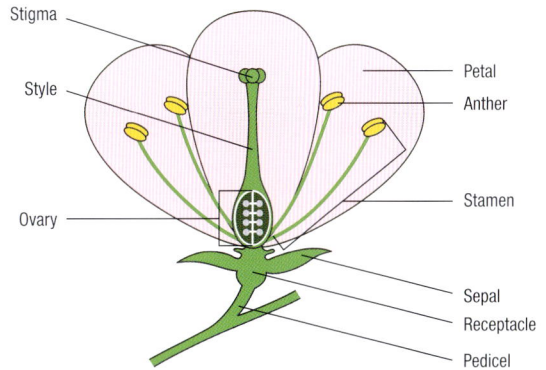

*The yellow flowers of the peeling plane are on slender stalks and are sweetly scented to attract pollinators.*

*Lowveld star-chestnut flowers are waxy, yellow and beautifully marked with brown or crimson.*

## SEEDS AND FRUIT

All trees reproduce with **seeds**, and most encase those seeds in some sort of **fruit**. In some cases, as with the marula, the fruit contains only a single large seed; in other species, such as the lowveld star-chestnut, the fruit contains many seeds. When ripe, seeds may fall to the ground and germinate beneath the mother tree, or they may be transported by wind, water or animals to germinate in other locations. Because animals feed on wild seeds, only a small number survive to germinate. Therefore, it is advantageous for a tree to produce large quantities of seeds to ensure their survival.

*A hard shell envelops the fruit of the snuff-box tree.*

*The fruit of kiaat is a circular pod with harsh bristles.*

*The bright red, fleshy fruit of the sourplum is edible but very sour.*

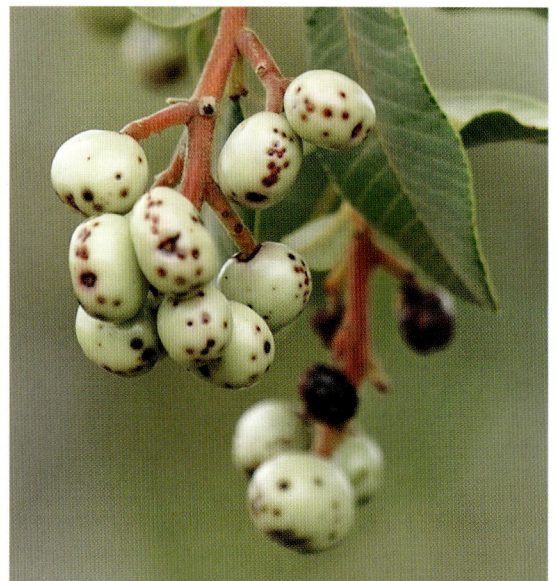

*The resintree's fruit is kidney-shaped and becomes black and wrinkled as it ripens.*

# TREES AS MODULAR ORGANISMS

One of the fundamental differences between plants and animals is that plants are modular organisms, while animals are unitary organisms. In unitary organisms, like humans and other mammals, the form is predictable and is not subject to significant variation. For example, humans have two arms, two legs, ten fingers, two eyes, and so on, and we all look roughly the same. An individual starts with a sperm fertilising an egg, whereafter a complex process of embryonic development commences. The foetus develops into a known form that will be retained after birth, except for growing bigger, until death.

A tree, however, is a modular organism. It grows by the repeated iteration of its parts (that is, the leaves, shoots and branches). Its form is not predictable and no two specimens of a species look exactly the same. Trees do not develop a foetus, but rather a module such as a leaf or a branch, which then produces further similar modules. Individual specimens thus consist of a highly variable number of modules, the development of which is a function of the interaction with the environment. Unlike unitary organisms, trees grow continuously at the tips of shoots and roots, as well as in a thin layer of cells (the cambium) immediately underneath the bark.

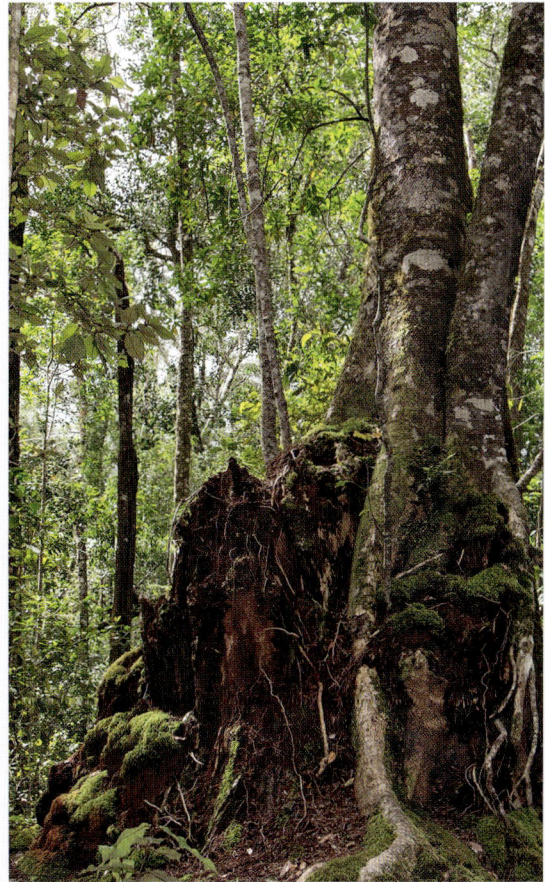

*Trees can overcome disasters and setbacks with greater ease than unitary organisms. On the left, the entire top section of a leadwood was lost, perhaps owing to lightning or wind. However, the tree pushed out new shoots and is still growing strongly. On the right, a white-alder resprouted after its trunk was damaged. The tree can regenerate time after time, enabling it to get very old.*

## HOW TREES GROW

Four hundred years ago, trees were believed to eat soil – because they are rooted in soil and get bigger and bigger every year. Leonardo da Vinci suspected that this was not true, but it was a Belgian, Jan Baptista van Helmont, who concluded from his experiments that trees 'eat water, not soil'. This was, of course, not correct either and it took almost two centuries before Swiss scientists figured out that leaves absorb carbon dioxide during daylight hours, and that it is this gas, plus water, that is responsible for the growth of plants. This was the birth of the concept of photosynthesis.

Tree growth begins with a seed. A seed contains an embryo and enough nutrients to grow a root and the first leaves. In the wild, seed germination varies significantly among species. Some seeds require little more than a few rain showers to sprout within weeks. Trees like *Vachellia* and *Senegalia* species, on the other hand, have developed a more conservative approach suited to the harsh, dry conditions in which they live. Their seeds are produced in vast quantities and have an outer coating that is hard and tough enough to protect the seeds within until moisture arrives, ensuring a built-in dormancy period.

Germination is triggered by external conditions such as contact with moist soil or with acids from browsers' stomachs or from dung, but also by heat and chemicals. The seeds of many species may germinate in the first rainy season, while others need disturbance such as trampling by wildlife or tumbling among rocks in a stream bed. Yet others may bide their time for several years. While the hard, protective coating of some tree seeds serves to protect the seed, it may also inhibit germination as water and air cannot penetrate the coating. As a result, some tree seeds require at least two winters before the coating is broken down sufficiently to allow germination.

When conditions are right, the seed germinates and the process of growth begins. First, as the seed begins to absorb water, the root emerges from the bottom of the seed and begins to grow down into the soil. As the root grows downwards, a shoot emerges from the top of the seed. This shoot contains the embryonic stem and leaves, covered in a sheath that helps to protect the delicate tissues as they emerge.

The shoot begins to grow towards the light, which is driven by the hormone auxin in the stem. As the tree continues to grow, more branches erupt from the main stem and new leaves grow out from the branches. The leaves are arranged in a specific pattern that allows them to capture the maximum amount of sunlight.

The growth in trees is caused by specialised dividing tissues called 'meristems'. These are found in the tips of shoots, roots and lateral buds, as well as at the tips of any branches or lateral stems. The cells in these meristematic tissues actively divide, making the plant grow bigger. This is known as 'primary plant growth'.

There are meristematic cells inside the vascular tissues (xylem and phloem) that run up and down inside the plant stems, roots and leaves. The major reason trees are able to grow so large is their ability to create woody tissue as they grow. This process is called 'secondary plant growth'. Wood contains the chemical lignin, which is a complex polymer that makes plant cell walls rigid. In trees, the xylem and phloem grow sideways around the inside of the plant stem and join up as the plant grows. They become the bands of vascular tissues that one can see in a stem cross section. Each year, the woody stem grows wider due to the production of new xylem in the woody interior and new phloem towards the exterior, which pushes the old phloem out to become bark. As a tree reaches maturity, it continues to grow and produce seeds. However, the rate of growth slows down and the tree begins to focus more on reproduction than on growth. Eventually the tree will die, but its legacy will live on through its seeds.

With age, xylem becomes increasingly lignified or woody. The rings in a tree trunk show the yearly growth of xylem, which, by the time it has become wood, is largely just lignin and cellulose. Not surprisingly, some tree species count among the most massive and longest-living organisms on Earth.

The rings in a tree trunk show the yearly growth in xylem.

The fruit of the bushveld red-balloon is a red, bladder-like capsule, with three seeds inside each lobe.

# THE UPTAKE OF WATER

Trees have a complex network of roots that can extend deep into the soil and spread widely around the trunk; and, like most plants, trees rely on their root systems to harvest nutrients from the soil. The root system has several specialised structures, such as root hairs, that increase its surface area, allowing for more efficient uptake of water and nutrients. Among these nutrients are nitrogen, phosphorus, potassium, iron, calcium and magnesium, and a host of other minor elements such as boron, cobalt, copper, iodine, manganese and zinc.

The uptake of water occurs through the process of osmosis. This is the diffusion of water molecules through a semi-permeable membrane (the outer membrane of the roots) from a region of higher to lower concentration of water molecules. Osmosis allows water and disolved nutrients to penetrate and pass through the membrane.

Water moves into the xylem (the tree's main water-conducting tissue) and upwards through the roots, trunk and branches to the leaves. The main driving force of the uptake and transport of water is the loss of water from the leaves.

*The roots of plants, including trees, are responsible for the uptake of water and nutrients.*

# TRANSPIRATION

Stomata (singular 'stoma') are openings or pores found in the outermost layer of leaves, as well as that of stems and other parts of the plant. Typically, there are thousands of stomata, which occur mainly on the lower surface of leaves, although in some plants they occur on only the upper surface and in others on both surfaces.

The pores are bordered by pairs of specialised bean-shaped cells ('guard cells'), which regulate the opening and closing of the stomata, based on variables such as light, temperature, humidity and the water status of the plant.

The main functions of stomata are to allow the uptake of carbon dioxide, which is needed for photosynthesis, and to limit the loss of water due to evaporation when conditions are hot and dry. Stomata generally remain open during the day when photosynthesis occurs. They close up at night when sunlight is no longer available and photosynthesis is not happening, thus preventing water from escaping through open pores.

Transpiration is the process in which water vapour is lost through the stomata. It serves to cool plants down when it is very hot, and enables water uptake by creating negative pressure in the leaves.

When water is less readily available for plants, hormones cause the stomata to close, reducing the loss of water that occurs during oxygen release and carbon dioxide intake. This helps to maintain a balance between water uptake and water loss, ensuring that the plant has enough water to survive and grow.

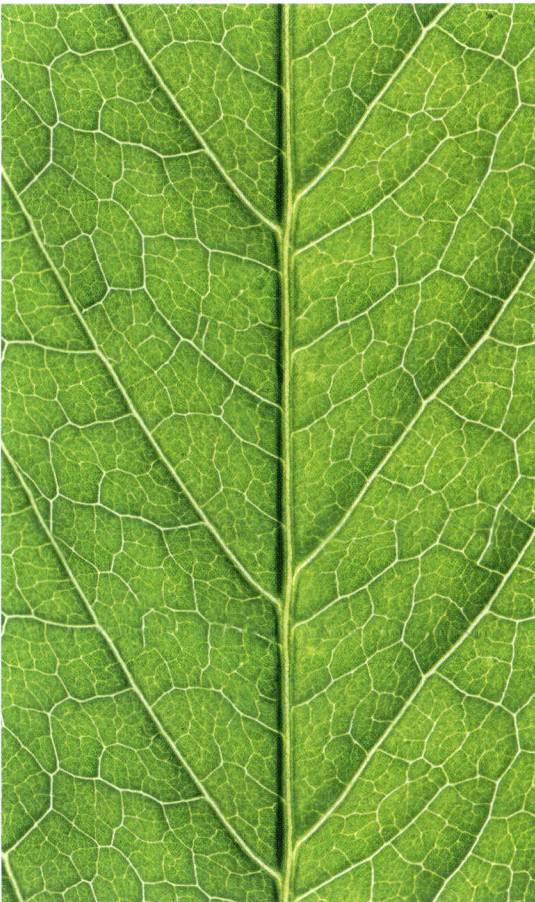

_Trees lose water vapour through pores in the leaf surface._

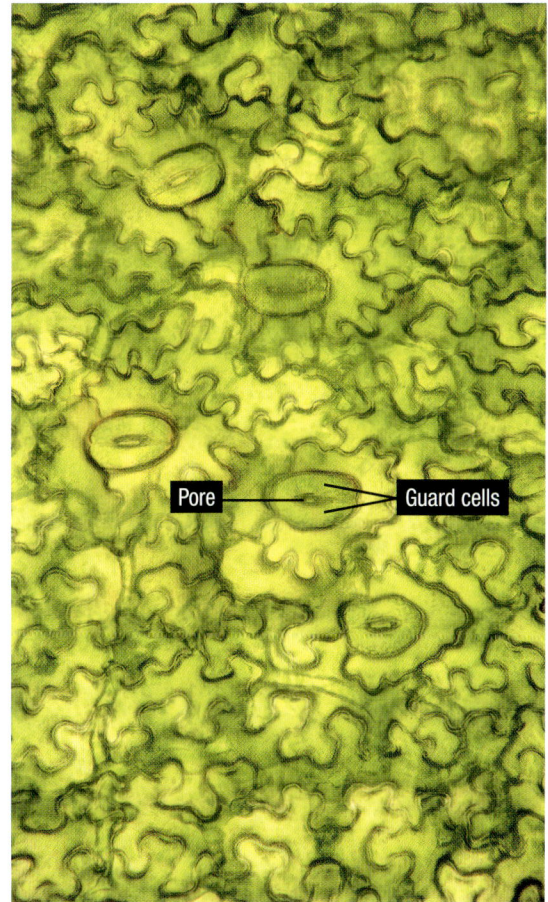

_Bean-shaped guard cells border the stomata._

## POLLINATION

Pollination is the process by which both cone-bearing and flowering plants reproduce. Most trees have both male and female parts in the same flower, although in some tree species the male and female flowers occur on different trees and, in some cases, separate male and female flowers grow on the same tree.

The male flower part, the stamen, is a long slender stalk with pollen at the end. Several stamens may be found in one flower. The female part of a flower, the pistil, consists of a stigma, style and ovary situated at the centre of the flower. The ovary contains the ovules (eggs) that will develop into seeds once they have been fertilised. Each tiny grain of powdery, yellowish pollen carries a plant's male genes in a single cell, encased in a tough coating.

The process of pollination begins when a pollen grain is deposited on the stigma of the flower and releases a sperm cell, which moves down through the style. The style is connected to the ovary, which contains one or more unfertilised ovules. Once fertilisation has taken place in the

TOP  *A butterfly visits the flower of a wildpear.*

ABOVE  *The delicate, pollen-rich blooms of the showy plane attract many insects, especially bees.*

ovary between the sperm cell and an ovule of the same species, the seed starts developing.

Flowering trees attract and compete for the attention of pollinators through their colourful, showy flowers, their pleasant (but sometimes not-so-pleasant) scent and by producing nectar, a sugary liquid that is high in energy. The plant–pollinator relationship is an example of 'mutualism', with both parties benefiting from the relationship.

Bees, birds, bats and other pollinators – often exclusively visiting only particular species – will land on a flower and, in the process, pollen is brushed off onto their body. When they move on to the next flower, the pollen is transported with them and some of it finds its way onto the stigma, setting the reproductive process in motion.

Some plants can self-pollinate when pollen finds its way from the stamens onto the stigma of the same flower.

Most plants, however, need to be cross-pollinated by pollen from another plant of the same species.

Conifer species (gymnosperms) bear cones rather than flowers and many rely on wind for pollination. Male cones produce pollen, which is carried by the wind to female cones, where sperm cells fertilise the seeds. Wind pollination is most effective in open habitats with stands of the same species growing near each other, and where the wind is likely to blow. It is not surprising to find that the tallest forest trees, whose flowers or cones are exposed to wind, rely on wind pollination. Pollination by wind is, however, almost non-existent among understorey plants that live in less windy conditions.

The flowers of trees pollinated by the wind are usually small and inconspicuous. They also do not produce nectar and have no need for bright colours to attract any pollinators.

A honey bee gathers pollen while foraging for nectar on a Cape hollyhock flower.

Weeping boerbean flowers produce copious amounts of nectar, which attracts birds such as this Cape white-eye.

ABOVE LEFT *The African green pigeon feeds on a variety of different fruits, but also eats seeds.*

BOTTOM LEFT *Dung beetles transport balls of dung, which often contain seeds.*

RIGHT *Vervet monkeys are important seed dispersers.*

# SEED DISPERSAL

One of the main priorities for all living organisms, including trees, is to ensure that their own kind persists into the future. In the case of trees, it is also important that the offspring disperse over a wide area. Being crowded in one area can result in too much competition for food, water and other essentials, and the species as a whole may suffer. In addition, if trees of one species are concentrated in one location, they are more at risk from potential disease or fire.

However, trees face some challenges in this regard, such as ensuring that their seeds end up in suitable soil, that at least some seeds survive the onslaught by seed predators and are able to germinate, and that their offspring have enough energy reserves to give them a good start in life.

In South Africa, seed dispersal by mammals and birds seems to be the most common form of dispersal, followed by wind dispersal and other mechanical means. Elephant, with their poor digestive systems, are particularly useful as seed dispersers. Studies have found that elephant consume more seeds from more plant species than any other large vertebrate. Although these studies focused largely on forest elephant, savannah elephant are also known to be important seed dispersers. Their expansive home ranges enable widespread seed dispersal.

Hippopotamus are essentially grazers, but they are among the few animal species that feed on the large fallen fruits of the sausagetree (*Kigelia africana*), and so play a key role in dispersing its seeds through their dung. Browsing antelope, giraffe and black rhino also play a role in seed dispersal for a number of tree species.

Primates eat fruits and are important seed dispersers for both forest and savannah trees, such as red currant (*Searsia chirindensis*), sourplum (*Ximenia caffra*) and fig (*Ficus*) species. They consume the fruits of a large variety of plant species and disperse the seeds through defecation or by carrying food in their cheek pouches and spitting and dropping seeds as they go.

Fruit-eating birds are numerous in South Africa, and include trumpeter and crowned hornbills, forest weavers, Cape white-eyes, black-headed orioles, sombre greenbuls, Meyer's parrots, African green pigeons, pale-winged starlings, Knysna turacos and red-fronted tinker-barbets. They disperse seeds by swallowing and defecating them or by dropping them, either beneath the tree or having carried them off some distance.

Some trees rely on wind for the dispersal of their seeds, including Cape-beech (*Rapanea melanophloeos*), wildpear (*Dombeya rotundifolia* var. *rotundifolia*), African-wattle (*Peltophorum africanum*), mountain cypress (*Widdringtonia nodiflora*) and species of the protea family. For effective wind dispersal, seeds need to be light enough and must have wings, plumes or hairs to slow their rate of fall.

Seed dispersal by water is uncommon in South Africa and is largely restricted to the Indian Ocean coastal belt biome. Water dispersal is found across four tree families, namely Apocynaceae, Avicenniaceae, Lecythidaceae and Fabaceae. About half of the species appear to be adapted for fresh-water dispersal, usually within swamp or mangrove environments, such as quininetree (*Rauvolfia caffra*), while those existing on the verge of the tidal zone are adapted for oceanic dispersal, such as grey nicker (*Caesalpinia bonduc*).

Seeds may also be propelled explosively by a tree's own fruit (usually a pod) that suddenly bursts open, for example mountain mahogany (*Entandrophragma caudatum*), Lowveld star-chestnut (*Sterculia murex*) and various *Senegalia* and *Vachellia* species. This phenomenon is largely restricted to species that occur in the savannah biome.

# MASTING

Masting is the irregular periodic production of larger than normal seed or fruit crops in perennial plants such as trees. This happens in synchrony with other trees of the same species in a region. The difference between a mast-seeding year and a normal seeding year can be thousands of fruits.

A popular explanation for mast seeding is 'predator satiation'. This hypothesis suggests that by producing excessive quantities of fruits and seeds in mast years, a tree may over-satiate the fruit- or seedeaters to the point where a larger than usual proportion of seed escapes consumption and is eventually able to germinate. Reduced seed production in the intervening years, resulting in inconsistent availability of the particular food source, may effectively control predator populations.

Very little research on masting has been done in South Africa and our knowledge is largely based on extrapolations of research elsewhere in the world. It has, however, been determined with a high degree of certainty that masting occurs among some of our cycads (*Encephalartos*). The quantity of fruit produced by some of our trees has been observed to fluctuate considerably over time, especially in species whose seeds are parasitised by insects. Casual observations also indicate that camel thorn (*Vachellia erioloba*) and umbrella thorn (*Vachellia tortilis* subsp. *heteracantha*) trees produce an abundance of seed in years of drought. Clearly, more research is required.

ABOVE *During some years, camel thorn trees may produce copious numbers of pods.*

TOP RIGHT *Some tree species, such as the bitter false-thorn, produce an abundance of seed in years of drought, most likely to ensure that a sufficient proportion of seed will escape consumption by browsers and germinate.*

# PHOTOSYNTHESIS

Earth's plants and animals cannot exist without energy from the sun. Plants have the ability to use energy from the sun in a process known as 'photosynthesis' – truly one of the great wonders of nature. Photosynthesis is the process by which plants, algae and certain bacteria utilise energy from the sun to synthesise nutrients from carbon dioxide and water, which can be used to fuel their own growth.

In a series of biochemical processes, the compound chlorophyll, present in the tree's leaves, captures light energy in the form of photons. These photons react with water and carbon dioxide (collected through the tree's leaves and roots) and are transformed into simple sugars such as glucose. Oxygen and water vapour are released into the air through pores in the leaves as byproducts.

Photosynthesis plays a key role in the carbon cycle, the process by which carbon is cycled through the Earth's atmosphere, oceans and land. During the process of photosynthesis, carbon dioxide from the atmosphere is absorbed and converted, along with water, into organic matter, which is then consumed by organisms or stored in the soil. Carbon is released back into the atmosphere as carbon dioxide when animals breathe (or when they die and decompose), completing the cycle.

Photosynthesis not only helps to mitigate the effects of global warming by using carbon dioxide (a greenhouse gas), but also provides the basis for most of the food chains and ecosystems on our planet.

During photosynthesis, trees 'inhale' carbon dioxide and 'exhale' oxygen, while we humans and other animals do the opposite. (However, when plants metabolise sugars, they use oxygen and release carbon dioxide, just like humans do.) Photosynthesis is responsible for all the breathable oxygen in the atmosphere. It is therefore safe to say that there would be no animal life on Earth, as we know it, without plants and the process of photosynthesis.

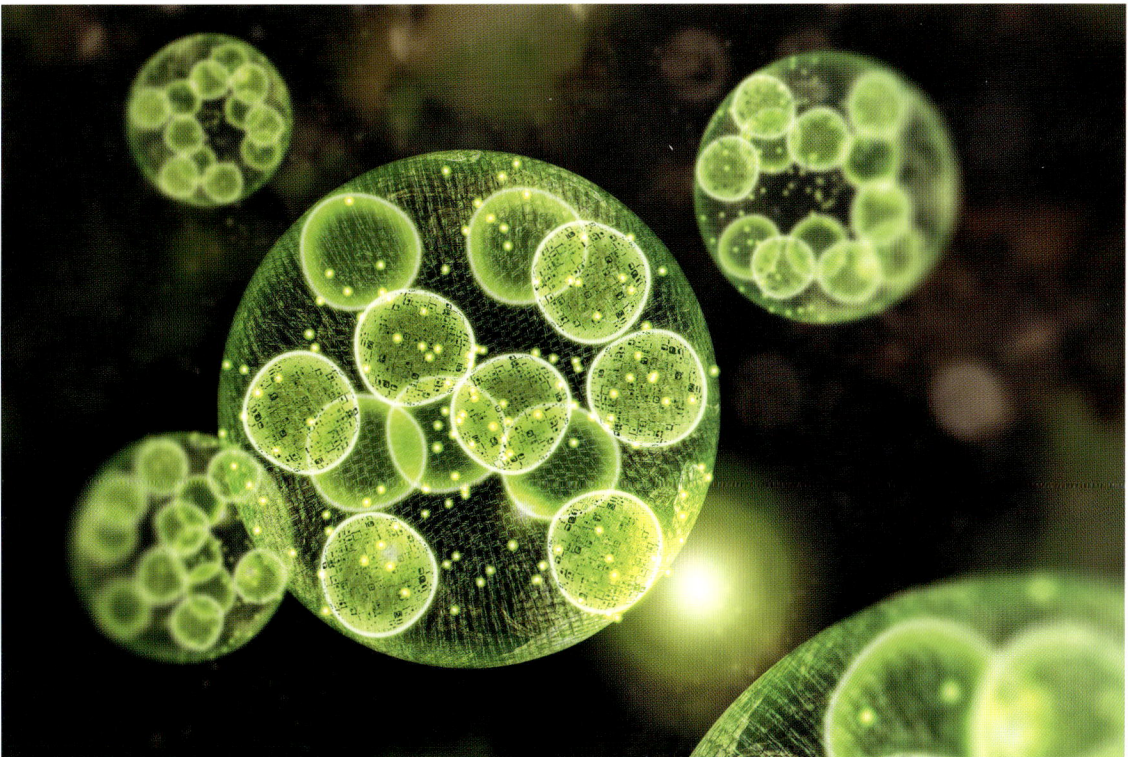

*Each cell in a colony of green algae contains chlorophyll that is used for photosynthesis.*

Trees likely evolved their typical form, characterised by very large external surface areas, to be able to intercept the maximum number of photons before they reach other plants or before they are lost as 'energy wastage'. The size and shape of a tree is also important: it is necessary to expose a relatively large surface area (the canopy) to the sun all day long to maximise photon absorption.

Trees allocate the carbohydrates generated by photosynthesis to their growth, maintenance, reproduction, reserve storage and protection. Defoliation by browsers may disturb this balance, as the removal of a photosynthetically active leaf causes reserves to be diverted to promoting new growth. This has been found to increase the photosynthetic ability of the remaining leaves, which have to supply resources, together with carbohydrate reserves, to repair the damage caused by defoliation.

As trees grow bigger, they take in and store more carbon. As they gain girth around their trunk, their leaf mass increases by the square of their trunk's diameter, resulting in many more leaves to remove carbon from the atmosphere. So, larger trees play a significant role in storing carbon.

## Why are trees green?

Chlorophyll is the pigment responsible for the green colour of leaves. All materials absorb light differently and reflect it back differently, too. If chlorophyll were able to absorb all the colours of visible light, trees would appear black, or almost black, because there would be no light reflected back to our eyes. Chlorophyll, however, strongly absorbs light from the blue and red portions of the light spectrum and green light is thus reflected back. Consequently, almost all plants look green to us for most of the time.

We often see new leaves on a tree as red, such as the red-leaved fig (*Ficus ingens*). This is due to a substance called anthocyanin, which protects the new leaves from ultraviolet light. Anthocyanins reflect red light and we see the leaves as red. As the leaves develop, the anthocyanin is broken down and the leaves appear green to us.

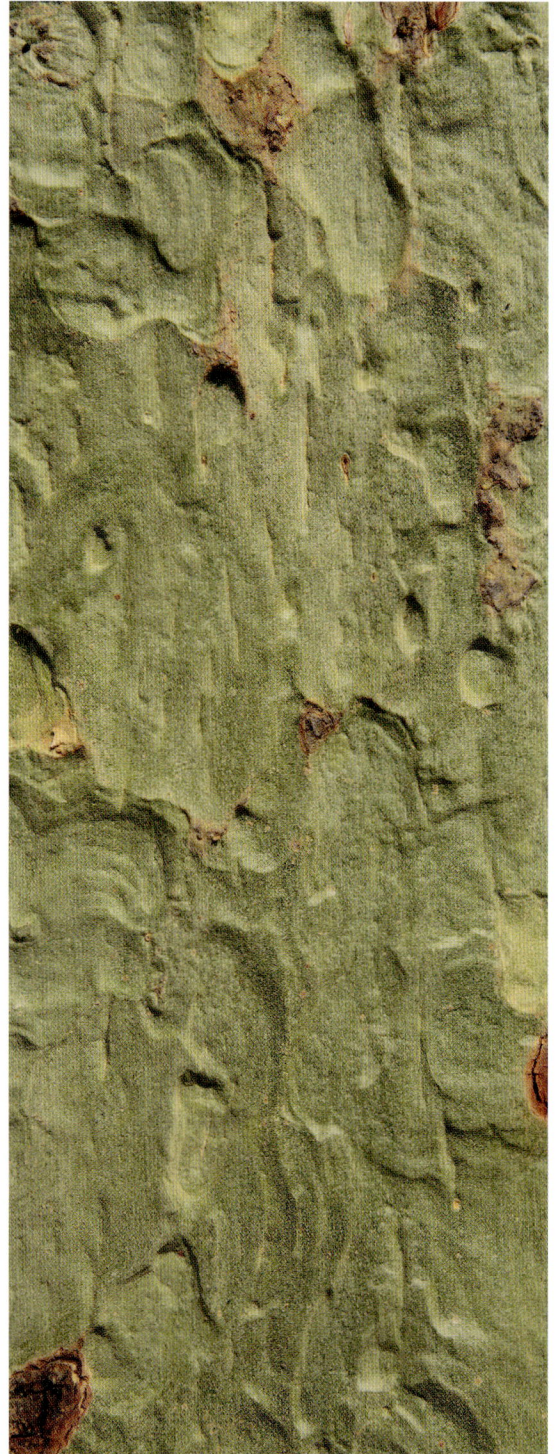

*In what is likely to be an adaptation, the fevertree is one of very few trees that use both their leaves and bark for photosynthesis.*

*White-syringa in summer, autumn and winter*

# THE SHEDDING OF LEAVES

In autumn, deciduous trees drop their leaves as part of their preparation for winter dormancy. This process is known as 'abscission' and is controlled by two hormones – auxin and ethylene.

Many tree species throughout South Africa, and specifically in the more arid savannah regions where the winters are dry, drop their leaves in autumn to conserve water and energy. Some need to shut down certain processes in anticipation of very cold weather, in which water in the soil could freeze. This shutdown also forestalls water in the plant tissues freezing and rupturing cells. Evergreen trees do not shed their leaves and so remain green and functional throughout the year. In areas with warmer winters and higher rainfall, trees are mostly evergreen.

Some trees, like the mitzeeri (*Bridelia micrantha*) and the sycamore fig (*Ficus sycomorus* subsp. *sycomorus*), can be either evergreen or deciduous, depending on the prevailing temperature in which they grow: in cold areas they are deciduous, but in warmer areas they will most likely be evergreen. The Cape-ash (*Ekebergia capensis*), nyalatree (*Xanthocercis zambesiaca*), apple-leaf (*Philenoptera violacea*) and the weeping boerbean (*Schotia brachypetala*) are semi-deciduous, that is, they are usually deciduous for only a very short period of time: in spring they shed their leaves and immediately sprout new ones.

The process of leaf shedding is triggered by the changing seasons: as winter approaches, daylight shortens and temperatures drop, the flow of the hormone auxin in the leaves slows, and levels of ethylene rise. This signals to some cells at the base of the leaves to weaken their cell walls, and others to expand and break connections between the weakened cells – causing the leaves to drop to the ground.

Some deciduous trees remobilise nitrogen and carbon from the leaves before shedding them, transferring the nutrients in the form of proteins to the roots and inner bark. In spring, these proteins fuel the growth of new leaves and flowers. Chlorophyll, which we see as the green colour of the leaves, is one of the first molecules to be broken down for its nutrients. This is why the leaves of some species turn yellow, orange or red during autumn.

At the end of the abscission process, when the leaves have been shed, a protective layer of cells grows over the exposed areas. Abscission seems to be triggered mostly by day length, but the conditions for leaf drop and the sprouting of new leaves and flowers are not the same for all genera and species. Some are triggered by changing air or soil temperatures. Others, especially trees with frost-intolerant foliage, rely on day length before dropping leaves or sprouting new ones. They will wait until days are long enough before producing new leaves. In this way the risk of a sudden cold spell in spring is minimised. This variation in triggers explains why some deciduous trees drop their leaves earlier in autumn than others, and why some are so quick off the mark in spring, while others hang back before producing new leaves or flowers.

Leadwood

Zebra-barked corkwood

## THE SHEDDING OF BARK

The process by which a tree loses its bark is known as exfoliation. It is a natural phenomenon and can happen for a number of reasons. It is not necessarily an indication that anything is wrong. The most common cause is that the tree is 'growing out of its skin', which must be shed to allow the trunk to enlarge.

Trees grow from the cambium, just below the bark, causing their outer layers to expand. Although the bark of most young trees is smooth and thin and can withstand growth with relative ease, as trees grow older, their bark layer loses its elasticity as it hardens and thickens, which then causes the outer layers to crack and split. In some trees, the outer dead layers peel and drop off, revealing the inner layer of bark. Examples are some corkwood (*Commiphora*) species, paperbark false thorn (*Albizia tanganyicensis*), quivertree (*Aloidendron dichotomum*), paperbark thorn (*Vachellia sieberiana*) and peeling plane (*Ochna pulchra* subsp. *pulchra*).

Exfoliation can be exacerbated by extreme temperatures, either cold or heat, causing cracks in the bark. A healthy tree can heal such blemishes, but damage by animals such as porcupines and elephant can be so severe that the tree may not be able to recover (see also 'How trees defend themselves', page 58).

Even very slow-growing trees such as leadwood (*Combretum imberbe*) can undergo exfoliation, exposing the thin inner bark of the tree. This exposure of fresh inner bark allows a higher level of gas exchange and transpiration to occur, thereby increasing the tree's metabolic rate. In the case of leadwood, exfoliation seems to lead to faster and more successful growth.

Another theory suggests that exfoliation may have a protective function, as the shedding of bark prevents the build-up of parasites, fungi, mosses and lichens.

Some trees, such as the fevertree (*Vachellia xanthophloea*) and green-stemmed corkwood (*Commiphora neglecta*), photosynthesise through their bark. Here, exfoliation may allow the removal of a light-blocking layer of lichen, enabling the tree to take advantage of sunny winter days to create carbohydrates even when no leaves are available.

*Quivertree*

# SYMBIOTIC RELATIONSHIPS

Living organisms all compete for food, light and water, but there is evidence of fascinating cooperation among them, often, but not always, for mutual benefit.

Symbiosis is a term derived from Greek and means 'living together'. Symbiosis can take different forms. In **parasitism**, one organism (the parasite) feeds on another, harming but not necessarily killing the other (the host). **Commensalism** occurs when an organism lives on a host without causing it harm, but not benefiting it in any way. In **mutualism**, both organisms benefit from the relationship. In some instances, the symbiotic relationship is a prerequisite for the organisms to survive. This is known as 'obligate symbiosis'. In other cases, the symbiotic relationship gives each organism a greater chance of survival, known as 'facultative symbiosis'. Symbiotic relationships aren't always symmetrical – they can, for instance, be obligate for one organism and facultative for the other.

Many trees are involved in symbiotic relationships, often depending on them for survival. A good example is the relationship between all fig trees and their dedicated wasp species. Individual wasp species are associated with individual fig species, breeding only in the fruit of their specific fig host. The fig tree in turn depends entirely on its wasp for pollination. When a fig is ready for pollination, it releases a chemical unique to its species. The associated wasps are able to detect these chemical releases and fly long distances to reach the trees. This cosy relationship between the fig and wasp species is host-specific: each fig species is pollinated by its own wasp species and prevents hybridisation between different fig species. Both figs and wasps depend on one another for survival in a classic example of obligate mutualism – neither party can survive without the other.

A fig fruit is nothing more than an inside-out bunch of small flowers. The pollination process begins when the female fig wasp burrows into an unripe fig through a tiny hole known as an ostiole, usually losing her wings and antennae as she goes, so narrow is the passageway. Inside the fig, she lays her eggs, moving from internal flower to flower and fortuitously spreading pollen from the fig in which she was born. Once her work is done, she dies.

After pollination, the ostiole closes up to seal the inside of the fig from the outside world. In due course the internal flowers, now pollinated, will produce seeds; the eggs laid in the flowers will hatch, the wingless males emerging first, ready to feast on the fig tissue and mate with their 'sisters' by cutting holes through the walls of the floral ovaries where the females are still confined. Once fertilised, the pregnant females, loaded with pollen, leave the fruit through the tunnels cut by the males. They are now ready to find another fig in which to start the process all over again.

Once the female wasps have escaped from the fig, it ripens and then attracts fruit-eating birds, bats and monkeys, setting in motion another set of inter-relationships between the tree and animals.

There are many other examples of symbiosis, such as the relationship between the mistletoes commonly found in the canopy branches of knob thorn trees; the relationship between spittlebugs and apple-leaf and African-wattle trees; the mutualistic relationship whereby fruit bats pollinate baobabs while feeding on the flowers;

LEFT *Fig trees depend entirely on wasps for pollination, and these insects breed nowhere else but inside the figs.*

Right *Many trees have symbiotic relationships with lichens (above) and fungi (right).*

*The mopane moth can lay up to 300 eggs. Its caterpillars, known as mopane worms, produce droppings that fertilise the soil and fuel tree growth.*

*As epauletted fruit bats move from tree to tree in search of flowers and nectar, they spread pollen and enable cross-fertilisation. These bats also distribute seeds.*

the mutually beneficial relationship between *Rhizobium* soil bacteria and leguminous plants; and the soil enrichment caused by dung beetles.

Another well-known relationship, and a classic example of mutualism, is that between the marula tree (*Sclerocarya birrea*) and the savannah elephant. Elephant consume large quantities of marula fruit, as well as leaves and bark, and excrete undigested seeds in their dung. This not only spreads the seeds over a large area, but also provides a nutrient-rich environment in which the seedlings can grow – to the benefit of all.

Mutualism is also found between the mopane tree (*Colophospermum mopane*) and nitrogen-fixing bacteria in the soil. Mopane trees have adapted to the nutrient-poor soils in which they grow by forming a symbiotic relationship with bacteria that are capable of fixing atmospheric nitrogen into a form that they can use. The bacteria live in nodules on the trees' roots and provide their hosts with essential nutrients. Both species benefit from the interaction; the bacteria are provided with a source of energy and a safe place to live, while the mopane tree is enabled to grow and thrive in nutrient-poor soils.

The symbiotic relationships between the roots of trees and fungi in the soil are highly developed, allowing the fungus to obtain carbohydrates from the plant, while the plant obtains mineral nutrients from the fungus. There

is thus a three-way relationship between the plant, the fungus and the soil, called a mycorrhizal association. The term is derived from the Greek *mukes* ('fungus') and *rhiza* ('root'), and literally means 'fungus root'. Some trees will only form a mycorrhizal association with a particular species of fungus, while others associate with a broad range of fungi.

Research has shown that the shortage of minerals in the soil (especially of nitrogen and phosphorus) can limit tree growth. Compounds containing phosphorus are usually insoluble in the soil and this limits the ability of the tree to take up phosphorus. Consequently, a tree would require an extensive root system to maximise its ability to harvest phosphates from the soil. Fortunately, there are large numbers of different fungi species in the soil that form extensive networks of thread-like cells called hyphae. These hyphae grow quickly and are effective at accessing large soil volumes and mobilising insoluble phosphates. The growth of the fungus is limited by the availability of free carbohydrates, which are known to be quite scarce in the soil. But the ability of fungi to obtain minerals from the soil is augmented by the ability of trees and other plants to synthesise carbohydrates. Thus, the fungus obtains carbohydrates and the tree, phosphates. The majority of plant species benefit from this particular symbiotic relationship.

# THE FASCINATING LEGUMES

Legumes belong to the family Fabaceae, a large group of plants that have pods for fruit. Thorn trees are legumes in the Fabaceae and the subfamily Mimosoideae. They are known for hosting *Rhizobium* bacteria in their roots.

The availability of nitrogen is often referred to as a primary limiting factor in plant growth and is a major challenge to world agriculture. Nature has an immense reserve of nitrogen in the atmosphere, which consists of approximately 80 percent nitrogen gas, but this is not directly available to plants. Some bacteria, however, are able to transform nitrogen gas into other forms of nitrogen in a process known as 'nitrogen fixation', and accumulate it biologically for their use.

*Rhizobium* bacteria, which are normally free-living in the soil, infect the root hairs of legumes and are housed in small root nodules. Energy is provided by the plant to feed the bacteria and fuel the nitrogen fixation process. In return, the plant receives nitrogen for growth. As nitrogen accumulates in the roots of the trees, new nodules grow, allowing for increased nitrogen fixation.

There are thousands of strains of *Rhizobium*. Some of these will infect many hosts; certain hosts will accept many different strains of *Rhizobium*. Although hosts may be nodulated by several strains of *Rhizobium*, growth may be enhanced only by particular strains.

There are hundreds of nitrogen-fixing tree species in the family Fabaceae and many of them are pioneer species, spreading in habitats such as wastelands or burned and overgrazed veld. Some of them, like certain *Albizia*, *Vachellia* and *Senegalia* species, as well as *Dichrostachys cinerea*, may become nasty invaders. Legumes also include some very fast-growing, high-biomass and deep-rooted species. Their constant leaf drop nourishes soil life, which in turn can support more plant life. The deep, extensive root system of these trees allows access to nutrients in subsoil layers while also stabilising the soil. Many species of nitrogen-fixing trees can also provide a range of uses for people, including food, wind protection, shade, animal fodder, firewood, fences and timber.

*Rhizobium bacteria packed tightly together. These bacteria infect the root hairs of legumes, and play a role in nitrogen fixation.*

The lantana shrub competes with indigenous plants and is poisonous to both humans and animals.

Browsing mammals, such as kudu, may over-utilise trees during times of drought.

Elephants can be destructive feeders, stripping bark, breaking branches and even uprooting entire trees.

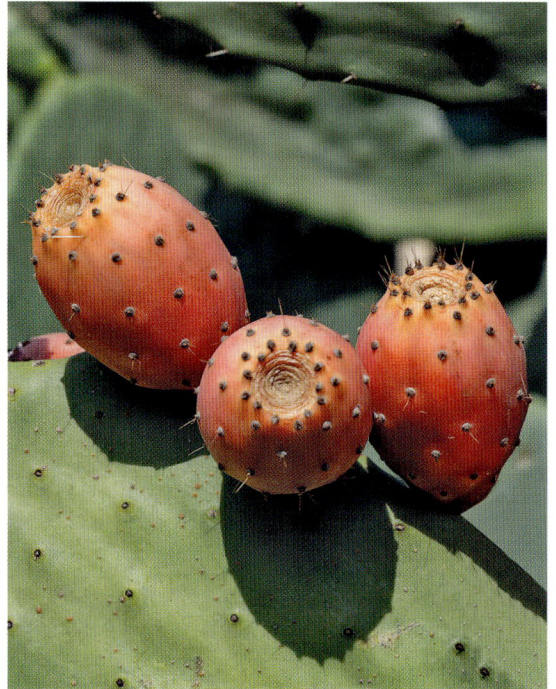

Prickly pears not only displace indigenous vegetation, but also impede the movement of wildlife.

# THREATS TO TREES

Although over-exploitation of forests and deforestation have become significant concerns globally, most of southern Africa is savannah or arid land, with very little by way of high-canopy forests, and these areas are not of much interest to logging or agricultural companies. The threats to our trees are somewhat different and usually take the form of botanical pollution and bush encroachment.

Botanical pollution is the result of exotic invasive species (grasses, sedges, reeds, shrubs, trees) that establish themselves in pristine areas and then start dominating indigenous plant life. Examples of invasive problem plants are: syringa (*Melia azedarach*), jacaranda (*Jacaranda mimosifolia*), castor-oil bush (*Ricinus communis*), lantana (*Lantana camara*), starbur (*Acanthospermum* species), American agave (*Agave americana*), queen-of-the-night (*Cereus jamacaru*), pepper tree (*Schinus molle*), and a number of *Opuntia* species, but there are many more, including a number of grasses.

Alien plant invasions can result in indigenous species being suppressed or displaced, to the point of local extinction. They may also negatively affect indigenous species diversity. Botanical pollution is not only a regional problem; increased international traffic and trade has turned this into an international headache. It now seems impossible to rid any country of alien invasive species. We should, however, limit the trend as best we can – and learn to manage those species that are now, unfortunately, permanent features of our world.

Bush encroachment presents another major conservation headache, especially on cattle ranches that consist essentially of grasslands with a variable density of trees and shrubs. Under ideal conditions, the grasses, trees, shrubs and animals all exist in harmony. However, mainly as a result of overgrazing, some indigenous tree species increase in density to such an extent that they suppress and displace almost all other vegetation. As a consequence, the once open savannah is replaced by an impenetrable mass of bushes (some with thorns) that seriously reduce the carrying capacity of the land for livestock and game. Some of the main culprits are black thorn (*Senegalia mellifera*), wild-syringa (*Burkea africana*), various raisin bushes (*Grewia* species), silver clusterleaf

(*Terminalia sericea*), common corkwood (*Commiphora pyracanthoides*) and sicklebush (*Dichrostachys cinerea*), but others such as mopane (*Colophospermum mopane*), red bushwillow (*Combretum apiculatum* subsp. *apiculatum*) and some of the guarri (*Euclea*) trees can also become invasive.

Like alien plant invasion, bush encroachment is not a uniquely southern African problem, and results from our ever-expanding human populations with ever-growing numbers of livestock. Fortunately, bush encroachment can be combated by physical or mechanical means or herbicides, or sometimes even with fire.

South Africa's few evergreen forests are not free of risk and trees like matumi (*Breonadia salicina*) and Outeniqua yellowwood (*Afrocarpus falcatus*) have been subjected to much over-exploitation. Larger forest complexes like the Knysna and Tsitsikamma forests are reasonably well managed and timber extraction is well regulated. In the more densely populated rural and coastal areas, however, illegal felling of trees, including forest trees and protected tree species, has increased significantly over the past three decades. The riverine forests and woodlands of Limpopo and Mpumalanga and the coastal forests of KwaZulu-Natal and the Eastern and Western Cape have been particularly affected, with the felling of matumi trees, in particular, causing the disappearance of rare riverine forest habitat. Much clearance is taking place for changed land uses, as well as trees being felled for a variety of purposes, or dying from the over-harvesting of their bark and roots for medicinal purposes.

Of the trees protected under the National Forests Act of 1998 and provincial ordinances, a handful of species are under serious threat. The pepperbark tree (*Warburgia salutaris*) was threatened by over-harvesting, and a project undertaken by South African National Parks, in collaboration with SAPPI, the Agricultural Research Council and the South African National Biodiversity Institute, has been highly successful in keeping populations stable. Thousands of seedlings propagated at Skukuza Indigenous Nursery have provided traditional healers with cultivated plants to grow, thereby reducing pressure on wild populations. The tree is now considered Vulnerable

Camel thorn trees are protected in South Africa because they are ecologically important in the habitat where they occur.

according to the Red List of South African Plants, an improvement from its previous status as Endangered.

Another tree under pressure of over-exploitation is Bushman's tea (*Catha edulis*), the leaves of which are used as a stimulant, also called *Khat*. This drug is mostly used by people from northeast Africa, but the use has spread to some local communities in the Eastern Cape. The harvesting and use of the leaves of this protected tree species are prohibited under narcotics legislation.

Many protected tree species, for example, camel thorn (*Vachellia erioloba*), which is used for braai wood, are actually abundant. These species are listed as protected because they play an important ecological role in local habitats. Research has shown that in the habitats where the adult trees of keystone species like camel thorn disappear, the diversity of fauna and ground flora is diminished significantly. Habitats are impoverished by the loss of ecosystem services contributed by larger trees, such as their microclimate impact, nesting possibilities and food for wildlife.

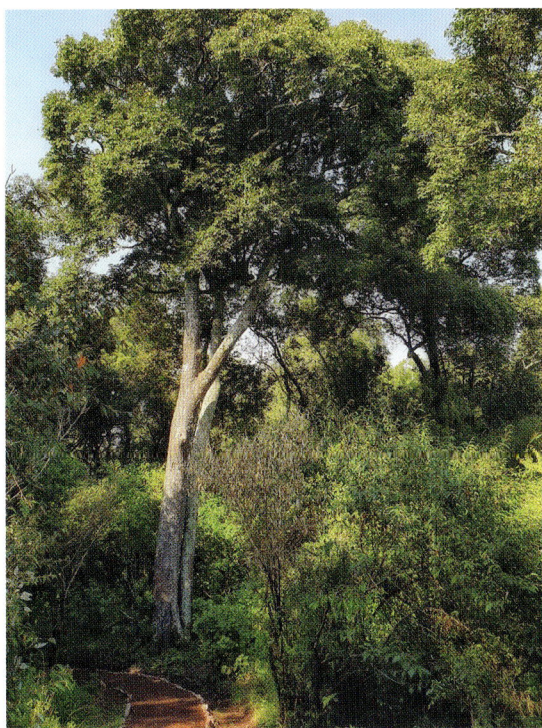

*The pepperbark tree is threatened by over-harvesting.*

## INVASIVE BORERS

At the time of writing, a major new threat for the country's trees is emerging: the spread of the invasive 'polyphagous shot hole borer' (*Euwallacea fornicatus*), an insect from Asia. The 2mm-long beetle burrows deep into living trees to make a nest for its eggs. It then cultivates a symbiotic fungus, *Fusarium euwallacea*, to feed its larvae. The effect of the fungus is to block the movement of water and nutrients in the vascular tissues of the trees. This causes die-back of the trees and, eventually, their death. Once matured, the larvae make their way out of the tree through the holes that resemble gunshot holes.

No cure or solution for this infestation has been found yet. Pesticides are ineffective because the beetle bores too deeply into the tree. Bringing in the beetle's natural predator – a Vietnamese wasp – is also too risky as it is not known what additional problems this may cause. Currently the only solution is to cut down infested trees and burn them. A single tree can host up to 100,000 beetles and infested trees have been observed from Mpumalanga to the western and southern Cape. This is a major threat to our floral heritage, as it seems that apart from exotic species such as oak trees (*Quercus* species), more than 30 indigenous tree species are particularly susceptible to this pest.

In towns like George and Knysna, where oak tree lanes have been decimated by this pest, indigenous trees, with some exceptions, generally fared better.

The little beetle has also spread to California, USA, Israel and Australia.

*Adult polyphagous shot hole borer*

Thorns, such as these on an umbrella thorn, deter or limit browsing.

## HOW TREES DEFEND THEMSELVES

While trees lack a central nervous system and, as far as we can detect, cannot feel pain, they are far from senseless and defenceless life forms. Trees may appear passive, fixed in one place, but they are constantly on the alert and have developed a multitude of defence mechanisms to deter potential threats to their survival. Trees' defence systems can be physical or chemical. As in all animal and plant species, this is a result of millions of years of mutations over countless generations that have survived external threats and succeeded in reproducing.

### PHYSICAL DEFENCE

A first barrier of defence is the outer structure of a tree and many species have developed physical defences to keep danger at bay. Some species have evolved thorns, spines or stinging hairs to ward of browsing herbivorous animals that seek out the leaves for their nutritious sugar and mineral content. Thorns may be present on trunks and branches, making access to leaves difficult, and spines may occur on leaf margins. The numerous needle-like spines on certain *Euphorbia* species are a significant deterrent to herbivores.

Some trees grow in a way that makes it physically difficult for browsers to reach the leaves. The umbrella shape of several African tree species not only maximises exposure of leaves to sunlight, but also limits browsing to taller animals and offers access to leaves at the edge of the umbrella only.

The leaves themselves can provide a barrier. A thick waxy cuticle, or outer layer, prevents penetration of the surface by insects and pathogens, and also helps to minimise the grip of insects. And while most leaves start out as soft and fragile, many harden as they develop and become unpalatable to browsing mammals.

Another physical line of defence is the bark of a tree, which may grow very thick and become reinforced, protecting more vulnerable inner parts and serving as an impenetrable barrier.

## CHEMICAL DEFENCE

Trees also have defences within their own tissues: chemicals that can prevent or reduce the extent to which animals feed on them. Some trees can increase the concentrations of toxic compounds such as tannins in their system, which make their leaves bitter and unpalatable. These tannins can also decrease the efficiency of a herbivore's digestive system, making it difficult for the animal to gain the nutrients it needs.

Although the softer parts of many trees are a ready food source for browsing mammals, it is insects (which outnumber humans alone by 200,000,000:1) that consume most plant matter. Insects are mostly undeterred by thorns and prickles because they can easily crawl between them, so this calls for defences on a cellular level. Specialised cells on the surface of some trees can instantaneously release unpleasant chemicals when they are threatened, making the taste unpalatable or even poisonous to the invader. Idioblasts are some of the most effective of these specialised cells. When surface cells are broken, idioblasts are able to release barbed crystals and toxins into the mouths of hungry attackers. These idioblasts cover much of the surface of the plant, acting as death traps for tiny herbivores.

Another form of chemical defence comes into play when, in response to an attack by insects, certain tree species release powerful airborne compounds that attract the predators of the attacking insects, luring them to the defence and protection of the tree. Wasps, dragonflies, lizards and small birds may be attracted by the released compound to the plant that is being eaten. Finding their preferred prey, they quickly dispose of the insects doing the damage, serving as allies to the affected tree.

Within the forest environment, it appears that a sort of chemical 'arms race' is fought by the plants and their insect pests. In response to chemicals that the plant produces to deter them, the insects evolve detoxification mechanisms as a means of overcoming the poisons. The plants, in turn, evolve new chemical defences. In time, the insects' remarkable adaptive abilities overcome these too, and so the escalation process continues. Consequently, there are ever more specialised relationships evolving between insects and plants.

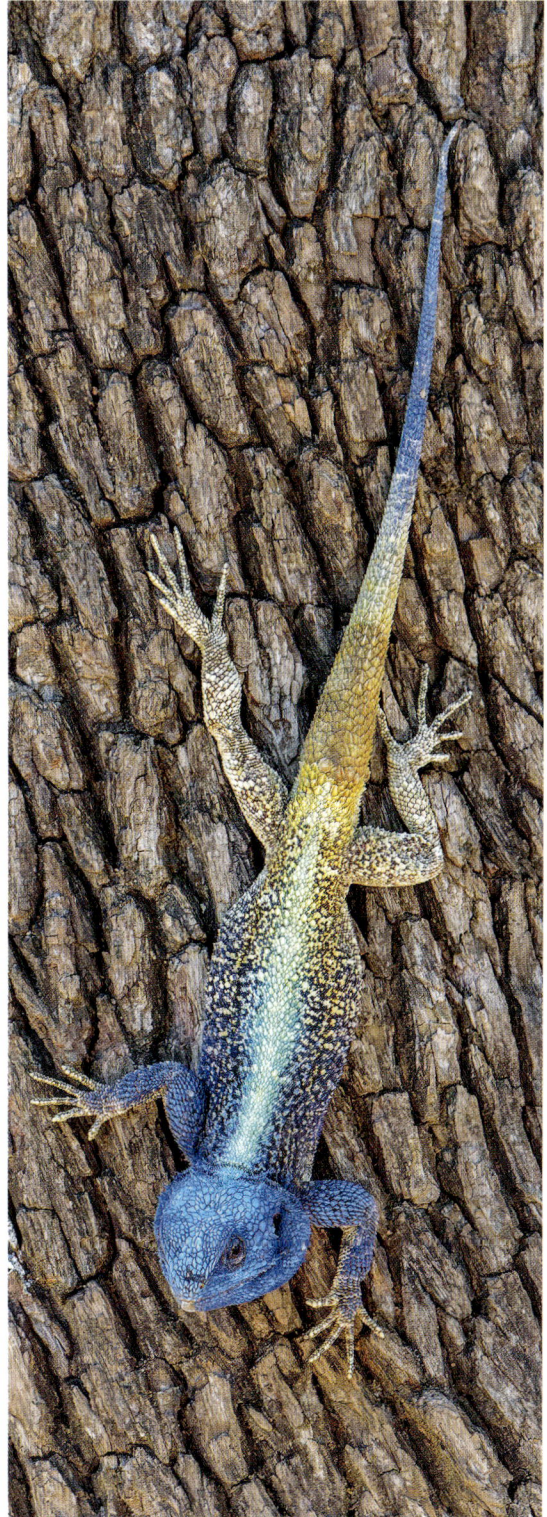

*Tree agamas feed on insects that are harmful to trees.*

## COLLABORATION

Another means of chemical defence is the remarkable ability of trees to communicate with other trees and plants. When attacked by browsers or insect pests, or when subjected to stressful conditions such as drought or microbial infection, trees may warn other trees of an impending crisis by releasing volatile organic compounds that cause physiological reactions in nearby plants. Recent experiments have shown that trees also communicate through chemicals released by their roots and even via networks of symbiotic fungi.

Tree species have developed individual mechanisms of defence, but they also collaborate with other species to defend the greater whole. In a forest, for example, different species growing side by side will produce different defensive chemicals. A herbivore may safely eat the leaves of one tree, but moving on to the species growing alongside it, may well be poisoned when eating its leaves. The forest thus has a communal defence strategy that will prevent even a small area of forest from being devasted.

### Trees and ants

Certain *Vachellia* thorn trees are known to house and feed aggressive stinging ants. The stinging little soldiers make their homes inside the trees' swollen thorns and feed on food specially produced by the plant for them. In exchange for housing and food, the ants will savagely defend their hosts to the death against all enemies, be they animal, vegetable or fungus. They even snip off the foliage of any other plants that happen to encroach upon their tree's 'personal space'. In experiments carried out to determine the effects of removing the ant colonies, the trees died, showing their dependence on the ants for defence and survival.

LEFT *The knob thorn's branches and trunk are studded with prominent knobs, which may deter elephants from damaging the bark.*

ABOVE *Some* Vachellia *thorn trees are host to stinging ants, which feed on the trees and defend them against herbivores and fungi.*

# FIGHTING BACK WITH CODIT

Though trees are unable to repair tissue damage, they have evolved a way of dealing with infections and diseases know as 'compartmentalisation of decay in trees' or CODIT. They have an amazing ability to generate new cells, and wall off any damaged or sick part from the living tissues.

The process begins with the tree minimising the spread of damage by strengthening the walls between cells. The cambium layer then changes the types of cells it produces around the damaged area so as to block it off from the surrounding vascular tissues – the beginning of the compartmentalisation process. The cells also produce more compounds to resist and potentially stave off the spread of troublesome microbes. Trees under attack continue to grow, especially around the infected or damaged compartment. If the tree is healthy enough, this growth will outpace further infection. Whether they are bacteria, fungi or viruses, microbes need living tissue to survive. By sealing off the affected area and saturating it with compounds that kill living tissues, the tree cuts off the food supply to the disease-causing organism. Only when the tree is severely weakened, will the infection outpace the growth of the tree.

CODIT is, however, not a cure-all. If a tree is not killed outright, it can face decades of repeated infections. Even if it is able to successfully fight these off, the accumulation of dead tissues over time can girdle and kill the tree.

*African hoopoes do not excavate their own hollows in trees. Since tree cavities do not heal and fill, these birds are able to reuse nests made by other species.*

*After a branch is pruned, fresh growth takes place around the damaged area, closing the wound to an extent. The scar, however, will remain.*

*A recently discovered dwarf suffrutex (underground tree),* Ochna babertonensis *was described in 2018.*

## UNDERGROUND TREES

Among the most remarkable botanical phenomena are underground trees. Also known as 'geoxylic suffrutices', underground trees are particularly common on the highveld plateaus of South Africa and on the plains of the Tongaland–Pondoland region of the Indian Ocean coastal belt. They are also known from the Kalahari sands of the Upper Zambezi basin, the central and eastern sandy plains of Angola, and in parts of Namibia, Botswana, Zimbabwe and Mozambique.

Almost all trees have roots that burrow through the soil in search of nutrients and water, and so, to some degree, can be said to live underground. However, underground trees are different. The only visible parts of the tree are green twigs and leaves that emerge from the ground. These twigs and leaves may constitute the entire canopy of a single vast plant whose large woody structures with branched networks of stems occupy a considerable area underground. The advantage for the tree of having the trunk and most branches underground is protection and safety from threats above ground. Those parts of the tree that are exposed – the above-ground shoots – are so small and thin that it does not matter if they are occasionally lost to wildfires, winter frost or even browsing. They can regrow quickly while the underground growth keeps spreading wider and wider. To top it all, the trees are largely drought resistant.

Underground trees are clonal, meaning that they reproduce asexually, without seed. They produce offspring by vegetative cloning – a form of reproduction in which a new plant grows from a part of the parent plant.

The oldest living trees in the world are underground trees. Being mostly impervious to above-ground threats, underground trees can reach ages well in excess of 10,000 years. The major threat to their longevity are pathogens. As clones, they lack the genetic diversity required to fight new diseases.

There are more than 200 species of underground trees in southern Africa, occurring in 39 families. Two of the best-known species are the aptly named ploughbreaker (*Erythrina zcyhcri*) and poison lcaf (*Dichapctalum cymosum*). Other examples include wild grape (*Lannea edulis* var. *edulis*) and sand apple (*Parinari capensis* subsp. *capensis*).

Poison leaf is found in the northern parts of South Africa and can cause lethal poisoning of livestock. Sand apple and poison leaf bear a superficial resemblance to one another and are frequently found in the same area.

Eland's bean (*Elephantorrhiza elephantina*) is a perennial suffrutex or subshrub; its unbranched, unarmed stems represent the canopy of a much larger underground tree. The leaves are dull green and doubly compound with 12–17 opposite or subopposite pairs of leaflets.

**TOP RIGHT** *Poison leaf is regarded as a toxic shrub, causing poisoning in livestock. It poses a major problem for stock farmers.*

**MIDDLE RIGHT** *Like other underground trees, the wild grape has a large subterranean rootstock. The fruit is edible and, in traditional communities, the roots are used to treat a range of maladies.*

**BOTTOM RIGHT** *Growing above ground, the simple branches and leaves of the sand apple can form a dense 'forest'.*

A quaking aspen forest in Utah, USA, comprises some 47,000 genetically identical trees.

# THE OLDEST AND LARGEST UNDERGROUND TREES

The oldest living trees in the world are underground trees. A stand of Huon pines (*Lagarostrobos franklinii*) at Mount Read in Tasmania is claimed to be more than 10,000 years old. Each of the trees is a genetically identical male that has reproduced vegetatively. None of the visible trees in the stand is anywhere near the age of 10,000 years, but the stand itself as a single organism has lived that long. The next oldest known living clonal tree is a Norway spruce (*Picea abies*) on the Fulufjället Mountain in Dalarna province in Sweden – carbon dating has shown it to be 9,550 years old.

In the Fish Lake National Forest, Utah, USA, there is a quaking aspen (*Populus tremuloides*) that covers some 43 hectares (107 acres) and appears as approximately 47,000 trees. Each of the apparently individual trees in the grove is genetically identical and shares the same massive lateral root system. It is likely one of the world's largest living organisms.

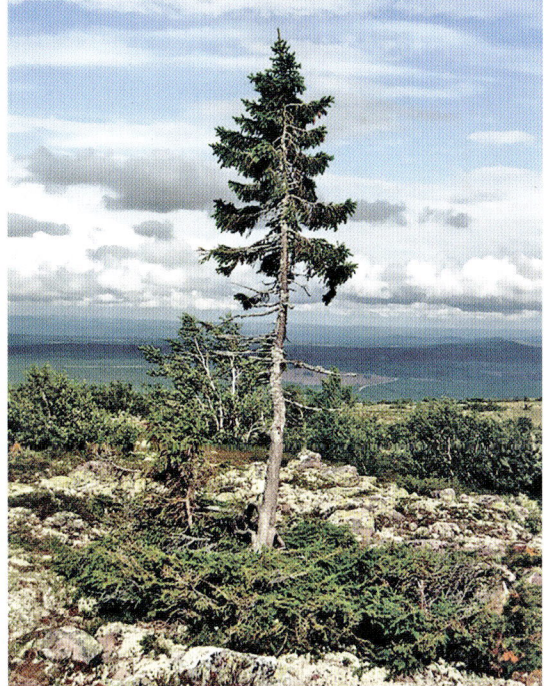

ABOVE *The second-oldest known living clonal tree is a Norway spruce.*

# MYSTICAL, MAGICAL AND CEREMONIAL TREES

There seems to be a direct relationship between trees and a sense of human well-being. Countless research projects have investigated this relationship, indicating that the sight of trees or shrubs evokes a deep unconscious response in us. Various studies show a range of outcomes and benefits of exposure to trees: a sense of calm, stress relief, positive and creative thinking, more rapid recovery from illness and reduced crime in neighbourhoods.

This connection between humans and trees goes back to the earliest times, and there is hardly a culture that does not attach some form of symbolic meaning to these plant forms. Trees are aesthetically pleasing, even majestical, and through the ages have inspired awe and admiration, serving as symbols of beauty, hope, life, protection and wisdom.

As elsewhere in the world, in southern Africa individual species are associated with different traditional and cultural practices, as well as medicinal uses, and these trees are thus bearers of localised meanings, significance and knowledge. Trees play a role in courtship, fertility and hunting rituals; ensure good fortune and good health; help to ward off evil; and are believed to influence natural phenomena such as rain, lightning, hail and drought.

Success in courtship can be ensured by the use of love charms or concoctions in which ingredients from trees such as wildpear (*Dombeya rotundifolia*), lavender feverberry (*Croton gratissimus* var. *gratissimus*), wild-pomegranate (*Burchellia bubalina*), spikethorn (*Gymnosporia buxifolia*), false horsewood (*Hippobromus paucifolus*) and woolly caperbush (*Capparis tomentosa*) are used.

Zulu traditions use the roots of the tasselberry (*Antidesma venosum*) in fertility medicine, while Xhosa traditions favour the jacketplum (*Pappea capensis*) for this purpose. Zulu and Tsonga people use the marula (*Sclerocarya birrea*) in cleansing ceremonies before marriage. This tree is venerated for its abundant fruits and has a place in many rituals.

In some communities, conception and birth are linked to certain tree species. The fruits of wild figs (*Ficus* species) and marula are widely used as fertility charms. The fruits of mustard trees (*Salvadora australis* and *S. persica*) are also believed to promote fertility. So are the large fruits of the baobab (*Adansonia digitata*).

The sex of unborn babies, it is believed, can be determined by the use of powdered marula bark. Furthermore, newborn baby girls are washed in water warmed on a fire of marula wood to ensure that they will be soft and kind. Boys are washed in water warmed on a fire made with Lebombo-wattle (*Newtonia hildebrandtii*) wood to make them strong and tough. In parts of Limpopo, boys are washed in water warmed on a fire of baobab bark in order for them to become great and mighty.

Trees such as puzzlebush (*Ehretia rigida*), sjambokpod (*Cassia abbreviata*), silver clusterleaf (*Terminalia sericea*), glossyleaf (*Rhamnus prinoides*) and Cape-chestnut (*Calodendrum capense*) all play a role as hunting charms or for materials for pre-hunt ceremonies.

Many people believe that good sleep and pleasant dreams can be ensured magically. Zulu charms use umzimbeet (*Millettia grandis*) and also Lebombo-wattle. White-milkwood (*Sideroxylon inerme* subsp. *inerme*) prevents bad dreams and dwaba-berry (*Monanthotaxis caffra*) is a charm against them.

Thorny trees, such as long-haired caperbush (*Capparis sepiaria*), woolly caperbush (*C. tomentosa*), common hook thorn (*Senegalia caffra*), buffalo-thorn (*Ziziphus mucronata*) and umtiza (*Umtiza listeriana*), are thought to have protective properties. The poisonous Maputaland ordealtree (*Erythrophleum lasianthum*) is believed to ward off black magic and to drive away hallucinations. Tree-fuchsia (*Halleria lucida*) is a charm against evil, as is the bark of sweet thorn (*Vachellia karroo*). The violet-tree (*Securidaca longepedunculata*) is regarded as a powerful charm against sorcerers and bad ancestral spirits. The roots of the broad-pod false-thorn (*Albizia forbesii*) and

In parts of southern Africa, the camel thorn tree is valued for its medicinal properties. The San are recorded as having used its roots to treat and chest and heart ailments. In other societies, the tree is regarded as sacred and may not be used by common people.

BOTTOM LEFT
A Zulu tradition is to use the smoke of burning green white-stinkwood leaves to deter enemies.

tamboti (*Spirostachys africana*) are also used to make an infusion to dispel evil spirits. In Zululand, cycads are planted near homesteads to protect them from harm.

Also in Zululand, the bark and roots of the greenthorn (*Balanites maughamii*), together with those of other plants, are used in a ritual to ward off evil spirits, while Ndebele traditions make use of the sourplum (*Ximenia caffra*). In some parts, medicine made from cheesewood (*Pittosporum viridiflorum*) is used for protection. The camel thorn (*Vachellia erioloba*) is also thought by some to provide protection against enemies and wild animals.

Crops can be protected by a number of different 'good' trees. Pegs made from the wood of these trees are often driven into the ground around fields of crops as protection. White stinkwood (*Celtis africana*) is one such tree. Smoke from the green leaves is also used to chase away enemies. A piece of baobab bark is often planted in fields to ensure a good crop.

Trees are also commonly used in rainmaking ceremonies and rituals. Examples are African-wattle (*Peltophorum africanum*), broom karee (*Searsia erosa*) and puzzlebush. Other trees such as buffalo-thorn, umtiza, glossyleaf, woolly caperbush and small-leaved willow (*Salix mucronata*) are used for protection against lightning when the rains eventually come. On the other hand, trees like black monkey thorn (*Senegalia burkei*), wild peach (*Kiggelaria africana*) and mopane are believed to attract lightning. The same goes for camel thorn and Lebombo-wattle, despite all their otherwise good properties.

Some trees are never called on for utility purposes; this is for varying reasons and differs from place to place. Some regard the wild custard-apple (*Annona senegalensis*) and the anatree (*Faidherbia albida*) as sacred and not to be cut or utilised. Other examples are shepherd's tree (*Boscia albitrunca*), velvet sweetberry (*Bridelia mollis*), black thorn (*Senegalia mellifera*), silver clusterleaf, and guarris like *Euclea schimperi*, *E. natalensis* and *E. divinorum*. Red-stinkwood (*Prunus africana*) is believed to be a sorcerer's tree. Probably the most feared tree in the country is Zululand's deadman's-tree (*Euphorbia cupularis*), with its highly toxic latex. It is believed by some that one can die by just looking at or getting too close to the tree.

# THE 'HEARTBEAT' OF TREES

While it would be absurd to suggest that trees have a heart, the idea that they have some kind of 'heartbeat' is not as far-fetched as people might think. Scientists have recently found that trees do in fact have a special type of regular internal pulse that can superficially be likened to the rhythmic beating of an animal's heart.

Researchers from Denmark and Hungary discovered this phenomenon by using terrestrial laser scanning to survey the nocturnal movement of 22 different types of trees. They observed that the canopies of trees seemed to change shape at night. The results, published in 2017, showed that all the test species underwent nocturnal movement, but that only seven had 12-hour 'sleep' cycles that involved the lowering and lifting of branches – up to 10cm in some cases.

It is well established that trees enter a 12-hour circadian cycle in response to light, a behaviour sometimes referred to as 'sleep motion'. During this time, they are believed to conserve energy by lowering their branches, which would otherwise be angled towards the sun. The branches of some species droop by about 1cm after sunset, before being raised after sunrise, with the movement possibly driven by changes in the tree's internal water pressure.

However, more remarkably, the scientists discovered that each of the species in the study experienced small pulses that create periodic, but smaller, movements throughout the night. These movements occur over shorter cycles, between two and six hours. Changes in movement were very slow, and in some instances measured only 1cm. In explaining the findings, the authors suggest that a type of 'pumping' mechanism is causing the water pressure inside the tree's tissues to change periodically, and that water is moved in pulses between parts of the organism – all of which suggests that movement and water transport in trees are more complex than originally thought.

# TREES AND RELIGION

For thousands of years, trees have stood at the heart of civilisations, and stories about them have shaped societies, their beliefs and their relationship to the cosmos and nature itself. The tree as a metaphor for life – and the interconnectedness of all living things – is a central feature of many religions, spiritual traditions and mythologies across the world.

In the Christian tradition, the first book of the Bible, Genesis, refers to the Tree of Life and the Tree of Knowledge of Good and Evil, both of which grew in the garden of Eden. Once Adam and Eve, the first humans said to have been created by God, ate from the Tree of Knowledge, they were expelled from the garden and prevented from eating from the Tree of Life, the source of immortality. The Bible mentions trees more than 200 times, often assigning a spiritual meaning to them.

The reference to trees and their association with life, death or immortality is not unique to Christianity. In fact, this concept is found in other sacred works, including the Quran, the Kabbalah and Buddhist and Hindu scriptures.

According to the Quran, a sacred tree, the Tuba, grows in Paradise, its branches representing a link between the righteous on Earth and heaven above. *Tuba* roughly translates as 'a beautiful place for those who believe and work righteousness'. Other trees of religious significance in Islam are the date palm tree and the olive tree.

In Buddhism, it is under a wild fig tree, the sacred Bodhi tree, that the Buddha meditated and attained Enlightenment. Descendants of the original fig tree are found in India and other parts of the world, including one that was planted in the botanical garden at the University of Pretoria.

In Hindu religious texts, trees are presented as living beings, with a conscience and the ability to experience feelings such as happiness. The fig tree, in particular, is one of the most sacred. Known as the peepal tree in India, it is associated with three Hindu divinities: Brahma, Vishnu and Shiva.

The story of trees is central to many other ancient belief systems. For example, the Sumerian, Babylonian and Assyrian civilisations, which dominated Mesopotamia between 3100 BC and 539 BC, all believed in a Tree of Life growing in the centre of Paradise, guarded by a snake and eagle-headed gods and priests. The ancient Egyptians are also known to have revered certain trees, particularly the sycamore fig and the date palm, and in ancient Greece the olive tree was regarded as a symbol of peace. In Norse cosmology, Yggdrasil, an enormous ash tree, stands at the centre of the universe. Yggdrasil is linked to both life and death, and connects all nine worlds of the universe, including earth, the underworld and heaven.

In the Americas, Mesoamerican civilisations, notably the Mayans, Aztecs, Izapans and Olmecs, left numerous depictions of trees. One such tree, the kapok or ceiba tree, was believed to have provided a link to the spiritual world, with its thick vines enabling souls to ascend to and enter this realm.

In Australasia, some Australian aboriginal societies believe trees to be, like humans, beings that emerge from the earth, and in their mythologies there are many examples of humans transforming into trees. In some tribes, a sacred plant is associated with each clan, and the fruits of this tree are not consumed.

In Africa, various societies have assigned mystical and spiritual powers to elements of the natural world, for example, trees, forests, rivers, lakes and the sky. These natural features are said to be inhabited by spirit beings – either the ancestors or non-human beings. These envoys of the spirit world can be benevolent or malicious, and need to be treated with reverence.

*The Tree of Life is recalled in this ancient Mesopotamian artefact.*

# PLANT INTELLIGENCE

Plants are capable of highly sophisticated behaviours that to some might seem similar to human functions – such as learning, memory, communication, problem-solving and intelligence.

- Plants are able to perceive the environment and respond by adjusting their form, the way in which they function, and aspects such as leaf shape and size.
- Plants react to certain wavelengths of light. They have ways of telling whether if it is day or night, how much light is available and where the light is coming from. As a result, shoots grow towards light and roots normally grow away from light.
- Plants are aware of seasonal changes, and know when to flower, produce fruit and discard their leaves.
- Plants have complex ways of communicating threats.
- In certain contexts, plants actively compete for resources, both above and below ground level.

But whether one can describe the functions that plants perform in terms usually restricted to human behaviour is a topic under debate. Some researchers have pointed out that plants can 'make decisions' that will affect their growth and ensure their survival. They can sample and use many varied parameters, such as humidity, light, gravity, temperature, nutrient patches, microorganisms in the soil, and availability of resources to 'make decisions' and modify their growth accordingly. They seem capable of self-recognition and territoriality, and can distinguish between interlopers and their own kind, enabling them to take suitable action against intruders and competitors. They can differentiate between vibrations caused by herbivores and those caused by insects or wind, thereby triggering appropriate chemical defences. They also communicate with their own and other species by releasing volatile hormones (ethylene) into the air. Some can even communicate by means of 'clicking' noises. In a sense, plants can see, smell, hear and feel.

Examples of these behaviours abound. During a drought in the early 1990s it was found that many kudu on game farms in the South African bushveld were dying, even though they clearly still had enough browse available; in fact, many died with a full stomach. A research team under Professor Wouter van Hoven from the University of Pretoria discovered that when a tree or shrub is being browsed, it increases the tannin levels in its leaves significantly – to such an extent that the browser is unable to digest the food. The study focused on *Vachellia* and *Senegalia* trees, but there are many other species suspected of employing this defence mechanism, such as *Colophospermum mopane* and species of *Combretum, Albizia, Commiphora* and *Searsia.*

The research team also found that when a tree is beaten with a stick, or browsed by an animal, the tannin levels in the *surrounding* trees increase. The trees have not only developed a remarkable defence mechanism to over-browsing, but they also seem able to communicate 'danger' to their neighbours by releasing ethylene.

Professor Suzanne Simard of the University of British Columbia has found that trees share information and nutrients through a network of thread-like fungi, called mycorrhizas that envelop and connect their roots. She likes to refer to this network as the 'wood-wide web'. These mycorrhizal filaments penetrate the soil, like fibre-optic cables, to extract water and nutrients on behalf of the trees. In exchange, they receive sugars made by the trees through photosynthesis. They are also able to transmit chemical alarm signals from one tree to another, thereby assisting in the distribution of information about threats such as browsing antelope, insects or other dangers. Furthermore, they are able to differentiate between threats, and adopt the most appropriate defence mechanism for each one. For example, the responses to a human breaking off a branch and an animal browsing the leaves are different: in the case of the former, the tree will seal off the break, but in the latter, poison in the leaves will act to deter the animal.

Simard's research has led to multiple discoveries about the subterranean workings of trees, and has spawned new lines of enquiry into the life of trees. If trees can 'learn' and 'remember', as some believe they do, we may have been misunderstanding and underestimating these majestic plants through the ages. This 'intelligence' may even give them the ability to adapt to climate change on their own. Could this be the ultimate form of intelligence: the ability to adapt one's life in order to survive? In any event, it seems we may have to rethink our understanding of intelligence – we may have been missing an entire universe of thought happening all around us all the time.

*Schematic depiction of an underground mycelium network*

# PART TWO

# SOUTH AFRICAN TREES

*Fevertrees*

## Family Achariaceae

# WILD PEACH

*Kiggelaria africana*

**A:** wildeperske **NS:** mphahlašilo **SS:** lekhatsi
**V:** mufhaṯa-vhufa **X:** umkhokhokho **Z:** isiklalu

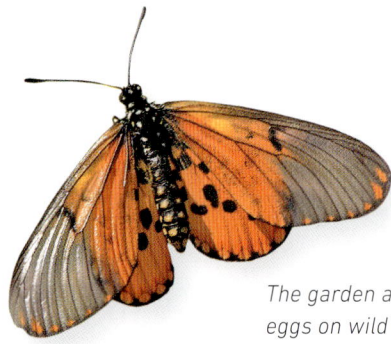

*The garden acraea lays its eggs on wild peach leaves.*

*Kiggelaria:* named after Franz Kiggelaer (1648–1722), a gardener and botanist from The Hague in the Netherlands; *africana:* 'from Africa'

This attractive tree occurs in the eastern parts of the country, from Limpopo to the Western Cape, and is well known for attracting butterflies and birds.

It is fast-growing and evergreen to semi-deciduous, with a rounded and spreading crown. Being both drought and frost resistant, the wild peach is a hardy species. It is found along streams and on rocky hills in bushveld and woodland, as well as in coastal and inland forests, where it can reach a height of 20m. The smooth, pale grey bark becomes rough with age.

From August to January, small yellow flowers are borne on separate male and female trees. Female flowers are larger and solitary; male flowers are smaller and borne in clusters. The fruit is a round, hard, knobbly, greenish-yellow capsule that splits open to expose the shiny black seeds in an oily, sticky, bright orange-red coating. The open seedpods form an attractive five-pointed star shape.

Despite its name, the wild peach is not related to the commercially cultivated peach tree. Their leaves are somewhat similar, but those of the wild peach are thicker, stiffer and have a thin coating of hair on the under-surface.

Wild peach leaves contain hydrocyanic acid and are not utilised by game or livestock, but are eaten by the larvae of various butterflies, such as the garden acraea

(*Acraea horta*), dusky-veined telchinia (*Telchinia igola*) and battling glider (*Cymothoë alcimeda*). The larvae can completely defoliate a tree, but as soon as they pupate, the tree bursts back into leaf, fertilised by the larval droppings left behind. Birds that prey on these larvae include cuckoos, such as Klaas's, red-chested, African emerald and black. Several fruit-eating birds, such as Cape robin-chats, Cape rock-thrushes, olive woodpeckers, crowned hornbills, Cape white-eyes, southern boubous and mousebirds are also attracted to the tree. As such, the wild peach is a must for butterfly and bird gardens. It is also a good shade tree.

The pink-brown timber is relatively hard and used for furniture, beams and floorboards. In the past, it was used for wagon wheel spokes.

# WILD PLUM

*Harpephyllum caffrum*

**A:** wildepruim **NS:** mothêkêlê **Z:** umgwenya

*Harpephyllum:* from Greek *harpage* ('hook') and *phullon* ('leaf'); *caffrum:* refers to the former colonial region of Kaffraria, now part of the Eastern Cape

This beautiful tree is often used for ornamental purposes and to attract birds and butterflies. It is a popular street tree in a number of South African towns and cities. With its thick crown and somewhat drooping leaves, the wild plum is a very good shade tree. It is hardy and fast-growing.

This evergreen tree has a roundish crown and can reach 15m in height. It occurs in riverine forests from the Eastern Cape northwards to Limpopo, where it is one of the largest forest species. The main trunk is usually clean, long and straight. Forest specimens may have buttressed roots, and very old trees often have heavily buttressed and deeply grooved trunks. An excellent specimen in Eshowe, KwaZulu-Natal, can be viewed from an aerial boardwalk in the forest subcanopy. The lowest branches are about 16m above the ground!

The bark is smooth and greyish when young, but becomes dark brown and rough as the tree matures. The branches are thick and grow in a candelabra-like formation from the trunk, but can be broken by strong wind. The tree has beautiful dark foliage with the odd red leaf in the crown. The compound, glossy, dark green leaves are distinctly sickle-shaped and crowded towards the ends of branches.

Wild plum trees flower in midsummer, with male and female flowers on separate trees. The insignificant greenish-white flowers are borne near the ends of branches. Larvae of the steel-blue hairtail butterfly (*Anthene definita definita*) live on the flowers and buds. It is also the host plant for a number of moth species.

The fleshy, plum-like fruit ripens from green to bright red and is popular among animals, including bushbabies, monkeys, baboons and forest antelope. Birds such as green pigeons, trumpeter hornbills, turacos, barbets, bulbuls and parrots also eagerly consume it. It can be eaten raw or cooked to make jams and jellies.

The bark and roots are used in various traditional medicines. The reddish wood is heavy, strong, hard and elastic, but not very durable. However, it is quite attractive when polished and can be used to make furniture.

*The fruit ripens from green to bright red. The leaves are sickle-shaped.*

*The isiZulu name,* umgwenya, *means 'resembling the skin of a crocodile', referring to the rough bark.*

# LIVE-LONG

*Lannea discolor*

**A:** dikbas   **NS:** morula-môpšane   **V:** muvhumbu

*Lannea:* from Latin *lana* ('wool'), referring to the dense, woolly hairs that cover young plants; *discolor:* a reference to the tree's distinctive leaves, whose upper and lower surfaces have different colours

*Live-long in autumn.*

Live-long is a typical bushveld tree found in North West, Limpopo and Mpumalanga. Like leadwood (*Combretum imberbe*), knob thorn (*Senegalia nigrescens*) and marula (*Sclerocarya birrea*), it typifies the bushveld landscape.

Its common name derives from its tendency to re-root – even fence posts made from wood have been known to take root and grow again. This deciduous tree rarely exceeds 15m in height, and has a rounded crown. Its leaves are distinctive, the upper surface being green while the lower surface is grey and densely hairy. Leaves turn bright yellow and are shed very early in winter, giving the tree a marula-like appearance for most of winter. However, the trunk is not as straight and thick as that of a marula.

Live-long trees grow on the slopes of mountains and hills, in open woodland and sometimes on termite mounds.

The wood has been used for household utensils and stamping blocks, but does not have much use otherwise. The bark has been used to make twine. Bushpigs, warthogs, monkeys, baboons and birds eat the fruit (which are edible for humans, too), and rodents feed on the seeds.

Family Anacardiaceae

# FALSE-MARULA

*Lannea schweinfurthii var. stuhlmannii*

A: valsmaroela  NS: mmopu  Z: umganunkomo

*schweinfurthii:* named after German botanist Dr Georg August Schweinfurth (1836–1925), who collected several species new to science while travelling in Africa

Though not as impressive as the marula (*Sclerocarya birrea*), the false-marula is an integral part of the bushveld landscape in the northern parts of the country. According to local tradition, a benevolent spirit resides in the tree, affording it the ability to protect and heal.

This deciduous tree or shrub (3–20m in height) has a straight trunk, a spreading but sparse crown and drooping branches. It occurs in woodland or riverine bush. In the winter, when the tree is bare, it can be confused with the marula, which grows in similar habitat.

From November to January, male and female flowers are borne on separate trees. The fruit – deep red to almost black when ripe – is borne in long bunches. They are eaten by bushpigs, monkeys, baboons and various bird species. Browsers, such as giraffe and kudu, eat the leaves, as do elephants, who also eat the twigs, bark, fruits and roots. The tree is also useful to feed cattle and game, who eat both the fresh and dry leaves. Purple dye can be extracted from the leaves and the bark is sometimes used in the tanning of leather. False-marula is fast-growing and can be easily propagated from cuttings and seed. It cannot handle frost.

Family Anacardiaceae

# MARULA

*Sclerocarya birrea* subsp. *caffra*

A: maroela  NS: morula  TG: nkanyi  V: mufula

**PROTECTED IN SOUTH AFRICA**

*Sclerocarya:* from Greek *skleros* ('hard, rough') and *karya* ('walnut'), referring to the hard kernel of the fruit; *birrea:* from the word *birr*, the tree's common name in Senegal

It is difficult to imagine the bushveld landscape without marula trees. This iconic deciduous species is found mostly in open woodland, reaching up to 20m in height, and has a wide, spreading crown. On young trees, the bark is smooth and grey, becoming cracked and flaking on older specimens.

It is probably best known for its popular fruit, which is fleshy and plum-like. Between February and April, the still-green fruit falls to the ground, later turning yellow. It has a pleasant scent and can be made into beer, brandy or liqueur, as well as a delicious jelly and jam. It is rich in vitamin C, containing up to four times as much as an orange. The single woody stone inside the fruit has two or three seeds containing an oily, rich protein. These seeds can be eaten raw or cooked.

Fallen fruits are eagerly eaten by a variety of animals. Elephant are famously fond of marula fruit, but will also eat the tree's bark. Various animals browse on marula leaves, including kudu and eland.

The wood is whitish with a reddish tinge and very light in weight. The coarse texture, however, makes it tough and difficult to work. It has been used for household items from spoons and bowls to grain pestles and drums. The inner bark has been used to make rope.

Family Anacardiaceae

# RESINTREE

*Ozoroa paniculosa* var. *paniculosa*

A: harpuisboom  NS: monoko
V: mubandulakhali  Z: isifico

*Ozoroa:* origin unknown, possibly from Arabic;
*paniculosa:* 'with loose flower clusters'

This species is known to attract numerous pollinating insects when in flower, including bees, ants and wasps. It is a stout, dioecious, evergreen or semi-deciduous tree with a round crown, reaching up to 7m in height. It occurs in deciduous woodland, often on mountain slopes and rocky terrain. The granular bark is dark grey and becomes rough with age. The narrow, simple leaves are bluish grey-green above, with prominent, parallel side veins; the undersides are silvery. Small, scented, creamy white flowers appear in small terminal heads from August to February. The fruits are small, fleshy, kidney-shaped drupes with reddish-brown spots, initially shiny green but turning black when ripe. Insect larvae often parasitise the fruit, feeding on the seeds inside. Elephant and black rhino browse the leaves and branches. The fruit has been used to dye leather.

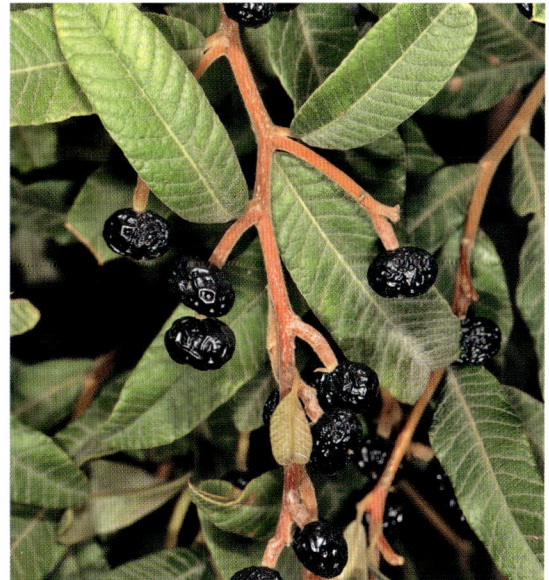

# RED CROWBERRY
## *Searsia chirindensis*

A: bostaaibos  NS: motha-thaa  V: muvhaḓelaphanga  X: umhlakothi

*Searsia:* named after Paul B. Sears (1891–1990), head of the Yale School of Botany; *chirindensis:* refers to Chirinda Forest in Zimbabwe, where it was found and described

Red crowberry can become an impressive, spreading shade tree with lovely reddish autumn foliage. It is a semi-deciduous shrub or tree, up to 10m high, although it may reach heights of 20m in forests. It occurs in a variety of habitats, from open woodland, rocky hillsides, mountain scrub and riverine bush to forest and forest margins – often along streams – and is found throughout the moister eastern parts of southern Africa.

Although the mature tree is spineless, the young and coppicing branches are usually armed with spines. The small yellow-green flowers are borne in clusters at the ends of branches during summer. Dark reddish-brown fruits grow in heavy clusters towards the end of summer, attracting various fruit-eating birds and monkeys. The tree is browsed by black rhino (who also eat the bark), kudu, nyala, bushbuck and red duiker.

The sapwood of the red crowberry is yellowish and the heartwood dark reddish brown. The heartwood is strong and hard and can be used for woodturning, small tools and implements, wagon wood and furniture.

Family Anacardiaceae

# KAREE
*Searsia lancea*

A: karee  NS: motšhakhutšhakhu  SS: mosilabele
TS: mošabêlê  V: mushakaladza  X: umhlakotshane

*lancea:* Latin *lancea* ('light spear, javelin'), referring to the narrow leaves that taper to a point

Karee is a common, popular tree that is particularly well known for its shade, fruit and wood. This graceful, evergreen tree is typically single-stemmed and has branches low down and a dense, round canopy. It rarely exceeds 8m in height. Karee occurs in a variety of habitats throughout most of the northern, central and southern parts of the country. It is often found in open woodland and along drainage lines, rivers and streams.

It produces fruit from September to January. These are small (up to 5mm in diameter), round, slightly flattened and covered with a thin, slightly sour, fleshy layer, which is glossy and yellowish to brown when ripe. The fruits are eaten by birds such as bulbuls, guineafowl and francolins, as well as by humans. The leaves are browsed by kudu and some grazers such as roan and sable antelope. In times of drought, karee can be an important source of food for these animals. Leaves also provide valuable fodder for livestock, though the high tannin content can taint the milk of dairy cows. The small, sweetly scented, greenish-yellow flowers appear in dense clusters and attract bees and other insects. The wood is reddish brown, close-grained, heavy, hard, tough and resistant to termites. It makes good fencing posts and can also be used for bowls, tool handles, bows and even furniture.

Karee is easily propagated from seed or cuttings and is fast-growing. It does not have an aggressive root system. As such, it a popular shade tree for gardens and parks and for hedges or for lining streets. It is a hardy species and resistant to drought and frost.

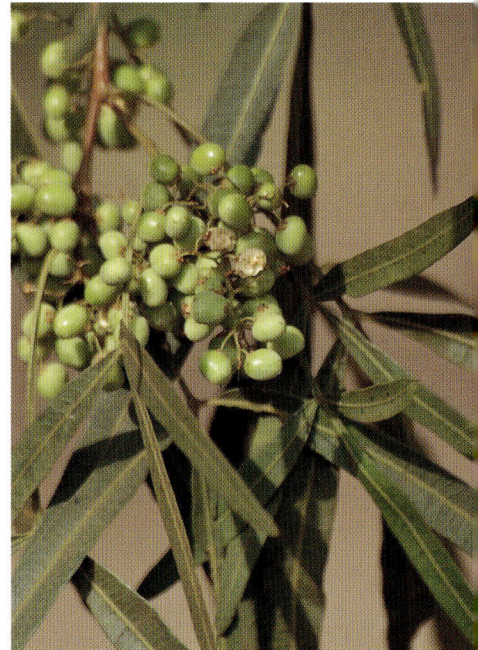

# SHAKAMA PLUM

### *Hexalobus monopetalus* var. *monopetalus*

**A:** shakamapruim, bastersuikerappel **V:** muhuhuma

*Hexalobus:* Greek *hexa* ('six') and *lobos* ('lobe') referring to the six fused petal lobes; ***monopetalus:*** 'with a petal'

This small tree is little known outside its natural distribution range in the northern parts of the country, but stands out owing to its beautiful flower display and delicious fruit, which is relished by monkeys, baboons and birds. As such, this species is also known as the 'baboon's breakfast'.

It is deciduous and slow-growing, with a rounded, dense crown and low branches, which are sometimes prostrate. It occurs in various soil types in low-altitude bush, scrub and stony hillsides – especially *Combretum-Terminalia* scrub, miombo woodland and open woodlands. Where it occurs in forests and relative wet conditions, it may grow up to 9m tall. Under drier conditions, it is much smaller.

The conspicuous, velvety, solitary flowers appear in October, borne as little balls in the leaf axils. Their petals are cream, long, slender and twisted, but not large enough to make individual flowers eye-catching. Nevertheless, when in full bloom in spring, the tree is an attractive sight.

The irregular oblong fruit is borne singly, has up to three cylindrical segments and is sparsely covered in short hairs. It is shiny, fleshy and orange to red when ripe (in summer), sometimes with green veins. Fresh fruit is tasty and can also be used to make jam. The wood is reddish, tough, durable and attractive, with a fine texture, which makes it suitable for ornaments, small utensils, tool handles, bows and gun stocks. It also makes for excellent firewood.

*The ripe fruit is red (left) but unripe fruits are green.*

Family Apocynaceae

# HORNPOD

## *Diplorhynchus condylocarpon*

**A:** horingpeultjieboom  **SH:** mutowa  **TG:** ntsowa
**TS:** moleye  **V:** muṱhowa

*Diplorhynchus:* from Greek *diplos* ('double') and
*rhunchos* ('snout'), referring to the paired beak-like fruit;
*condylocarpon:* from Greek *kondulos* ('knuckle') and
*karpos* ('fruit'), referring to the distinctive shape of the fruit

While relatively unknown outside of the Waterberg region
in Limpopo, where it is common, this tree has many
traditional and medicinal uses and can be planted for
its aroma alone. In Zimbabwe it is known as wild rubber
owing to its milky latex, which forms a soft, rubber-like
substance and is used as glue.

The hornpod tree is deciduous and multi-stemmed, with
a spreading, sparse crown and drooping branches.

This species is quite variable
in appearance and can grow up to 12m in
height, but is often no more than a woody
shrub. Instead of forming stands, scattered
individuals grow on stony hills and mountainous
terrain in hot, dry areas and also in sandy soil in
open woodland.

The trunk is covered with small lenticels and becomes
scaly and rough with age, cracking into small pieces. With
a bit of imagination, it may resemble crocodile skin. The
leaves are opposite, leathery and smooth, ranging in colour
between light green and somewhat darker green. The pale
yellow midrib and lateral veins are conspicuous. Small,

sweetly scented white flowers appear with the new leaves in spring and attract butterflies, bees and birds. The fruit consists of two woody, dark brown follicles with pointed tips and is covered in white lenticels. Each fruit carries two to four compressed, winged seeds.

Various browsers, including black rhino and elephant, eat the leaves. Rhino also eat the fruit, as do antelope. The wood is hard and heavy with a fine grain and is an attractive brown when polished. It is used for carvings and small utensils, such as spoons. Although it would be suitable for making furniture, it is very difficult to find large enough planks for this purpose. Wood from the branches have been used for assegais and arrow shafts.

Hornpod is also a good firewood. The tree is fire resistant and able to withstand repeated burning.

*Mature fruits split to expose yellowish pulp, which contains many seeds.*

# TOADTREE

## *Tabernaemontana elegans*

**A:** paddaboom, buffelbal  **SH:** mukashu
**Z:** umkhahlu

*Tabernaemontana:* named after Jacob Theodor von Bergzabern, a 16th-century herbalist, who Latinised his name to Tabernaemontanus ('hut or tavern in the mountain'); *elegans:* 'elegant' or 'neat'

With its large, glossy leaves and white flowers, this smallish tree has to be regarded as one of the more attractive trees of the subtropical and coastal forests in the eastern parts of South Africa.

The toadtree is deciduous and upright in form, with a rounded crown. It seldom exceeds 10m in height. It is recognised by its corky, pale brown bark with longitudinal fissures, as well as by its fragrant white flowers and unusual fruit.

The common name derives from the leathery to woody fruit, with its green, warty toad-like skin. The fruit is borne in pairs. Each has two lateral ridges and one dorsal ridge. When mature, it splits open along one side, often while still on the tree, displaying the yellowish pulp inside. Embedded in the yellow pulp are numerous small dark brown seeds. The fruit is eaten by humans, baboons, monkeys, black rhino and birds, such as hornbills and barbets.

The timber is whitish in colour, and while it is soft, light and easy to work, it is coarse-grained and does not finish very smoothly. It is used for making spoons, knife handles, bows, building poles and as firewood. The tree's latex is tapped to make birdlime or used as glue for arrowheads. The toadtree is fast-growing, but requires regular watering, needs to be planted in full sun and should be protected against frost. The corky bark makes it relatively resistant to fire.

The town of Lephalale in Limpopo has successfully planted toadtrees to line some of its streets.

# QUININETREE

*Rauvolfia caffra*

A: kinaboom  X: umjelo, umthundisa
Z: umhlambamanzi

## PROTECTED IN SOUTH AFRICA

*Rauvolfia:* named after Leonhart Rauwolf of Augsburg, a 16th-century medical doctor and collector of medicinal plants; *caffra:* refers to the former colonial region of Kaffraria, now in the Eastern Cape

This is an impressive species: graceful and upright, with a tall, straight trunk that reaches up to 30m in height under ideal conditions. The crown is round to upright but also spreading, making it a very attractive tree. It is usually evergreen, but can be semi-deciduous.

The quininetree is found in the eastern parts of South Africa, usually near water in riverine bush, evergreen forest margins, swamp forest and along riverbanks. Away from rivers and streams, this hydrophyte is a sure indicator of ground water.

The leaves, flowers and fruit are eagerly eaten by vervet monkeys, and throughout summer, the ripe fruit also attracts bushbabies and various fruit-eating birds, such as bulbuls, pigeons, barbets and hornbills. Herbivores do not appear to browse this tree, but insects and butterflies visit the flowers, in turn attracting insect-eating birds. Although the quinine is valued as a good bird and butterfly tree, its invasive root system makes it unsuitable for the smaller garden.

The pale cream wood is light and soft, but has been used for fruit boxes, household utensils and furniture. In the past, the bitter latex was used to treat malaria, but was found to be ineffective. It has since been determined that the tree does not contain any quinine, the substance used to treat malaria. The common name has stuck, however.

This tree resembles the matumi (*Breonadia salicina*) but the latter has no milky latex.

# CABBAGETREE

## Cussonia spicata

A: kiepersol  NS: motšhetšhe  SW, X, Z: umsenge

*Cussonia:* named after Pierre Cusson (1727–1783), a professor of botany at the University of Montpellier; *spicata:* 'spike-like', referring to the arrangement of the flowers

The cabbagetree is a strikingly beautiful species with evergreen foliage and an unusual form – it has a much-branched, rounded crown. It is a fast-growing yet relatively long-living.

It occurs on mountain slopes and rocky outcrops and along forest margins, montane grassland and montane forests. It is popular with gardeners and can be seen in parks and gardens throughout the country. It normally grows up to 15m in height, but under ideal conditions (especially along forest margins) it can grow much bigger. The largest known specimen in South Africa, in the Woodbush forest in Limpopo, is 35m high, with a trunk circumference of 11.6m and a crown spread of 22m (pictured opposite). This exceptional specimen is regarded as the fourteenth largest indigenous tree in South Africa and is estimated to be about 2,000 years old.

Cabbagetree bark is grey, thick and corky. The compound leaves are produced toward the ends of branches in large round heads. The leaflets are bluish green.

In the 19th century, the soft, whitish wood was used as brake-blocks on wagons. Today, it does not have much use, though the leaves and roots are still used in some traditional remedies.

Livestock and elephant eat the leaves. Through June to September, the ripe fruits attract bulbuls, turacos, starlings, mousebirds and barbets. It can withstand light frost and does not need a lot of water.

# QUIVERTREE

*Aloidendron dichotomum*

**A:** kokerboom

*Aloidendron:* from Greek *aloe* and *dendron* ('tree');
*dichotomum:* from Greek *dikhotomos* ('cut in half'),
referring to the way the branches fork into two

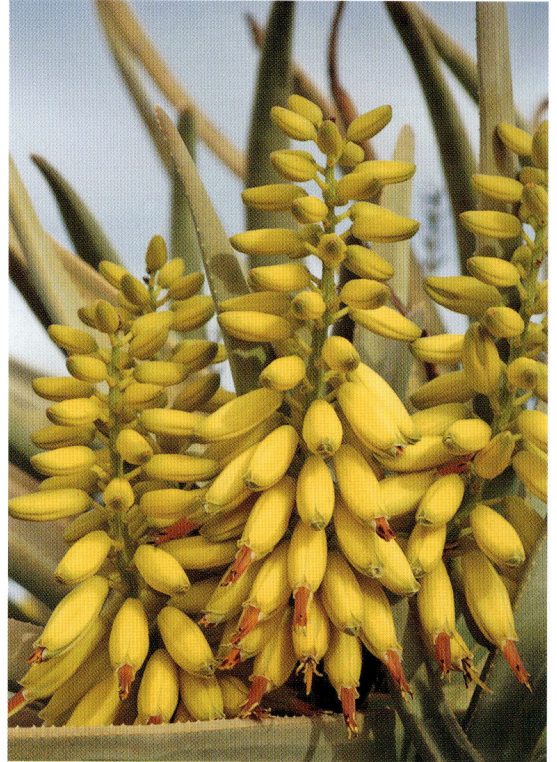

The quivertree is arguably the best-known desert plant in southern Africa, and the national tree of Namibia. This hardy, slow-growing tree aloe can reach 7m in height. The stout trunk, which can reach a metre in diameter, usually tapers from the base to the top, with the first branches appearing about halfway up. The branches fork repeatedly, resulting in a densely rounded crown. The blue-green leaves are borne in small terminal rosettes. The bark on the trunk forms razor-sharp brown scales. A thick layer of white powder on the branches reflects the sun's rays. The tree is drought and frost resistant.

Bright yellow flowers appear in June and July and attract many birds, especially sugarbirds, which feed on the copious nectar. When in flower, it is among the most striking flowering plants in its native Namaqualand and Bushmanland – the dry arid western parts of the country.

The quivertree does not have timber, but rather a soft pulpy, fibrous tissue in the trunk and branches. It is therefore not a true woody tree, but more accurately arborescent (tree-like).

Sociable weavers are known to build their massive nests in the branches of these trees, which are often the only trees available in parts of the arid west.

The name 'quivertree' is derived from the San practice of hollowing out the branches of this tree and using the bark as casing for storing their bows and arrows. It is believed that Governor Simon van der Stel named the tree *kokerboom* ('quiver tree') after observing this practice during an expedition to Namaqualand in 1685.

# GREENTHORN
## *Balanites maughamii*
A: groendoring  SW: umnunu  TG: nulu  Z: ugobandlovu

### PROTECTED IN SOUTH AFRICA

*Balanites:* from Greek *balanos* ('acorn'); *maughamii:* named after R.C.F. Maugham, the British consul in Lourenço Marques (now Maputo), who provided specimens of this tree to Kew Botanical Gardens in 1911

The greenthorn, a fairly common tree in KwaZulu-Natal, is sadly on the decline owing to habitat loss and excessive bark harvesting for the commercial medicinal plant trade in northern KwaZulu-Natal. It is a deciduous or semi-deciduous tree of up to 20m in height, usually with a spreading crown and a remarkably tall, straight trunk. It occurs in bushveld, sand forest, on sandstone outcrops, along riverbanks, near springs and sometimes around pans. The trunk is grey and smooth, and deeply folded and buttressed in large specimens, making it easy to identify.

The flowers are minute, inconspicuous and usually green. They appear in September, borne in the axils of the spines or leaves and occasionally on the spines. Some of the zigzagging branchlets are armed with spines, which are conspicuous and initially green with small brown tips. Elephant have been seen browsing on the branchlets.

Good quality oil can be extracted from greenthorn seeds, but is slightly bitter. This oil burns with a bright flame and the kernels are sometimes used as torches, giving rise to the alternate name, 'torchwood'. Warthogs, baboons, monkeys and antelope eat the date-like fruit. Although rather tasteless, the fruit is edible. These trees are not attacked by borers, making for good quality wood, which is pale yellow-brown. Being hard and heavy, it has been used for knife and implement handles and rifle stocks. The stones of the closely related *B. aegyptiaca* were found in Egyptian tombs, placed there as offerings to the dead.

# SAUSAGETREE

## *Kigelia africana*

**A:** worsboom  **NS:** modukguhlu  **SS:** lekgatsi  **V:** muphatavhafu
**X:** umkokoko  **Z:** umvongothi

*Kigelia:* derived from the tree's local name in Mozambique, *kigeli-keia*; *africana:* 'from Africa'

This tree is well known for its unique, sausage-shaped fruit, which dangles from a long stalk, can be up to half a metre long, and weighs up to 10kg. Elephant and giraffe pluck and eat developing fruit from the tree, and hippo, black rhino and porcupines eagerly feed on fallen mature fruit.

The flowers appear in August, and are unmistakeable: large, trumpet-shaped and wrinkled, with a deep maroon colour. They remain in bloom for up to two months, opening at night, when they are visited and pollinated by epauletted fruit bats. Nectar-feeding birds and *Charaxes* butterflies also frequent the flowers. Unpollinated flowers fall to the ground, where animals such as nyala, bushbuck, greater kudu and baboons are quick to eat them.

Sausagetrees are especially common along rivers. They are fast growing, reaching a height of about 20m. Depending on the rainfall, they can be deciduous, semi-deciduous, or evergreen. The leaves are seldom eaten by browsers, elephant and greater kudu being the exception.

The wood is tough and strong but easy to work, and has been used for fruit boxes, yokes, mortars, drums, tool handles and stools. In the Okavango, the trunks of large sausagetrees are hollowed out and turned into *mokoros* (canoes). The dried fruit can be used as firewood, but the wood itself is not good for this purpose. Sausagetrees are suitable for large gardens and parks in warmer climates, but cannot handle frost.

Family Bombacaceae

# BAOBAB

*Adansonia digitata*

**A:** kremetart  **TS:** mowana  **V:** muvhuyu

**PROTECTED IN SOUTH AFRICA**

*Adansonia:* named by the Swedish 'father of taxonomy' Carl Linnaeus after the French naturalist Michel Adanson (1727–1806), who saw the tree in 1749 in Senegal; *digitata:* from Latin *digitus* ('finger' or 'toe'), referring to the hand-like shape of the leaves

Baobabs are the oldest living organisms in Africa, with large specimens living well over a millennium. Some speculate that the most ancient of these giants are 4,000 years old, but radiocarbon dating estimates the oldest to be just over 2,000 years old.

This magnificent tree grows up to 20m tall. The enormous trunk is swollen with stored water, and can reach a circumference of close to 30m. Young trees are usually single-stemmed, but as the trees grow, they produce new stems from roots or fallen trunks. Over time, these stems grow and fuse with the older ones, producing the mammoth trees we find across Africa. False cavities sometimes develop: large empty spaces between several fused trunks, which have never been filled with wood. Thus, large baobabs often have multiple trunks, fused around a hollow core.

The baobab is deciduous, with hand-sized leaves divided into 5–7 'fingers'. When the branches are bare, they look like roots reaching into the sky – giving rise to folklore, which suggests that the first baobab was planted upside down.

Slow-growing and long-lived, the baobab starts flowering at around 30 years of age. Only a few of its large, white flowers open at a time, blooming for just one night between October and December. Each flower opens in the evening, then wilts and drops to the ground the next morning. The advantage of this staggered flowering is likely that pollinators, primarily bats, are forced to move from tree to tree in search of nectar, rather than feasting on a single tree. This improves the odds of cross-fertilisation.

Baobabs are a rich source of food, water and shelter. Various game species eat the leaves and fallen flowers. Baboons and monkeys crack open the large seed pods, weighing 2kg or more and containing over 400 seeds, to feed on the nutritious pith. Elephant eat the moist, calcium-rich bark, especially when water is scarce. They typically dig into the tree with their tusks, tearing the bark, then rip off strips with their trunk. Damage this severe would kill most tree species, but baobabs have impressive regenerative powers and grow new bark to cover the wound.

For centuries, humans have used the hollow stems of baobabs for shelter and storage – there are accounts of spaces even being used as a prison and a pub. The bark can be rolled into strong fibre to make ropes and baskets. The leaves and young sprouts are edible, the seeds are roasted as a coffee bean substitute, and the fruit pulp can be used to make a refreshing drink that is richer in vitamin C than orange juice. In the past, tartaric acid was extracted from the fruit, for use in food preparation. The leaves and bark have various medicinal uses. Like elephant, humans have been known to strip and chew the bark as a source of moisture during dry spells.

Since baobab tissue contains a lot of water, a dead tree will collapse into a mound of fibrous pulp. Worryingly, some of the region's largest and oldest baobabs have died in recent years. The cause is likely climate change, which has led to prolonged droughts in some areas.

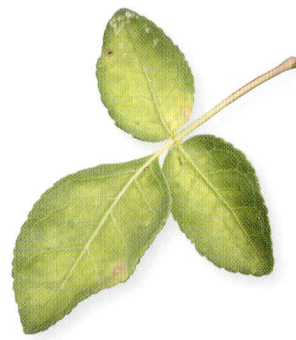

Family Burseraceae

# SAND CORKWOOD
## *Commiphora angolensis*
A: sandkanniedood  TS: morôka

*Commiphora:* from Greek *kommi* ('gum') and *phoros* ('bearing'); *angolensis:* from Angola

The *Commiphora* genus comprises about 18 species in South Africa. These somewhat strange-looking trees trees or shrubs usually have flaking bark and milky or watery sap. They are deciduous, standing bare for much of the year. One can hardly imagine an arid or bushveld landscape without these trees.

Sand corkwood is multi-stemmed and rarely reaches more than 7m in height. It occurs in hot, dry woodland on deep Kalahari sand, where it often forms thickets. The common name refers to the species' preference for sandy soils. The bark is grey with brown lenticels, peeling in yellowish papery pieces to reveal the green underbark. When the tree is without leaves, the green underbark stands in for the leaves, converting sunlight into sugars through the process of photosynthesis.

The leaves are trifoliate and often browsed by eland. The gum-like resin has a strong taste and probably deters herbivores. Nevertheless, *Commiphora* trees are utilised by elephant, and in areas with large elephant populations, these trees sustain great damage.

Sand corkwood is a host plant for the poisonous pupae of *Diamphidia nigroornata*, a beetle that is traditionally used by San hunters as arrow poison. The insects feed on the leaves of the sand corkwood and lay their eggs in the soil beneath it, where they develop into pupae. Hunters squeeze the contents from the cocoon and spread it on the arrow shaft just below the arrowhead. Interestingly, the poison is only active if it enters the bloodstream, not if it is swallowed.

*Commiphora* species have been used since biblical times for their aromatic resins and healing balms. In the sandy western bushveld of South Africa, game ranchers often use this tree, in conjunction with other substances, to prepare game feed in times of drought. The wood has been used to carve household items such as spoons and bowls. Like all corkwoods, this species is easily grown from truncheons or short thick branches that are stuck in the ground.

Family Burseraceae

# PAPERBARK CORKWOOD

## Commiphora marlothii

A: papierbaskanniedood  TS: mophaphame
V: mukarakara

*marlothii:* named after H.W.R. Marloth (1855–1931), a South African pharmacist and botanist

This impressive tree is one of the larger trees in the *Commiphora* genus, but is better known for the yellow papery flakes that peel off the green aromatic bark. These papery strips, although rather brittle, can be written on with a pencil if care is exercised.

It is a deciduous, dioecious tree with a short, heavy trunk and a sparsely branched, rounded crown, reaching up to 12m under ideal conditions. It usually grows on koppies and rocky mountain slopes and is relatively common in parts of the Waterberg in Limpopo.

The compound, elliptic to obovate, velvety leaves with short thick leaf stalks are diagnostic. The leaves turn mustard yellow before falling from the tree. Small, yellow flowers are borne in axillary compact heads and appear with the new leaves from October to November. The fruits are drupes and borne in tight, hanging clusters on long hairy stalks, appearing between November and March.

As is the case with all *Commiphora* trees, paperbark corkwood exudes a yellowish, aromatic, milky latex when cut. The wood is too soft for use in carpentry.

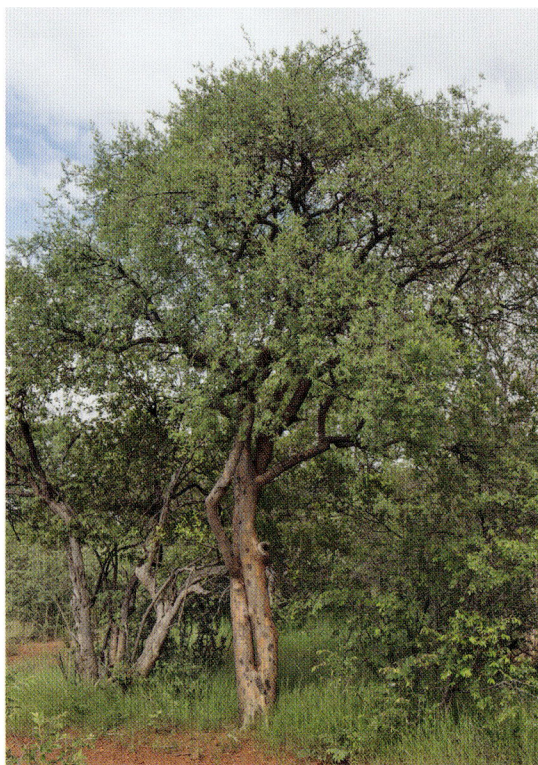

# VELVET-LEAVED CORKWOOD

## *Commiphora mollis*

A: fluweelkanniedood  NS: mmetlakgamêlô
TW: mokômoto  V: muukhuthu

*mollis:* 'soft', referring to the soft, silky hairs on the leaves

This hardy but frost-sensitive tree has many branches and a wide crown that may reach up to 8m. It is deciduous and dioecious. It occurs in dry bushveld or woodland, usually on rocky soil but also in sandy soils, and is widespread in Mpumalanga, Limpopo and North West. The trunk may be fluted and its bark may peel off in thick discs. Bark facing the sun is typically silvery and smooth, with wrinkles around the branches, whereas bark facing away from the sun is khaki to toffee-coloured and peels of in small discs to reveal the green underbark. Brown resin ducts are visible on the trunk and watery milky sap is exuded from the bark.

The alternate, compound leaves have 2–6 pairs of opposite leaflets. These leaflets are greyish green above but lighter and hairier below. In early autumn, the leaves turn yellow and fall to the ground. Small, yellowish to pinkish flowers appear in small axillary clusters before or with the new leaves. Male flowers are usually larger than female flowers. The fruit is pale green to brown and matures to a dull red drupe with a black seed. It is much sought after by fruit-eating birds.

Kudu and other browsers feed on the leaves and shoots, while elephant are known to dig up the succulent roots. The leaves are also eaten by the white-barred gypsy moth (*Palasea albimacula*). The wood is rather soft and has no functional use.

Corkwoods typically start shedding their leaves early in autumn. During winter they are completely bare.

Family Burseraceae

# WHITE-STEM CORKWOOD

## *Commiphora tenuipetiolata*

**A:** witstamkanniedood, poeierstamkanniedood, bloustamkanniedood  **V:** muṱahadzi

*tenuipetiolata:* 'slender leaf stalk'

Satin-bark corkwood is a dioecious tree with a single trunk. It occurs in dry woodland, usually on well-drained sandy soil or among rocks, and often alongside mopane (*Colophospernum mopane*). The bark is bluish green to white and flakes in yellow-grey strips to reveal the blue-green underbark. Sometimes, however, it peels in brownish discs, and in some areas the bark has a satiny sheen.

The leaves are usually trifoliate, but sometimes have 5–9 leaflets. The greenish-yellow flowers appear with the new leaves in small axillary clusters. The fruit is a round, fleshy berry, which is red when mature.

This tree is similar to, and can be confused with, the sand corkwood (*C. angolensis*). The latter, however, is usually multi-stemmed, with leaves and branches covered in velvety hair, and its leaflets are slightly larger.

The Himba people of northern Namibia make a soap and a perfume from the myrrh resin in the bark of this and other *Commiphora* species in the region. The soap is traditionally used as a hand soap or for cleaning clothes and other fabrics. The raw resin has a sweet, fruity smell similar to raisins and dates, but when heated, its aroma is reminiscent of cumin and chilli powder.

# ZEBRA-BARKED CORKWOOD

*Commiphora viminea*

A: sebrabaskanniedood  V: mutonyombiḍi

*viminea:* 'with long flexible shoots'

This single-stemmed, deciduous, fast-growing tree is found in dry deciduous woodland, often in association with mopane (*Colophospernum mopane*). Its bark is creamy grey or pale green, patterned with horizontal bands of large, black, warty lenticels, resembling zebra stripes – hence the common name. Resin ducts are present in the bark and often exude large quantities of gum-resin. The branchlets are initially pale green to red-brown before turning purple, and are spine-tipped. Simple leaves are tightly clustered on small lateral spur-branchlets; occasionally leaves are trifoliate. The yellowish-green flowers appear before or with the new leaves. Male flowers are usually much larger than female flowers. The fruit is an almost spherical fleshy berry, reddish brown when ripe. The trunk reportedly has some anti-cancer properties.

# POD-MAHOGANY
*Afzelia quanzensis*

**A:** peulmahonie  **SW:** umkholikholi  **Z:** inkehli

**PROTECTED IN SOUTH AFRICA**

*Afzelia:* named after Adam Afzelius (1750–1837) from Uppsala, Sweden, who lived in Somalia; *quanzensis:* refers to the Cuanza River in Angola, where this tree was first found

With its magnificent spreading crown and bright green leaves that turn a spectacular yellow in autumn, this relatively uncommon tree must rank as one of the most attractive in South Africa. In spring, the glossy new leaves are copper-coloured, becoming dark green as they age. Slow-growing and deciduous, this tree can grow up to a height of 35m. It occurs throughout southern Africa, preferring low-lying woodland and dry forest, but is absent from the dry western parts.

When in bloom from June to November, this species cannot be confused with any other as the flowers are unique, with a single large petal streaked red on the inside and green on the outside, and four green sepals. The flowers are strongly scented and attract not only a multitude of insects, but are also a favourite of many antelope, including Sharpe's grysbok, which seek out these trees during flowering time. Several butterflies, especially *Charaxes* species, breed on the tree. Various game animals – from duiker to eland and elephant – browse the leaves, but in small quantities only. The large, flat woody pods contain up to ten distinctive black-and-red seeds. The seeds are particularly popular items in the curio industry, and are often strung into lovely necklaces. The seeds are also a favourite food source among rodents.

The termite-resistant timber is attractively red-brown, heavy, works well and takes a fine polish. It has been used for furniture, panelling and construction. In Maputaland, the wood is used for dugout canoes. The tree is easily grown from seed, but is sensitive to frost.

# WILD-SYRINGA

*Burkea africana*

**A:** wildesering, rooisering  **NS:** monatô
**TG:** mpulu  **TS:** monatô  **V:** mufhulu

*Burkea:* named after Joseph Burke, who collected plants in the Magaliesberg area during the 1840s; *africana:* 'from Africa'

This beautifully shaped tree, with its flat-topped, rounded or spreading crown, was often depicted by the famous South African landscape artist J.H. Pierneef. It is a slow-growing, deciduous tree, reaching 8m in height but occasionally growing up to 20m.

It occurs mostly on sandy soils in the subtropical regions of southern Africa, where it may form stands, but it is absent from most of the lowveld. Locals may cut these trees down in order to harvest the caterpillars of the pallid emperor moth (*Cirina forda*), which is regarded as a delicacy when dried and roasted. Monkeys and birds such as parrots eat the flowers and pods.

Wild-syringa wood is heavy, moderately hard and durable, with light brown sapwood and reddish to dark brown heartwood. The grain is interlocked or wavy and the texture is relatively fine and even. While not difficult to work with power tools, and taking a fine polish, it tends to split on nailing. The wood has been used for fences, heavy construction, parquet flooring, railway sleepers, furniture, joinery, carving, turnery, interior trims, boat building, mine props and musical instruments such as xylophones.

The wild-syringa is not related to the syringa-berry (*Melia azedarach*), a species that hails from India and has invaded large parts of South Africa.

Family Caesalpinioideae

# MUSASA
*Brachystegia spiciformis*
**A:** msasa  **V:** mutsiwa

**PROTECTED IN SOUTH AFRICA**

*Brachystegia:* from Greek *brakhus* ('short' or 'flattened') and *stegos* ('roof'), but the allusion is uncertain; *spiciformis:* 'spike-like', referring to the shape of the inflorescence

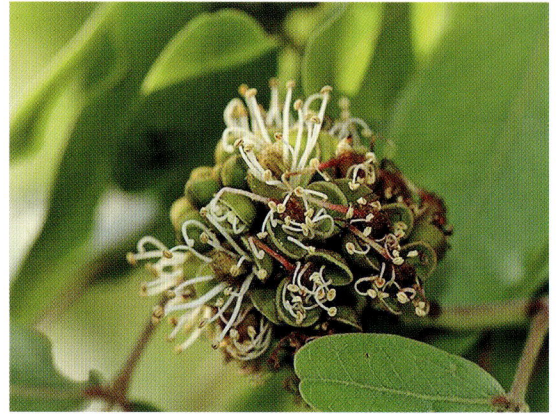

Musasa is the defining tree species of miombo woodland, the vegetation type that dominates the south-central African subregion. It has the widest distribution range of any *Brachystegia* species, ranging from near Mombassa in Kenya to the Soutpansberg in Limpopo in South Africa, where a small isolated population was discovered at the start of the 21st century. This slow-growing, usually deciduous tree grows up to 15m high, and has a beautiful wide shape and a flat crown. It occurs in a variety of soil types in areas with a minimum rainfall of 600mm per annum. In eastern Angola, this tree reaches up to 25m as a result of high rainfall during the growing season.

Musasa is well known for the amber to deep red or brown colours of its new leaves, which sprout during spring. Within three weeks, the colours shift to deep green. In southern Africa, flowering occurs from August to November and fruiting from May to August. The insignificant-looking flowers appear after the new leaves, and are popular with bees, which probably pollinate them. The flowers yield excellent honey.

After pollination, fruit development takes up to eight months. The pods split explosively and the flat seeds are flung up to 20m from the parent tree. The ground under the tree is often saturated with seedlings.

The pale brown to red-brown heartwood is hard, heavy and difficult to work. The wood is not durable and is generally regarded as an inferior general-purpose timber. It makes good charcoal, however, and is popular as firewood.

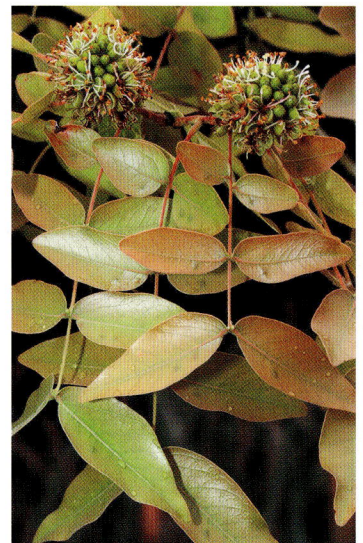

# FALSE-MUFUTI

## *Brachystegia utilis*

**A:** valsmufuti  **TG:** tzonzo

*utilis:* 'useful'

An extremely rare tree in South Africa, occurring as a very small population in a little-known valley in the Soutpansberg in Limpopo. It is a slender, deciduous tree with a dense, much-branched, roundish or flattish crown. This species can grow up to 15m high but occasionally reaches 20m. It favours deciduous woodland on ridges and hill slopes in shallow stony or gritty soils or sometimes in flat, sandy areas.

Like musasa (*B. spiciformis*), new leaves show a great range of red colours when immature, later turning to various shades of green. The common name suggests that it is similar to mfuti (*B. boehmii*), but it has far fewer leaflets, which are more rounded and more widely spaced. False-mufuti also has fewer secondary veins on the leaves.

The fibrous bark is used to make string and cloth.

# SJAMBOKPOD
## *Cassia abbreviata*
A: sambokpeul  TS: monêpênêpê, molepelepe
V: muvhonela-ṱhangu

*Cassia:* from Latin, referring to wild cinnamon;
*abbreviata:* 'shortened', but the allusion is unclear

Flowering sjambokpod is one of the bushveld's most spectacular sights – it produces an abundance of flowers even in years of low rainfall. This graceful, relatively slow-growing, deciduous tree usually has a straight bole and an open crown, and reaches up to 10m in height.

It occurs in the northern parts of Limpopo and Mpumalanga, where it favours open woodlands, low-altitude arid bushveld and hillsides.

The compound, velvety leaves, which droop slightly, are bright green initially and fade to dark green with age. The large, yellow, pea-like flowers appear in spring, before the new leaves, and are a valuable source of nectar and pollen for bees. Exceptionally long, cylindrical pods with a velvety texture may be seen hanging from the tree for months.

These contain numerous seeds, which are eaten by birds, monkeys and baboons. Game animals do not show much interest in sjambokpod, except kudu, which may nibble on the new leaves. Birds are fond of the seeds and fruit pulp.

All *Cassia* species are legumes, like *Senegalia* and *Vachellia*, and contribute nitrogen to the soil. Although sjambokpod does not form nitrogen-fixing root nodules, it has a high nitrogen content in its leaves, suggesting that it may fix atmospheric nitrogen in a different way.

Living trees are frequently infested by borers. This, and the fact that the wood cracks easily, makes it unusable as timber. Sjambok pod is popular with traditional healers and is harvested for roots and bark. This strong demand, coupled with the destructive manner in which it is harvested, is putting wild populations under pressure. It is a very attractive tree for the smaller garden in areas with little or no frost.

Gonimbrasia belina

## Subfamily Caesalpinioideae

# MOPANE

*Colophospermum mopane*

**A:** mopanie  **NS:** mohlanare  **TS:** mophane

*Colophospermum:* from Greek *kolophonios* ('resin') and *sperma* ('seed'), referring to conspicuous resin glands dotting the seeds

This deciduous species has a wide distribution range across the savannah woodlands of southern Africa. It is so dominant in this region that it has become the anchor species in a widespread ecoregion known as 'mopane woodland', which includes savannah, grassland and shrubland. Soil quality determines whether a mopane seedling becomes a shrub or a tree. On alluvial soils, it can grow into a magnificently large tree, but this is not common in the South African bushveld, where soils are often poorly drained. Here, mopane may develop into nothing more than a shrub or small tree.

The characteristic butterfly-shaped leaves open at night and close during the day to control moisture loss,

enabling the tree to beat the heat in its hot, dry habitat. The leaves start changing colour in autumn, shifting from green to various shades of yellow and brown. The colourful spectacle of mopane woodland in autumn can be considered Africa's version of the magnificent autumn display seen in New England in the USA. By the end of winter, most trees are bare.

Mopane leaves are high in protein and provide valuable browse for various game species. The leaves and bark are favoured by elephant, which feed rather destructively by breaking off branches and ringbarking the trunks. These trees are remarkably robust, however, and can survive even ringbarking.

Young leaves are more palatable than older ones, have more protein and nitrogen and contain less tannin. But even the dry, fallen leaves are eagerly picked up from the ground by animals such as eland, buffalo, nyala, impala, steenbok, grey duiker, kudu and Lichtenstein's hartebeest.

Mopane leaves and seed oil have a turpentine-like smell and the early Voortrekkers consequently named the species 'turpentine tree', a name that is no longer in use.

Caterpillars of the grey emperor moth (*Gonimbrasia belina*), commonly known as mopane worms, feed on the green leaves during summer. These caterpillars are high in protein and are regarded as a delicacy among locals,

who eat them dried and roasted. During the mopane worm season, bagfuls of the caterpillars are collected to be dried and stored for leaner times. Drying and retailing mopane worms has become a significant commercial operation in mopane country.

Mopane wood is dark reddish, durable, strong and excellent for furniture, although it is difficult to work. It has also found other commercial uses, such as railway sleepers and mine props. Some people regard mopane as the best firewood in Africa. Since its leaves close during the day, mopane is not a good shade tree.

# MAPUTALAND ORDEALTREE

## *Erythrophleum lasianthum*

**A:** Maputalandoordeelboom  **SW:** umkhanku  **Z:** umkhwangu

*Erythrophleum:* from Greek *eruthros* ('red') and *phloios*, ('bark'), referring to the red sap in the bark; *lasianthum:* from Greek *lasios* ('woolly') and *anthos* ('flower'), referring to the woolly flower spikes

The Maputaland ordeal-tree is a unique, attractive, evergreen tree with a tall trunk (6–15m), a spreading, rounded crown and drooping foliage. It is endemic to the dry sand forests of Maputaland and adjacent Mozambique. This tree contains one of the commonest African poisons, known to have killed stock and humans. It has a number of medicinal uses and features prominently in sorcery and magic.

The common name refers to the now-outlawed practice of 'trial by ordeal', which caused the deaths of many people. Someone accused of a serious crime, such as witchcraft, was given a mixture of water and powdered bark to drink as the village watched. An innocent person would drink quickly, with a clear conscience, inducing vomiting before the poison could be absorbed. They would live and be deemed innocent. However, if the person were guilty, they would drink the mixture reluctantly, enabling absorption of the poison. Death would almost certain follow, which would prove their guilt.

Young trees have smooth, grey bark that becomes red-brown, rough and fissured with age. The doubly compound, alternate leaves have glossy, dark green leaflets with a wavy smooth-edged margin. Small, creamy green flowers appear from September to November in honey-scented spikes. The fruit is a large, flat, dark brown pod, splitting on the tree to release large brown seeds. The pods can also persist on the tree for months and be found beneath the tree at all times.

All parts of the tree are toxic. The leaves are used to protect stored grain against insects. The bark, roots and seeds are extensively used medicinally as they have anaesthetic properties, despite also being poisonous. For example, the bark is used moderately as a fish poison, but also as snuff and for colds and headaches.

The wood is very hard, durable and termite resistant. The heartwood is a light reddish colour. It has been used in construction and furniture making.

This species has been listed as Near Threatened on the Red List of South African Plants: it has a restricted habitat; deforestation and crop farming are causing significant habitat loss outside of conservation areas; large volumes of bark are removed on an unsustainable basis; there is a vibrant market for bark and wood; the number of trees in the distribution range seems to be on the decline; and trees also seem to be harvested within conservation areas. It likely to become vulnerable if the destructive trends continue.

*Ptyelus grossus*

## Subfamily Caesalpinioideae

# AFRICAN-WATTLE

### *Peltophorum africanum*

**A:** huilboom, boerboon  **NS:** mosehla, mofehlo
**TG:** ndzedze  **TS:** mosêtlha  **V:** musese  **Z:** umsehle

*Peltophorum:* from Greek *pelte* ('small shield') and *phero* ('to bear')', referring to the shield-like shape of the stigma; *africanum:* 'from Africa'

Also known as the weeping wattle, this is one of Africa's 'rain trees' – during springtime, water often drips from its branches. This phenomenon is caused by the gregarious spittlebug *Ptyelus grossus*. Immature spittlebugs congregate on young shoots and suck the tree's sap. They excrete fluid as quickly as they ingest it, frothing it into a protective layer against the sun and predators. The secretion of large quantities of liquid causes an incessant drip, creating a 'rain' or 'weeping' effect.

The African-wattle is a hardy, semi-deciduous to deciduous, drought-resistant tree and is found in a variety of habitats. It has a sparse, spreading crown, reaching up to 10m in height, and is often multi-stemmed from ground level. The trees flower spectacularly in spring: masses of bright yellow flowerheads attract nectar-loving birds, insects and bees. The flowering season is unusually long,

from spring to midsummer, sometimes even into autumn. This tree is not popular with browsers and is only nibbled on in times of food scarcity, although elephant and giraffe may browse on it more regularly. Black rhino are known to strip and eat the bark.

In years gone by, many farmhouses had floors covered with cow dung. African-wattle branchlets made excellent soft brooms for applying the dung.

The heartwood is relatively hard and heavy with a fine grain, works easily and has been used for turning, tool handles, furniture and carvings. It is not borer-proof and therefore not suitable for use as fencing posts.

It is an ideal tree for larger gardens. Young trees grow easily and fast and become excellent shade trees with beautiful flowers.

# WEEPING BOERBEAN

## *Schotia brachypetala*

**A:** huilboerboon **NS:** molope **SW:** vovovo **TG:** chochelamandleni
**TS:** umutwa **V:** mulubi **X:** umgxam **Z:** umgxamu

*Schotia:* named after Richard van der Schot (1733–1790), originally from Delft, Holland, and a professor of botany and chemistry and director of the botanical garden at the University of Vienna; *brachypetala:* from Greek *brakhus* ('short') and *petalos* ('petal')

The weeping boerbean is another of South Africa's 'rain trees'. The flowers produce such quantities of nectar that it drips down to the ground, making the tree appear as if it is weeping. Like the African-wattle (*Peltophorum africanum*) and apple-leaf (*Philenoptera violacea*), this tree is also host to spittlebugs, which produce a protective froth.

This beautiful tree has a dense, dark, rounded spreading crown and hanging branches. It occurs in open,

warm, dry bushveld, deciduous woodland and scrub forest, often along riverbanks or on termite mounds. It is usually deciduous for a short period, but in warm, frost-free areas it may be evergreen. The leaves are discarded in early spring (September to October). The new coppery or reddish leaves appear shortly thereafter, but quickly change to a shiny light green before becoming dark green. The striking deep red flowers with their pink petals also appear in spring and produce copious nectar, which attracts various bird and insect species.

Giraffe, kudu, nyala and impala browse on the leaves, and black rhino may eat the bark. The hard, flat pods usually contain 14 seeds. While the pods are still on the tree, the flat sides split open inside a ridge on the convex side of the pod to release the seeds. Parrots and grcy go away birds are mostly responsible for seed dispersal.

The sapwood is pinkish grey and not durable unless treated, whereas the heartwood is hard and heavy with a fine texture, making for beautiful furniture that darkens with age if oiled regularly. Weeping boerbean is an excellent tree for gardens, parks and farms. It is easy to grow, though young trees need to be protected against frost.

# SHEPHERD'S TREE

## *Boscia albitrunca*

**A:** witgat, matoppie **SW:** siphiso **NS:** mohlôpi
**TS:** motlhôpi **V:** muṱhobi

**PROTECTED IN SOUTH AFRICA**

*Boscia:* named after the French professor of agriculture, Louis A.G. Bosc (1777–1850); *albitrunca:* from Latin *albus* ('white') and *truncus* ('trunk')

This attractive, evergreen tree can usually be identified from a distance by its stout trunk and rounded olive-green crown. The trunk is usually white or greyish, but occasionally yellowish in colour. It is a stocky tree that grows up to 8m in height, favouring dry, open woodland.

In more arid areas, the shepherd's tree is a valuable resource as it provides nourishing fodder for game and livestock. Furthermore, it is believed not to increase the levels of unpalatable tannin as a defence against over-browsing. Kudu and eland eat the leaves in the dry winter months, when there is very little food available in the form of green leaves. As a result, shepherd's trees often have straight browse lines. The leaves are also a food source for the larvae of several butterfly species.

The shepherd's tree has an impressive root system, and is arguably one of the deepest in the world. In one

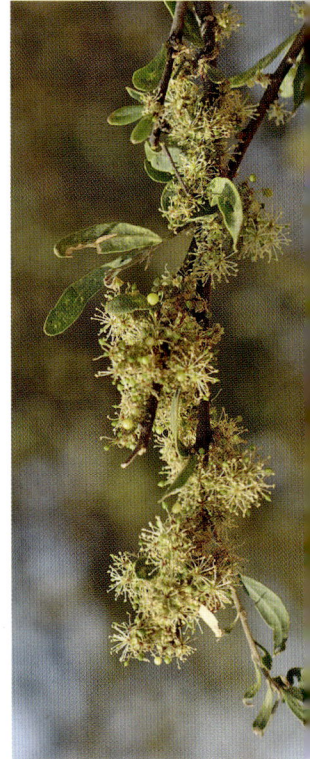

particular study in the Kalahari, a tree was found with a taproot of 68m, making it at least eight times as tall as the tree itself. This remarkable adaptation enables it to survive and flourish in the harsh, arid western parts of the sub-continent by reaching water deep under the ground.

The English name 'shepherd's tree' comes from the fact that herdsmen use the tree for shade when tending their goats or sheep. The origin of the Afrikaans name *witgat* (meaning 'white hollow') is uncertain. Some believe it refers to the pale trunk, or to the colour of the hollow excavated around the taproot and lateral roots by the wind and rain. Another explanation comes from the white holes left in the trunk of older trees once the sapwood has become hollow. These holes make excellent nesting sites for bees. Others believe that *witgat* is derived from an old Dutch word that means coffee. The early white pioneers used to sweat, dry, roast and grind the roots to make a substitute for coffee. It is not exactly a drink for the connoisseur, but when mixed with ordinary beans, it at least makes the coffee lasts longer.

The shepherd's tree also features prominently in African folklore and superstition, and some tribes traditionally regard the *matoppie* as a sacred tree that should not be damaged.

The fruit is edible and utilised by humans, primates and birds. Although the wood is heavy, it has very little commercial use. It is an excellent shade tree.

# STINK SHEPHERD'S TREE

*Boscia foetida* subsp. *rehmanniana*

A: stinkwitgat, mopiepie, noeniebos, mapipi  NS: mopipi
TS: mopipi  V: tshibibi  Z: umvithi

*foetida:* 'bad-smelling' referring to the unpleasant smell of the flowers; *rehmanniana:* named in honour of Joseph Rehmann (1788–1831), a physician from St Petersburg

This tree's shape and size are similar to that of the shepherd's tree (*B. albitrunca*), but the leaves are much smaller. Like the shepherd's tree, it is evergreen. This extremely slow-growing species is common in the more arid western parts of the subcontinent, where evergreens are uncommon. It favours hot and dry open bushveld, often growing on termite mounds.

The rounded crown is quite dense. The small leaves are in tight clusters on small, angled spurs along the branches.

This species is unusual in that it relies on blowflies as pollinators. The flowering season lasts for about a month in early summer, when an abundance of small yellow-green flowers stink to high heaven in order to attract as many blowflies as possible. From midsummer onwards, the tree is covered in masses of colourful little berries.

Browsers tend to avoid this species, and the wood has no functional use. Yet it remains one of the more attractive trees in its arid home range.

# BEADBEAN

*Maerua angolensis* subsp. *angolensis*

A: knoppiesboontjie  SW: umenwayo
V: mutamba-na-mme  Z: umenwayo

*Maerua:* likely from the Arabic word *meru* ('high'), as some species can reach 9m or more; *angolensis:* 'from Angola'

This beautiful tree is evergreen to deciduous, with a slender, upright trunk and a somewhat spreading, rounded crown that reaches 10m in height. It is a common trcc in Limpopo, North West and Mpumalanga, where it is found in hot and dry open woodland in low-altitude areas but absent from high-rainfall areas.

The fragrant, pincushion-like flowers are without petals and are produced in abundance at the beginning of the rainy season. The fruit is a long, slender pod, which is usually irregularly constricted between the seeds. It is not edible. The leaves are browsed by game animals, especially kudu, nyala and bushbuck.

This tree is often home to caterpillars and butterflies, which attract insect-eating birds.

In terms of timber, the tree is not highly regarded. The wood is whitish yellow, hard and dense, but also brittle. It has been used for cabinet work and tools, as well as hut posts. It makes for good firewood and charcoal.

The beadbean is an attractive ornamental tree for gardens in drier areas, especially since it is easily propagated from seed. This species is both frost and drought resistant.

# BUSHMAN'S TEA

## Catha edulis

A: boesmanstee  X: igqwaka  Z: umhlwazi

**PROTECTED IN SOUTH AFRICA**

*Catha:* derived from the Arabic name *khat*;
*edulis:* 'edible' in Latin

This attractive, deciduous to evergreen tree has a straight trunk, upright crown, somewhat drooping branches, and bright green leaves that turn yellowish in autumn. It grows up to 15m in height, and is found in and at the margins of high-altitude forests and in woodland or on rocky outcrops, often in mist belts.

In northeastern Africa and the Arabian Peninsula, this plant is known as *khat* or some derivative thereof, and is grown and used as a stimulant that causes excitement and euphoria and supresses appetite. People chew the fresh leaves or brew tea from dried leaves. The World Health Organization has classified the plant as a 'drug of abuse' that can result in psychological dependence. Although it is a controlled or illegal substance in some countries, it is cultivated as a cash crop in Uganda, Ethiopia, Somalia and Yemen. In South Africa, the tree is also regarded as a drug, but it is not widely used. Bushman's tea was known to the ancient Egyptians, who used it ritually. The chewing of *khat* pre-dates the drinking of coffee.

The wood of bushman's tea is golden-brown or brown, moderately hard, fine- and straight-grained and is suitable for furniture, utensils, fence poles and firewood. Dry logs are insect-proof and very durable.

The tree is fast-growing, frost tolerant, does not need much water, and attracts insects and birds.

Family Celastraceae

# BUSHVELD SAFFRONWOOD

## *Elaeodendron transvaalense*

**A:** bosveldsaffraan, lepelhout  **TG:** ximapana
**TS:** monamane  **Z:** ingwavuma

**PROTECTED IN SOUTH AFRICA**

*Elaeodendron:* 'olive wood', from Greek *elaia* ('olive') and *dendron* ('wood'), referring to the fruit's resemblance to those of *Cassine orientalis*, found in Mauritius, Réunion and Rodrigues and locally known as *bois d'olive*; *transvaalense:* 'of the Transvaal'

The most widespread of the saffron trees, this is a slow-growing, deciduous or evergreen tree with a wide, spreading crown. In South Africa it is usually bushy and no more than 8m in height. It is found along streams, on rocky hillsides and often on termite mounds in deciduous woodland.

The bark is pale grey and may be finely fissured horizontally. The leathery and smooth leaves are simple and either alternate or spirally arranged. The leaf stalks are very short. Leaves may appear in groups of three. The greenish-white, bisexual flowers are very small and borne in the leaf axils. Although they are borne in clusters, individual flowers have long, slender stalks. The hard-shelled, edible fruit is fleshy with a central stone containing the seed.Leaves and young shoots are browsed by giraffe, kudu, impala and elephant, and the fruits are eaten by primates and birds.

The wood is whitish, cross-grained, brittle and insect resistant. It has traditionally been used for making spoons, ladles, headrests and tobacco pipes. The bark has some medicinal uses, especially for treating fever and stomach problems.

Although this tree has a wide distribution across southern Africa, it is not common. It is heavily harvested for medicine, and repeated bark removal is putting the species at risk, making it increasingly rare.

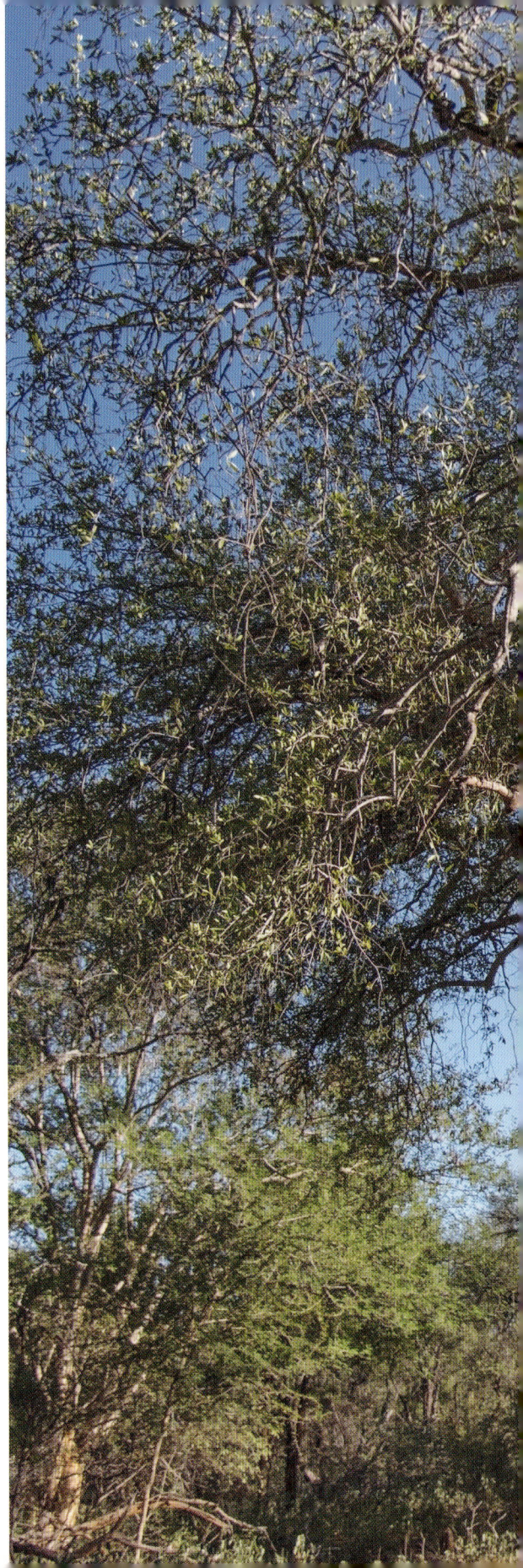

Family Celtidaceae

# WHITE-STINKWOOD

*Celtis africana*

**A:** witstinkhout **S:** modutu **TS:** modutu
**V:** mumvumvu **X:** umvumvu **Z:** umvumvu

*Celtis:* Latin name used by Pliny the Elder; also the ancient Greek name for one of the plants reputed to be the 'lotus of the ancients'; *africana:* 'from Africa'

This upright, deciduous, spreading tree can reach a height of close to 30m under ideal conditions. It occurs in a variety of habitats throughout much of South Africa (excluding the more arid western parts), growing in dense forests, on rocky outcrops, in bushveld and open grassland, on mountain slopes, along riverbanks and in kloofs.

This tree is known as white-stinkwood owing to its white or creamy white colour and the unpleasant smell of freshly cut wood. It is not related to black stinkwood (*Ocotea bullata*) and unlike that species has no commercial value.

The smooth trunk with its pale grey to white bark is diagnostic. The bark sometimes has horizontal ridges and in old trees may be loosely peeling. The wood is tough and strong, but difficult to work. It can be used for a variety of household articles, shelving and even furniture.

It grows fast, is drought and frost resistant to some degree, and is a popular species for lining streets and for large gardens or parks. The fruit is eaten by a variety of birds, such as the African olive pigeon, bulbuls, mousebirds and barbets.

# MOBOLAPLUM

## Parinari curatellifolia

A: grysappel  NS: mmola  TG: mbulwa  TS: mobola  V: muvhula  Z: amabulwa

*Parinari:* unknown; *curatellifolia:* refers to the leaves, which are similar to *Curatella americana*, a tropical American tree

This attractive evergreen tree has a straight trunk and a wide crown ranging from roundish to mushroom-shaped. It occurs from Eswatini through Zimbabwe, and is found in well-drained sourveld with sandy soil in open deciduous bushveld. It is particularly common near rivers and in areas of poor drainage.

The leathery leaves fold upwards and are green above and grey-yellow and hairy underneath. The rust-coloured inflorescences are rich in nectar and release a sweet scent. A variety of game animals eat the leaves and fruit, including primates, elephant, antelope and porcupines. Similar to marula fruits, the fruits of mobolaplum drop before they are quite ripe, and ripen fully while on the ground. Humans eat the fruit fresh or make a porridge from it. It also makes excellent syrup and beer. The single seed is eaten as a nut.

This species is popular with beekeepers as it produces large quantities of pollen and nectar. The bark can be used for tanning leather.

The wood is hard but very difficult to work – as such, these trees are seldom cut down.

While mobolaplum can be grown as an ornamental, to provide shade and for its fruit, propagation can be quite challenging. It is also sensitive to frost and cold wind.

# AFRICAN MANGOSTEEN

*Garcinia livingstonei*

**A:** Afrikageelmelkhout  **NS:** mokongono  **TG:** himbi  **Z:** umphimbi

## PROTECTED IN SOUTH AFRICA

*Garcinia:* named after Laurent Garcin (1683–1751), a French botanist who collected plants in India; *livingstonei:* honours Scottish explorer David Livingstone (1813–1873), one of the first naturalists to record the tree

This much-branched tree has a rather rigid crown and whorls of blue-green leaves. Its branches grow at right angles to the trunk, and the branchlets are short and thick. Dioecious and evergreen, this erect tree can reach up to 20m in height in ideal conditions (typically 6–12m). Found in hot, drier areas, it grows in riverine woodland or forest, along riverbanks, in coastal grassland and on rocky outcrops.

The scented flowers are greenish to whitish or yellowish and appear in groups of 5–15 in leaf axils on old wood. They are rich in nectar and attract a variety of insects, especially bees. The fruit is a smallish, thin-skinned, fleshy, bright orange berry with a single large seed. This edible fruit is pleasantly sweet and somewhat acidic, but contains latex that some people find unpleasant. It is commonly harvested from the wild to make syrup, jelly and jam. The wood is fairly hard and has a fine texture, but is prone to borer attack and is not commonly used.

These slow-growing trees can handle drought and heavy rain quite well, but are sensitive to cold weather.

# RED BUSHWILLOW

*Combretum apiculatum subsp. apiculatum*

**A:** rooiboswilg **NS:** mohwelere **SW:** imbondvo lemnyama **TG:** mugavi **TS:** mofudiri **V:** musingidzi **Z:** umbondwe omnyama

*Combretum:* Latin name used by Pliny the Elder for a climbing plant in a different genus; *apiculatum:* 'ending abruptly in a short point', referring to the sharp tip of the leaf

Five genera and 41 species of *Combretum* occur in South Africa. These plants can be shrubs, climbers or trees. The majority of species in this genus are pollinated by insects and birds, but a few are pollinated by mammals, such as bats. *Combretum* species are also known to have a wide range of medicinal uses.

Red bushwillow is a common, single- or multi-stemmed deciduous tree that grows up to 10m in height. It occurs in Limpopo between the Crocodile River in the west and the Lebombo Mountains in the east. Once established, this slow-growing tree is frost and drought resistant and makes for an excellent shade tree. It can form large dominant stands in less sandy areas.

The green leaves are eaten by most browsers, including giraffe and elephant, and the dry leaves are picked up from the ground by a variety of mammals, such as impala, duiker and kudu. The common name is derived from the reddish colour of the leaves in the dry winter months.

The four-winged fruit is typical of *Combretum* trees, the fruit is four-winged, almost round to egg-shaped, yellowish green and often tinged with red. It has a single seed in the centre, believed to be poisonous, but eaten by brown-headed parrots. The wood is of a good quality, being strong, heavy, hard, dark and fine-grained, but it is difficult to get planks of a useful length. It is often used for fencing posts.

# FOREST BUSHWILLOW

## *Combretum kraussii*

A: bosvaderlandswilg  NS: modubu  SW: imbondvo lemhlophe
V: muvuvhu-thavha  X: ulandile  Z: umdubu wehlathi

*kraussii:* named after Dr F. Krauss of the Stuttgart Museum, who collected plants in South Africa from 1837 to 1840

This fast-growing, deciduous or semi-deciduous shrub or tree reaches up to 12m in height. It occurs on rocky or wooded hillsides, in evergreen forest and along forest margins in Limpopo, Mpumalanga, KwaZulu-Natal and the Eastern Cape.

The bark of young trees is smooth but becomes furrowed and dark grey as the tree grows older. The simple leaves are shiny, dark green above and paler green below, and are borne on short lateral twigs. The leaf veins are conspicuous; the leaf margins are smooth, wavy and rolled under. During autumn, the leaves turn bright red and purple before being shed, resulting in a colourful display. In spring, the new leaves appear as a white flush, which can be equally spectacular. The small, creamy white flowers are borne from September to January on dense, short spikes in leaf axils. The leaves surrounding the flowers may lose their chlorophyll and turn white while the tree is flowering. The small, characteristic four-winged fruit stays on the tree for a long time, drying to a reddish brown.

*Combretum* trees are pollinated by various insects, including bees. This species has adapted to wind dispersal by developing winged fruit that can carry the seed on wind or air currents. Some browsers eat bushwillow fruit and thus also assist in seed dispersal.

The wood is yellowish in colour, tough and hard, with a straight grain and a fine texture, but its sawdust can cause skin irritation. The timber has been used for flooring, joinery, ship building, furniture, turnery, cabinet work, agricultural implements and mine props. It is also good firewood.

This is an attractive tree for gardens and parks, as the changing leaf colours delight throughout the seasons. It is an ideal container tree or for planting along driveways or in paved areas, since the roots are not aggressive and are unlikely to lift paving. It is grown easily and quickly from seed. Young trees should be protected against frost, but once established, they are reasonably frost and drought resistant. It tolerates shade well.

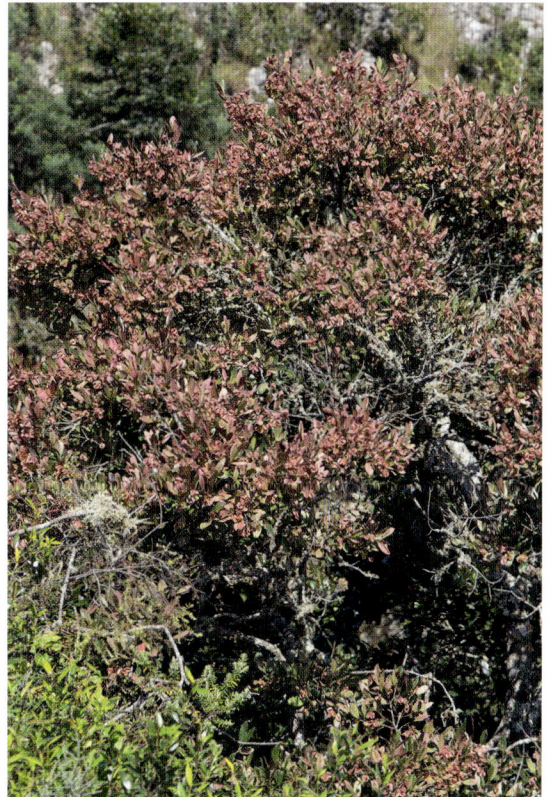

# RIVER BUSHWILLOW
## *Combretum erythrophyllum*

**A:** riviervaderlandswilg  **NS:** moduba-noka  **V:** muvuvhu
**ND:** umdubu  **X:** umdubo  **Z:** umdubu wehlanze

*erythrophyllum:* from Greek *eruthros* ('red') and *phullon* ('leaf')

River bushwillow is a low-branching, single or multi-stemmed deciduous tree with a dense spreading crown that can reach up to 10m in diameter and up to 12m in height. It is hardy and fast-growing, occurring along rivers or where underground water is readily available.

This tree is known for its delicate green spring foliage, which darkens and becomes glossy in summer. In autumn, the leaves turn spectacularly red, yellow and orange before being shed in preparation for winter. In spring, small, inconspicuous, sweet-scented, greenish-yellow flowers appear in dense, almost spherical, axillary heads that attract bees and other insects.

The fruits are four-winged and initially greenish brown, drying to an honey-brown. They remain on the tree for a long time and are reputed to be poisonous. The leaves are browsed by elephant, giraffe, nyala, kudu, eland and bushbuck. Wasps lay their eggs in the walls of the fruit and the larvae feed on the seed inside. The larvae, in turn, are eaten by the southern black tit, which opens the fruit to get at the larvae. River bushwillow is also the larval host plant for several butterfly species, such as the light ciliate blue (*Anthene liodes*), red-tab policeman (*Coeliades keithloa*) and two-pip policeman (*C. pisistratus*).

The timber is undifferentiated, bright yellow when cut and pale yellow when dry. It is soft yet tough, but the grain is coarse and it is difficult to achieve a smooth finish. Nevertheless, it has been used for carpentry, household items, and in times gone by for yokes and yoke-pins. With its non-aggressive root system, this excellent shade tree is often planted along streets, in parks and in gardens. It is remarkably frost resistant.

The Luvuvhu River in Limpopo was named after the river's bushwillows, locally known as *muvuvhu*.

# RUSSET BUSHWILLOW

## *Combretum hereroense*

**A:** kierieklapper **NS:** mokabi **V:** mugavhi **Z:** umhlalavane

*hereroense:* from Hereroland in Namibia

This slow-growing, deciduous tree has a roundish crown. Found throughout much of southern Africa, it grows in dry savannah woodland of various types, including mopane, where it is found on termite mounds, along the fringes of pans, marshes and dambos, along riverbanks and in flat or rocky terrain. It seems to thrive on sandy or silty substrates.

Russet bushwillow is sometimes multi-stemmed, with arching branches, and can reach up to 12m in height (though it is sometimes only a shrub). The horizontally growing branches often have vertical branchlets, which are ideal for knobkieries, hence the Afrikaans name *kierieklapper*. Russet bushwillow is browsed by game and cattle and is valued as fodder. Elephant sometimes push the trees over to get at the roots. Leaves can be dried as a substitute for tea, but the seeds are considered poisonous.

The wood is undifferentiated, though the colour intensifies from pale yellow to brown in the centre, hard, durable and easy to work. It is a general-purpose timber. In the past it was used as supports in mineshafts. Like most *Combretum* species, it makes for exceptional firewood.

# LEADWOOD

*Combretum imberbe*

**A:** hardekool  **H:** omumborombonga  **NS:** mohwelere-tšhipi
**TG:** mondzo  **TS:** motswiri  **V:** mudzwiri  **Z:** impondondlovu

## PROTECTED IN SOUTH AFRICA

*imberbe:* refers to the lack of hairs on the tree

Leadwood is one of the most impressive icons of the African savannah and is found throughout southern Africa. It is the tallest of the region's *Combretum* species and seems to do particularly well on alluvial soils, where it can grow up to 20m in height. This semi-deciduous tree has a spreading canopy, and is easily identified by the distinctive whitish to pale greyish bark, which is deeply fissured lengthwise and has irregular horizontal cracks that give it a coarse-grained appearance.

Leadwood is browsed by impala, kudu, grey duiker, red lechwe, giraffe and elephant. The common name refers to the heaviness of the wood. The heartwood is very dark (almost black), but fades with age, and is durable, close-grained, termite resistant and extremely heavy and hard. It makes excellent furniture, but is difficult to work and frequently breaks wood-working tools. It is a legendary firewood and the white ashes have traditionally been used as a whitewash for homesteads. Leadwood has also been used as props for large thatched-roof buildings at game lodges and as fencing posts, railway sleepers and mineshaft props.

Having such a hard wood, the tree grows very slowly. It has been suggested that leadwood growing under ideal conditions can take up to 1,000 years to reach maturity, another 1,000 years to die and another 1,000 years to decay and return to the soil – representing a life cycle of 3,000 years. The oldest tree identified in southern Africa is a leadwood cut down in 1972 in the Hlane Royal National Park in Eswatini. Carbon dating has put the age of this tree at about 1,040 years. Another large leadwood near Letaba in the Kruger National Park is estimated to be about 900 years old.

Family Combretaceae

# VELVET BUSHWILLOW

## *Combretum molle*

A: fluweelboswilg, basterrooibos
NS: mokgwethe  SW: imbondvo lemnyama
TG: xikukutsi  TS: modubatshipi
V: mugwiti  Z: umbondwe omhlope

*Hamanumida daedalus*

*molle:* from Latin *mollis* ('soft'), referring to the velvety leaves

This is a variable species – it can be evergreen or deciduous and have either a straight or crooked trunk. It is a hardy, fast-growing, cold-sensitive tree, rarely exceeding 10m in height, usually with a single trunk or branching relatively low down.

It prefers open woodland and bushveld, often occurring on mountain slopes or in rocky places, on termite mounds and in semi-evergreen thickets. It is a common tree of the Magaliesberg, Waterberg and Soutpansberg mountains. The crown is roundish, yet rather narrow, and the autumn foliage has a red to purplish tinge. The leaves are densely covered with velvety hairs (hence the common name) and yield a red dye.

A variety of antelope species browse this tree, and it is also a source of food for the larvae of the guineafowl butterfly (*Hamanumida daedalus*) and Morant's orange (*Parosmodes morantii morantii*). The strongly scented, greenish-yellow flowers are in dense axillary spikes and attract bees and other insects. The four-winged fruit is light green with a reddish shade, turning red-brown when dry. The wood is yellowish, hard, termite-proof and durable, and has been used as fencing posts, hut poles, for household utensils and for carved ornaments.

# LARGE-FRUITED BUSHWILLOW

## *Combretum zeyheri*

A: raasblaar  NS: moduba-tšhipi  TS: modubana, moduba-tshipi
V: mufhaṱela-ṱhunḓu  Z: umbondwe wasembudwini

*zeyheri:* named after Carl L.P. Zeyher (1799–1858), a German naturalist who collected the first known specimen in the Magaliesberg range

Large-fruited bushwillow is a common, slow-growing, deciduous bushveld tree with a short or crooked trunk and a round crown. It is sometimes no more than a shrub, but can grow up to 15m tall. This drought-resistant, frost-sensitive tree occurs on a variety of soils, and is regarded as an indicator of sourveld. It often grows with velvet bushwillow (*Combretum molle*), wild-syringa (*Burkea africana*) and broad-pod robust thorn (*Vachellia robusta*). The fragrant, yellowish flowers are stalkless and produced on axillary spikes that appear with the new leaves. When in bloom from September to November, the profusion of flowers can be quite impressive. The conspicuous orange-brown fruit is four-winged and about 8cm in diameter, larger that that of other *Combretum* species. The Afrikaans name *raasblaar* ('noisy leaf') refers to the sound made by the leaves and fruit when the wind blows.

It is the larval food plant for several butterfly species. Elephant, giraffe and kudu are known to eat the leaves, and baboons and hornbills feed on the ripe fruits.

When cut, the timber is bright yellow, but fades to pale yellow to brown as it dries. The wood is hard and tough, but difficult to work. It is not durable and inclined to warp and crack. As such, its uses as a general-purpose timber are limited. The fibrous roots were used to make baskets.

# PURPLEPOD CLUSTERLEAF

## *Terminalia prunioides*

**A:** sterkbos, bloedvrugboom  **TG:** xaxandawu
**TS:** motsiyara  **V:** muţwari

*Terminalia:* derived from the Latin *terminus*, referring to the leaves clustered at the ends of branchlets; *prunioides:* refers to the bright, plum-coloured fruits

This single- or multi-stemmed, semi-deciduous to deciduous, frost-sensitive shrub or small tree has a dense, rounded crown and drooping branches. It occurs in sandy areas and on stony slopes in semi-arid zones, and in poorly drained clay soil, reaching up to 12m under ideal conditions. The leaves are borne in clusters on short spur-branchlets, dark green above and paler green below, softly hairy when young but later almost hairless.

The white to creamy yellow flowers are borne in clustered spikes on the spur-branchlets and are unpleasantly scented. The pod is bright red to purple-red, hence the common name. This tree may flower more than once during a season and will then have fruit and flowers at the same time, making it one of the striking trees of the northern and north-eastern parts of the country.

A variety of game animals, such as elephant, kudu, impala and giraffe, browse the leaves and fruit. Brown-headed parrots are also partial to the fruit and aid seed dispersal.

The timber is evenly brown, heavy, hard, tough, undifferentiated and durable, and has traditionally been used for fencing, hut construction, implement handles and knobkieries. Being such a hard wood, it makes for excellent firewood.

# SILVER CLUSTERLEAF

## *Terminalia sericea*

A: vaalboom, sandgeelhout  V: mususu

*sericea:* 'silky', referring to the dense silky hairs on the leaves

This deciduous, straight-boled tree may grow up to 15m tall under ideal conditions. It occurs in woodland and mixed bushveld on sandy and well-drained soils, where it can form dominant stands. It is often a pioneer and is common throughout much of southern Africa. In sandveld, it is usually associated with wild-syringa (*Burkea africana*).

The common name refers to the silvery, silky leaves, which form clusters at the ends of branches. The silvery colour of the foliage makes this tree conspicuous and easy to identify from a distance.

New leaves appear in spring. Eland are particularly partial to these, and are known to break young trees and the branches of older trees to get at the juicy, fresh leaves. Kudu also eat the young leaves.

The wood is yellow, hard and resistant to attack by wood borers and termites and is used as a general-purpose timber. It has also been used for furniture, although it is difficult to find planks that are long enough.

The bark is rich in tannin and the tree is an important medicinal plant, possessing anti-HIV, antifungal, anti-bacterial, anticancer, antiparasitic, anti-inflammatory and antioxidant qualities. The bark or roots are, for instance, used in the treatment of syphilis and gonorrhoea and illnesses related to HIV. The leaves and roots are boiled in water and the infusion is taken orally for the treatment of coughs, diarrhoea and stomach ache. The leaves can also be used as an antibiotic for wounds. A pharmaceutical company in Europe has patented an extract from the leaves that is used in skin treatment. This attractive tree is slow-growing and fairly resistant to drought and cold; it could be planted more often for decorative purposes.

# WHITE-ALDER

## *Platylophus trifoliatus*

A: witels

*Apis mellifera*

> *Platylophus:* from Greek *platus* ('broad') and *lophos* ('fringe') – a reference to the fruit capsules, which appear to have a fringe; *trifoliatus:* refers to the leaves, which have three leaflets

This South African endemic is the only species in its genus. It is a slow-growing, evergreen tree that typically grows up to 30m tall. It occurs in the forests of the western and southern Cape between Piketberg and Humansdorp, usually along stream banks or near rivers. It needs plenty of moisture, and favours habitat that is sufficiently wet and humid.

White-alder may live for hundreds of years owing to its ability to resprout when the trunk or branches are damaged. It is often multi-stemmed, as coppice shoots frequently grow from an old stem. Single clean-stemmed trees are rare. The bark of young trees is whitish grey, with sparse longitudinal fissures, becoming brown and rough with age and sometimes taking on a gnarled appearance. The compound leaves are dark green above and pale green below. Veins are clearly visible on both sides. This is the only tree in South Africa with opposite leaves that have three leaflets with toothed edges, making it easy to identify.

In December, the small white or cream bisexual flowers appear in clusters in the axils of leaf stalks. The flowers produce copious amounts of nectar to attract bees, which also pollinate the tree. It is generally regarded as an excellent 'bee tree'.

The fruit is a small capsule, containing two seeds, borne in clusters among the leaves.

The timber is variable in colour, medium-hard and medium-heavy and easily worked. It has been used for boat keels, fence posts, window frames, boxes, picture frames and even furniture, as it has a beautiful grain, polishes well and has a pleasant fragrance. The gnarled old trunks have a particularly lovely grain.

# JACKALBERRY
## *Diospyros mespiliformis*
**A:** jakkalsbessie **TG:** ntoma **V:** musuma

*Diospyros:* from Greek *Dios* ('Zeus') and puros ('wheat');
*mespiliformis:* resembling *Mespilus*, the common medlar

The jackalberry tree has symbiotic relationships with a number of living organisms. Various insects, such as bees and wasps, pollinate the flowers. It is not unusual to find snakes residing close to or around the tree, as they prey on the rodents and certain birds that feed on the fruits. Seeds are dispersed either through wash-off by rain or in the droppings of animals that feed on the fruits. The jackalberry grows in mutualism with termites, which aerate the soil around the roots in return for protection by the tree. Since termites live on dead organic matter, they do not eat the living wood. Jackalberry wood is termite resistant after the tree has been felled.

This tree reaches up to 25m in height, with a rounded crown and a distinctly dark (almost black), straight trunk, occurring in woodland and along rivers and riverine fringes.

It is often seen on termite mounds. This is an excellent shade tree with a dense, dark, evergreen crown. It is believed that jackalberries can reach an age of more than 200 years.

The fruit is edible, either fresh or as a preserve. It is also used to make traditional beer and brandy. Jackals eat the fallen fruit, hence the common name. The leaves are browsed by elephant, giraffe, kudu, eland and buffalo. Baboons favour jackalberry groves as sleeping sites, as they apparently feel relatively safe from predators in these tall, straight-boled trees.

The wood is dark brown to almost black with a fine and even texture, strong, heavy, durable and termite- and borer-proof. It has many uses including the making of furniture, bowls, household utensils, flooring, canoes, stamping blocks and pestles. The wood is, however, difficult to saw and work.

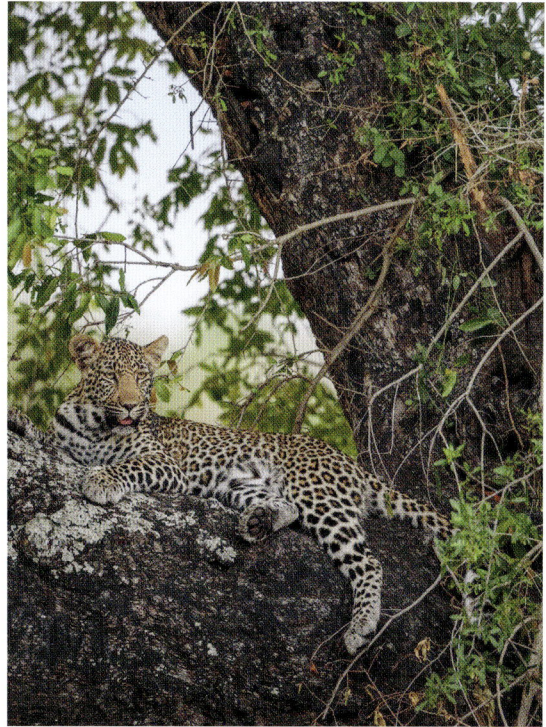

Family Euphorbiaceae

# LAVENDER FEVERBERRY

## *Croton gratissimus* var. *gratissimus*

**A:** laventelkoorsbessie, bergboegoe, makwassieboom
**NS:** mologa  **V:** mufhorola  **Z:** umahlabekufeni

> *Croton:* derived from Greek *kroton* ('ticks'), referring to the seeds' resemblance to ticks; *gratissimus:* 'most pleasing'

Lavender feverberry is a slender shrub or small tree, seldom reaching more than 10m in height, with drooping terminal branches and drooping foliage, often with a few bright red-orange leaves in the crown. It is hardy, fast-growing, drought resistant and frost tolerant, occurring in a variety of woodland vegetation types, mostly on rocky inclines. In South Africa, this species is found only in the northern parts of the country.

From September to November, this attractive tree has an abundance of small cream to yellow flowers in spikes about 10cm long. The small buds stay on the tree for months before the flowers open. Male and female flowers are borne on the same spike: one or two female flowers at the bottom of the spike, while the rest are all male.

The fruit is a three-lobed capsule that turns yellow as it ripens. In late autumn, the capsule dries out, then

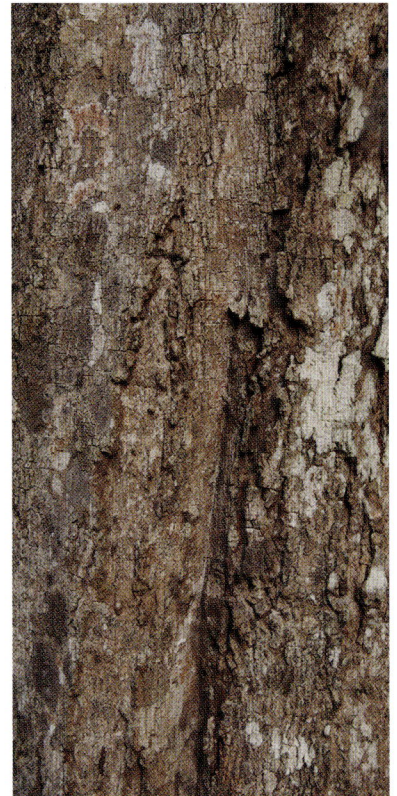

bursts open, flinging the seed away for further dispersal by the wind.

The upper surface of the leaves is shiny and dark green. The lower surface is a striking silvery colour and is covered by dense scales. Scattered cinnamon-coloured glandular scales dot the leaves. Lavender feverberry (var. *gratissimus*) has smooth leaves, distinguishing it from hairy lavender feverberry (var. *subgratissimus*), which has leaves with a hairy upper surface.

The leaves contain an aromatic oil and is only occasionally eaten by kudu and elephant. As the fragrance of the crushed leaves is quite pleasant, this tree has been used for making perfume.

A San name for this species is *maquassi* and the small town of Makwassie is named after it. Boegoeberg in the Northern Cape is also derived from one of the common Afrikaans names for the tree.

Although the lavender feverberry is generally believed to be toxic, is has been planted in gardens and parks.

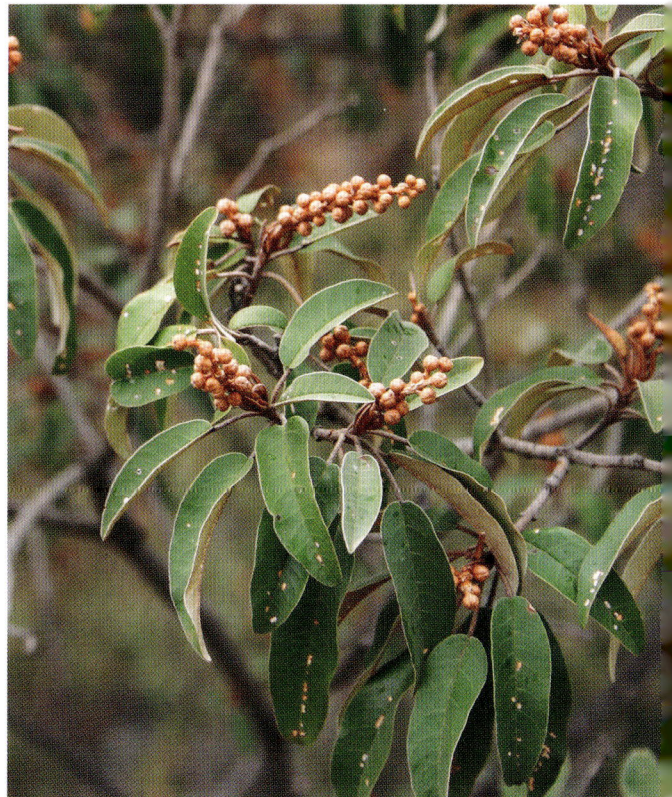

Family Euphorbiaceae

# FEVERBERRY

*Croton megalobotrys*

**A:** grootkoorsbessie  **NS:** motsibi  **V:** muruthu

*megalobotrys:* from Greek *megalos* ('large') and *botrus* ('bunch of grapes'), referring to the bunches of large fruits

The feverberry reaches up to 15m in height. It occurs in riverine bush on alluvial flats, along the banks of rivers and seasonal watercourses, and in understorey vegetation under of larger trees. It is a fine shade tree, common along the Limpopo River from Rooibokkraal to Pafuri, and also occurs in Mpumalanga. A good place to view it is Letaba Camp in the Kruger National Park.

This tree is usually multi-stemmed or branches quite low down. The densely leafed crown is roundish to conical. This tree is typically deciduous, with the leaves turning dark yellow to golden-brown before being shed. If well watered, it may be semi-deciduous. The pale greenish-yellow flowers are borne on separate male and female trees and inflorescences are situated either at the tips of branchlets or in leaf axils. They attract a large variety of insects, which in turn attract insect-eating birds. Impala, nyala, kudu and bushbuck browse the leaves, as do black rhino and elephant, which eat the young branches too. Tree squirrels eagerly open the three-lobed fruits to get at the seeds.

The larvae of the green-veined butterfly (*Charaxes candiope*) also feed on the leaves.

The bark and seeds are sometimes used as a fish poison. The seeds are believed to be effective in treating malaria, hence the common name 'fever-berry', and an oil can also be extracted from them to make soap.

Dry wood is white to off-white with a yellow tinge and distinct buff-brown annual rings. It is light, easy to work, polishes well, does not crack and is used as a general-purpose timber and for carving household items.

# BUSHVELD CANDELABRA-TREE

## *Euphorbia cooperi* var. *cooperi*

A: bosveldkandelaarnaboom, noorsdoring  NS: mohlohlo
V: mukonde-ngala  Z: umhlonhlo

*cooperi:* named after Thomas Cooper (1815–1913), an English plant collector and grower who travelled in South Africa from 1859 to 1862

This spiny, succulent tree has a candelabra-like shape, and grows up to 7m in height. It is found in woody grassland and on rocky outcrops in sandy and loamy to clay soils.

The trunk is stout, cylindrical and unbranched for up to 3m. It is usually also scarred from fallen branches, which leave black holes in the trunk. The branches, which curve upward, have 4–6 wings and resemble a string of large triangular beads. The spines are arranged in pairs along each ridge on the branches. Yellowish-green, bisexual flowers are clustered between the spines along the ridges toward the tips of the branches. The fruit is a maroon three-lobed capsule. Ripe fruits burst open on the tree, flinging seeds several metres away.

All *Euphorbia* species possess toxic latex. The milky latex of the bushveld candelabra tree is probably the most poisonous of all euphorbias, and can cause serious irritation of the skin and eyes, even causing blindness. Taken internally, it can cause death. The latex is used to paralyse fish. The plant is not utilised by game or livestock, but birds eat the seed. Typical of the genus, the wood is soft and fibrous, rendering it unusable, although the tree trunk is sometimes used to make fence poles.

# NABOOM

*Euphorbia ingens*

**A:** gewone naboom  **NS:** mohlohlo-kgomo  **TS:** nkondze

*Euphorbia:* given in honour of Euphorbus, a 1st-century physician to King Juba of Mauretania; *ingens:* 'huge'

This iconic bushveld tree is conspicuously cactus-like, with a short trunk and a large, rounded crown consisting of numerous branches, the ridges of which are set with short spines. It reaches about 10m in height.

Naboom occurs in various types of dry woodland and often on koppies. It is the largest of the *Euphorbia* species and is relatively common in the central parts of South Africa's bushveld.

From autumn to winter, this tree produces small, greenish-yellow flowers on the ridges of its branches, attracting butterflies, bees and insects, which pollinate the flowers. Many fruit-eating birds eagerly feed on the fruit – a round, three-lobed capsule that turns red to purple when ripe. Giraffe and black rhino also utilise this species during the dry season. It provides a home for hole-nesting birds such as woodpeckers.

Naboom is known for its toxic latex. It causes irritation to the skin and damage to eyes – even permanent damage. It is an ingredient in fish poison.

The wood is light but tough and fairly good planks can be obtained from it. Being resistant to wood borer, it has been used as roof struts.

Since 2000, a worrying trend has emerged: these trees are dying off in increasing numbers. An afflicted tree starts turning grey, then its branches rot. This is typically followed by beetle attack and death. Research has revealed that the die-off phenomenon is caused by poor habitat management, such as overgrazing by livestock and bush encroachment, which places the trees under severe stress and enables certain insects to thrive and eventually kill the trees.

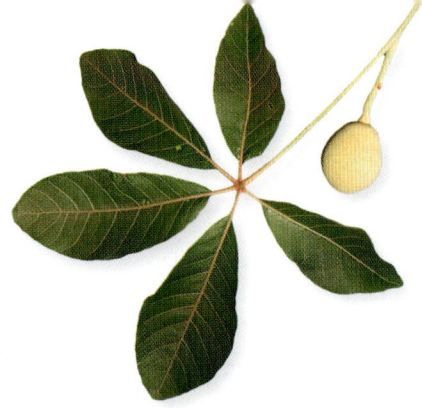

Family Euphorbiaceae

# MANKETTI

*Schinziophyton rautanenii*

A: mankettiboom, spikkelneut, wilde okkerneut
H: omungete  ND: umgoma  SH: mungongoma
TS: mokongwa, monghônghô

*Schinziophyton:* in honour of Swiss explorer and botanist Hans Schinz (1858–1941); *autanenii:* named after Finnish missionary Martti Rautanen (1845–1926)

Manketti, also known as mongongo nut, is an attractive tree with a straight trunk and a spreading canopy, reaching up to 20m in height. It prefers hot and dry climates and grows in deep sand throughout Africa. It is well adapted to its tough environment: the long taproot can reach water deep in the earth; the trunk stores water; the thick bark is resistant to veld fires; and the deciduous leaves enable the tree to retain moisture. A single population in the Lephalale district is the only known occurrence of this species south of the Limpopo River – likely a relic from a time when these trees had a much wider continuous distribution range. As the Limpopo mankettis are in a conservation area, they are not utilised by humans. In the manketti's northern ranges, however, it is valued for its fruits and nuts. The nuts yield a yellow oil, which is used as food or for cosmetics. Finely crushed nuts can be used to make soup or a gravy and are enjoyed with meat or vegetables. The fruits ripen on the ground, turning from yellow to reddish brown, and can be eaten fresh, dried or cooked. They are also used for making alcoholic beverages, soap and sweet porridge. The yellowish wood is light, soft and durable, and is used in the curio trade.

Cheetahs seem to have developed a special affinity for this tree. The trunks of the Limpopo mankettis often show scratch marks made by cheetah claws. Cheetah scat is often found on dead trees that have fallen over.

# KUDUBERRY

*Pseudolachnostylis maprouneifolia*
var. *maprouneifolia*

**A:** koedoebessie  **ND:** umqobampunzi
**SH:** mutsonzowa  **V:** muṭonḓowe

*Deudorix dinochares*

*Pseudolachnostylis:* resembling the genus *Lachnostylis;*
*maprouneifolia:* with leaves resembling those of the
magic-nut *Maprounea*

Kuduberry is an attractive, deciduous tree with a roundish
crown, growing up to 12m in height. It is found on rocky
slopes and in frost-free woodland, riverine fringes and
sandveld, and grows best in deep, well-drained soils in
Limpopo. It is usually single-stemmed, with a straight trunk
that branches relatively high up. In autumn, the leaves
change to a spectacular fiery red colour before being shed.

Kuduberry is a larval food plant for the butterflies
paradise skipper (*Abantis paradisea*) and apricot playboy
(*Deudorix dinochares*). The flowers are known to attract
bees, but the tree is also pollinated by a variety of other
insects such as wasps. From April onwards, the still-green
fruits start falling and then ripen on the ground. Kudu
eagerly feed on these, hence the tree's common name.
While other antelope also eat the fruit, it is not palatable to
humans. Some fruits may remain on the tree year round,
and old fruits from the previous season can sometimes be
found next to new ones.

The seeds are dispersed by elephant and antelope.

The wood is moderately heavy and smooth, with an
even grain. It is used for turning and handicrafts, as well
as for making charcoal.

Although this slow grower can handle drought and hot
climates quite well, it cannot tolerate frost.

In Zimbabwe, this tree is known as duikerberry.

Family Euphorbiaceae

# TAMBOTI

*Spirostachys africana*

A: tambotie  NS: morekuri  SW: umtfombotsi
TG: ndzopfori  TS: morukuru  V: muonze  Z: umthombothi

## PROTECTED IN SOUTH AFRICA

*Spirostachys:* from Greek *speiros* ('coil, twist') and *stakhus* ('ear of grain') referring to the spiral arrangement of the flowers on the spike; *africana:* 'from Africa'

Tamboti is a slow-growing, deciduous tree of up to 15m in height, with a rounded crown. The thick, rough bark is dark brown to black, and characteristically cracked into regular rectangular blocks, which are arranged in longitudinal rows.

The fruit is a three-lobed capsule. When ripe, it bursts open, and these 'explosions' can often be heard on hot summer days. Tamboti is one of South Africa's 'jumping bean' trees – when its seeds become infested with the larvae of the snout moth *Emporia melanobasis*, the seeds jerk and jump centimetres into the air.

The sapwood is creamy, but the heartwood is a beautiful rich brown. The wood is very popular as it is hard, durable and resistant to termites and wood borers – ideal for making high-quality furniture. Many a bushveld homestead proudly displays lounge and dining-room suites made of tamboti, but it is becoming increasingly difficult to obtain timber of decent size.

Although the wood is very hard, it is not used as firewood as the smoke causes headaches and nausea and makes food unpalatable. The milky latex is poisonous and causes extreme irritation to skin, as well as pain and damage to the eyes. Great care should be taken when living trees are cut down or sawn. It is not surprising that tamboti is sometimes used as a fish poison. Insects avoid the wood – in fact, pieces of wood can be placed among clothes as a repellent.

Kudu, nyala, impala, vervet monkeys, elephant, bushbuck, giraffe and eland browse on fresh leaves, while black rhino eat the young branches. Duiker, impala and nyala also feed on dry fallen leaves.

*Flowering spikes: female flowers arered, while male flowers are gold-coloured owing to the pollen.*

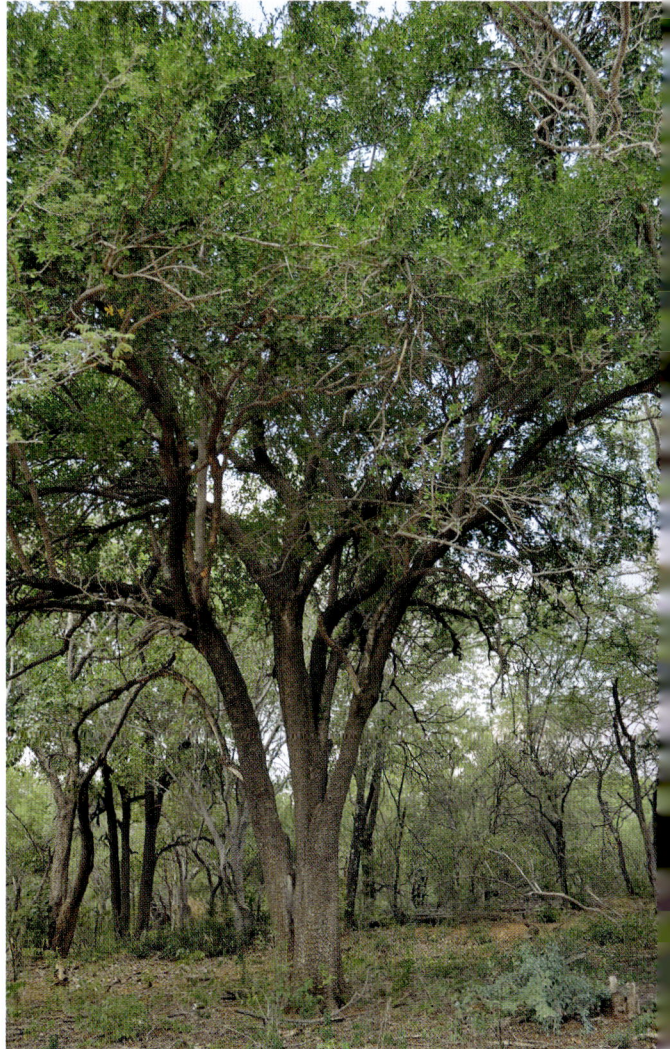

# LEBOMBO-WATTLE

## Newtonia hildebrandtii var. hildebrandtii

**A:** Lebombowattel  **Z:** udongolokamadilika, umfomothi

### PROTECTED IN SOUTH AFRICA

*Newtonia:* named after Francisco Xavier Oakley de Aguiar Newton (1864–1909), who collected plants in Angola from 1885 to 1886; *hildebrandtii:* named after Johan Maria Hildebrandt (1847–1881), a German plant collector, biologist and explorer

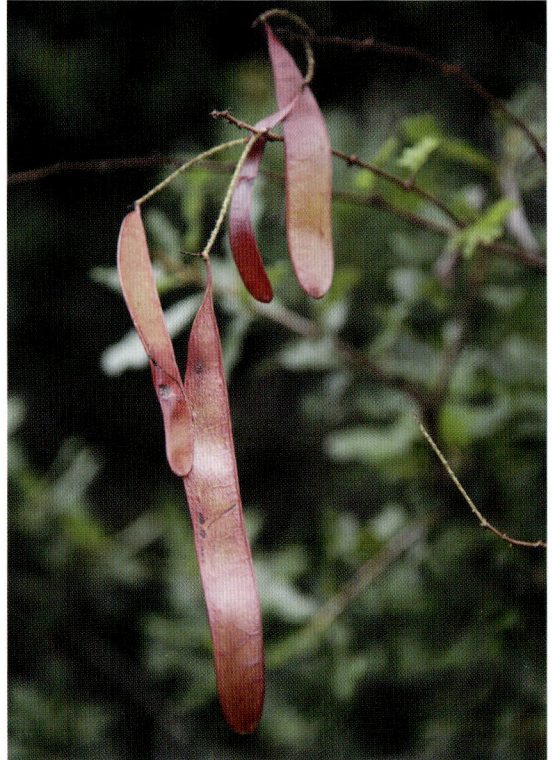

Lebombo-wattle is an icon of the Maputaland sand forest: an impressive deciduous tree of up to 25m in height, with a rounded spreading crown. The bark is dark grey to almost black, cracked and longitudinally flaking. The leaves are doubly compound. The flowers are arranged in long, creamy white spikes, appearing in clusters in December and January. The long, red pods develop from April to September in bunches, splitting on the tree to reveal the large, flat, pinkish-brown seeds, which are surrounded by a brownish papery wing.

This magnificent tree is the host of nearly all sand forest epiphytic orchids (such as *Cyrtorchis praetermissa* subsp. *zuluensis, Aerangis mystacidii, Mystacidium venosum* and *Mycrocoelia exilis*). It also hosts the hanging wild cactus (*Rhipsalis baccifera*), South Africa's only indigenous cactus, as well as some epiphytic ferns that are endemic to the sand forest.

Since there are usually no seedlings or young trees in the immediate vicinity of the Lebombo-wattle, this tree is suspected of releasing chemical compounds that inhibit the growth of surrounding plants.

The wood is very hard, heavy and dark reddish brown. It is used in construction and for poles, implements and carving. It is also very popular as firewood and for making charcoal and is sold in bundles in Maputaland, especially along the road between Jozini and Kosi Bay.

Family Gentianaceae

# FOREST BIGLEAF
*Anthocleista grandiflora*

A: boskoorsboom, grootblaarboom  NS: mophala
SW: umhobohobo  TG: geludzu  V: mueneene

*Anthocleista:* from Greek *anthos* ('flower') and *kleistos*, ('closed'), likely a reference to the stamens closing off the floral tube by forming a ring around its mouth; *grandiflora:* 'large-flowered'

Forest bigleaf is a pioneer species characteristic of the high-rainfall forests of the Drakensberg Escarpment and does not occur further west. It is a slender, evergreen tree of up to 30m, with a tall, straight trunk. Its leathery leaves are clustered at the ends of branches and are the largest simple leaves of any tree in southern Africa. The longest leaves are found on young trees and can be well over a metre in length.

The fragrant, creamy white flowers appear in September. They turn yellow and then brown with age. They attract many different insect species, which in turn attract insect-eating birds. The fruit is a fleshy, smooth berry, soft and yellowish brown when ripe, with many small, dark brown seeds. Birds, samango monkeys and fruit bats visit the tree to feed on the fruits, while bushpig and some of the forest species of duiker eat fallen fruits. Elephant are known to eat the tree's leaves and branches.

This species grows fast and the wood is soft and brittle, with little practical use. Forest bigleaf is a striking, attractive tree for the large garden, provided it gets plenty of water and is not subjected to frost.

# FOREST LAVENDERTREE

### *Heteropyxis canescens*

**A:** boslaventelboom  **SW:** inkunzana

*canescens:* 'whitening', referring to the ash-grey colour of the hairs on branches and the under-surface of leaves

This dioecious, evergreen or semi-deciduous tree is fairly rare, with a small distribution range along the Drakensberg escarpment in Mpumalanga. It is found in semi-moist conditions along streams in forests and forest margins. Under ideal conditions, it can grow up to 20m in height, but is usually much smaller, especially under garden conditions. It has attractive, pale orange to beige bark that flakes off in patches to leave distinctive blotches.

The narrowly elliptic, simple, large, leathery leaves are alternate or spirally arranged. Their upper surface is dark green above and the underside is paler green with grey hairs. In winter, the leaves turn deep red and persist on the tree for most of the cold months. When crushed, the leaves produce a pleasant lavender smell, hence the common name. Small, yellow-green flowers appear in clusters on the ends of branches and attract butterflies, bees, wasps and other insects.

The root system of this rather poorly known species is not aggressive and the tree does not get very big. It is also somewhat frost tolerant (though not drought tolerant), making it suitable for gardens and landscapes. It is easily propagated from fresh seeds, hardy and fast-growing. Since it is not a common tree, there are no known traditional uses of the tree or its wood.

# LAVENDERTREE

## *Heteropyxis natalensis*

**A:** laventelboom  **SW:** inkunzi  **TG:** thathasani
**V:** mudedede  **Z:** inkhuzwa

*Heteropyxis:* from Greek *heteros* ('different') and Latin *pyxis* ('small box with lid'), referring to the fruit, which may look as if it has a lid; *natalensis:* refers to its place of origin, KwaZulu-Natal

This deciduous tree has drooping foliage and a neat, small crown. It grows to about 10m in height, occurring in the eastern parts of South Africa along forest margins and on rocky hillsides.

The main trunk is usually crooked and sometimes fluted. Initially, the bark is smooth and pale with tawny, silvery hues, darker grey patches and a papery grain. As the tree matures, the bark develops a rich texture and flakes off in large scales, leaving craggy, apricot-coloured patches that provide shelter for a myriad tiny insects and ants.

The leaves are shiny dark green above and paler green below. The midrib is prominent but the lateral veins are

inconspicuous. There are domatia (small cavities that house arthropods) in the axils of the lateral veins. Crushed leaves and twigs produce a strong lavender scent.

In autumn, the leaves turn red or purple. Depending on how cold it is, the tree may hold onto them during winter and drop them only a few weeks before the new leaves appear.

The minute, yellowish-green and sweetly scented flowers appear in summer and are borne in clusters at the ends of twigs. The masses of flowers attract many insects, which attract insect-eating birds. The fruit is a small, shiny, brown oval capsule and eventually splits into two or three valves to release the numerous seeds inside it.

The bark and leaves are eaten by black rhino, while kudu and bush duiker feed on the leaves. The wood is pale pinkish brown, tough, hard and very fine-grained, and is used mainly as fencing posts and for making charcoal. The tree is also ideal for clustered or boundary plantings, or as a feature plant on its own.

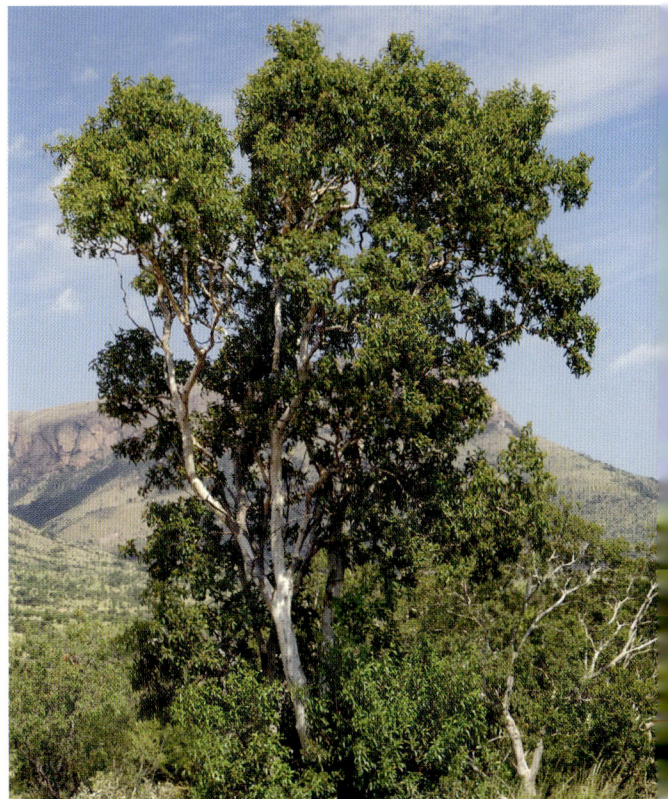

# WHITE-SYRINGA

## *Kirkia acuminata*

A: witsering  TG: mvumayila  TS: modumêla  V: mubvumela

*Kirkia:* in honour of Sir John Kirk (1832–1922), a Scottish explorer and naturalist who accompanied David Livingstone on his Zambezi expedition in 1858–1864; *acuminata:* refers to the narrowly tapering leaf tip

This tall attractive, straight-boled, deciduous tree reaches up to 20m in height, with a large, rounded, spreading but somewhat sparse crown. It is very drought resistant and grows on sandy soils or rocky hills throughout the northern parts of South Africa. In autumn, the leaves turn yellow with tinges of red. During the dry winter, the tree is completely bare and all the branches, branchlets and fruit seem to reach for the sky in a beautiful symmetry. The trunk generally branches high up and is bare and straight.

Elephant and antelope browse on the foliage and bushbuck have been observed eating the fallen leaves. White-syringa is, however, not tolerant of destruction by elephant.

The heartwood is brownish with attractive dark brown veining and a straight grain, giving it a fine texture. It is easily sawn, but will rapidly blunt tools owing to the presence of silica crystals. It also planes easily and turns and polishes well. The wood has many uses: poles, planks, household utensils such as bowls and spoons, carving, curios, boxes and crates, novelties, turnery, flooring, furniture, cabinet work and light construction. Strong rope can be made from the plaited inner bark, although this rope loses much of its strength when dry.

# MOUNTAIN-SYRINGA

## *Kirkia wilmsii*

**A:** bergsering **NS:** modumela

*wilmsii:* named after Friedrich Wilms (1848–1919), a German pharmacist, botanist and plant collector who lived in Lydenburg

This smallish, graceful tree has an irregular spreading canopy and grows up to 15m tall. It prefers granite and dolomitic soils in dry places and is usually found on mountain slopes. This deciduous species is endemic to Limpopo and Mpumalanga.

The trunk is short and often branches near the base. The leaves turn yellow to bright red in autumn and can provide a spectacular sight. The sprays of greenish-white flowers appear in spring and are pollinated by small insects. The seeds are mainly distributed by wind.

Mountain-syringa is browsed by elephant, kudu, klipspringer and bush duiker, and impala are known to eat fallen leaves.

The timber has no heartwood, is light and soft, with many small conspicuous pores. Whereas the wood has no functional use, good rope can be made from the inner bark.

The roots are thick and contain water, enabling the tree to survive brief periods of drought. Humans have harvested these roots in times of drought as well.

# TINDERWOOD

### Clerodendrum glabrum

**A:** tontelhout, bitterblaar, stinkboom  **NS:** mohlokohloko
**SW:** umphehlavatsi  **TG:** xinhun'welambeva  **V:** munukha-tshilongwe
**X:** uqangazane, uqangazani  **Z:** ifamu

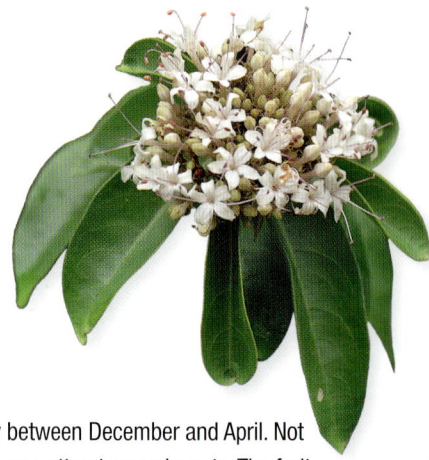

*Volkameria:* named after botanist Johann Christoph Volkamer (1644–1720); *glabra:* 'hairless'

Tinderwood can be a shrub or a smallish deciduous tree up to 12m in height. It is widely distributed in Limpopo, where it occurs in open woodland, on rocky hillsides and in riverine thickets.

The crown and leaves are often drooping and the stems and branches are covered in white lenticels. The leaves are opposite or, mostly, in whorls of three or four, and are folded up on either side of the midrib. They produce an unpleasant scent when crushed. The tree is known for its profusion of white to pale pink flowers, with pink to purplish protruding stamens. The flowers are borne in dense, rounded terminal heads – with inflorescences of up to ten flowers – and make for a showy display between December and April. Not surprisingly, the flowers attract many insects. The fruit is a cream to yellow fleshy drupe when ripe and remains on the tree for months. It is eaten by a variety of birds. The leaves are also a food source for the butterfly larvae of the Natal bar (*Cigaritis natalensis*) and the purple-brown hairstreak (*Hypolycaena phillippus*). Spittlebug nymphs feed on the sap from the tree and produce a protective foam, which drips from their bodies to the ground.

The wood is whitish to light brown, hard and close-grained but somewhat brittle. It is often used as tinder-wood to start fires, hence the common name. It has also been used for fish kraals and in hut construction. Its magnificent flower display makes this fast-growing species a popular garden tree.

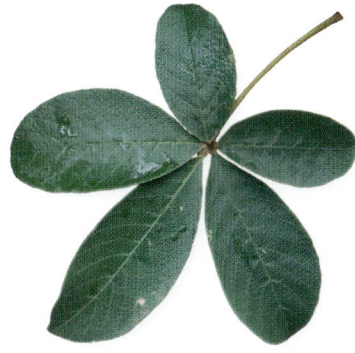

# POORABERRY

## *Vitex pooara*

**A:** poerabessie, stinkbessie **X:** inunkisiqaqa

*Vitex:* from Latin *vieo* ('to weave' or 'tie up'), referring to the flexible stems of some species in this genus

One of seven *Vitex* species in South Africa, pooraberry is a small deciduous tree of up to 5m in height with spreading branches and a rounded crown. This somewhat rare species is thought to be a South African endemic, with a limited distribution range in the northwestern parts of the country – Limpopo and North West.

It occurs on rocky ridges and outcrops, on Kalahari sand and in deciduous woodland. The sour bushveld of the Waterberg is a particularly good place to see them, but they are also found in the vicinity of Rustenburg and Modimolle.

The bark of mature trees is brown, ribbed and cracked, and peels in strips. The leaves are opposite, with five leaflets and velvety on both sides. The leaf stalks are 3–8cm long, but there are small petiolules on the leaflets. Pooraberry produces only a few small bisexual flowers from late November to December. These are pale blue or mauve and whitish, and borne in axillary heads. The small, round fruit is fleshy and black when ripe, with a persistent calyx forming a saucer at the base. It is edible, either raw or cooked, but not particularly pleasant. The tree is also known as smelly-berry fingerleaf.

Family Lauraceae

# STINKWOOD

## *Ocotea bullata*

A: stinkhout, swartstinkhout  X: umnukane
Z: umnukane

### PROTECTED IN SOUTH AFRICA

*Ocotea:* probably derived from the indigenous name for
*Ocotea guianensis* in French Guiana; *bullata:* from Latin
bulla ('bubble'), referring to the swellings on the leaves

This valuable species, famed for its beautiful timber, occurs in the high forests of South Africa. Its distribution range stretches from Table Mountain to the montane forests of Limpopo, though it is quite rare in the Eastern Cape, where it is replaced by sneezewood (*Ptaeroxylon obliquum*).

Stinkwood is a tall, slow-growing, evergreen tree that reaches up to 30m in height under ideal conditions. It usually has a single, long, straight trunk, but shoots sometimes develop at the base and these may grow into additional trunks. The trunk can develop fluting and buttresses when mature. The simple, alternate, leathery leaves are dark glossy green, with wavy smooth-edged margins. Distinctive 'bubbles' or swellings are present on the upper surface of the leaves, in the axils of lateral veins. Young leaves and leaf stalks are often red.

The small yellowish-green or creamy flowers appear in loose clusters in midsummer in the axils of leaf stalks near the tips of branches. They are often dioecious, but may be monoecious. The fruit resembles an acorn. It matures from yellowish green to purple when ripe, and is eagerly eaten by birds such as African olive pigeons, eastern bronze-naped pigeons and Cape parrots.

Stinkwood timber is highly sought after by furniture manufacturers. Along with real yellowwood (*Podocarpus latifolius*), it was used extensively to make traditional Cape furniture. In days gone by it was also used for wagons, boats, gunstocks, doors and window frames. The wood is reddish brown to black with a yellowish sapwood. The texture is fine and smooth. The timber is moderately hard and heavy with a beautiful lustre and takes a fine polish.

Although stinkwood is easy to saw and turns well, it can be demanding on tools. The sawdust is reported to be an irritant, causing sneezing. The common name is derived from the unpleasant smell of the freshly cut wood.

Traditionally, the Knysna forests have been the primary source of stinkwood timber and it did not take long for these forests to become depleted of large specimens. The timber is now almost unobtainable and extremely expensive. Today, a well-run programme is in place to manage the recovery of stinkwood in the Knysna forests. Unfortunately, this species has been extirpated on the slopes of Table Mountain and replaced by pine plantations.

# CAPE-ASH

*Ekebergia capensis*

**A:** essenhout  **NS:** mmidibidi  **SW:** umnyamatsi  **TG:** nyamarhu

*Ekebergia:* named after Captain Carl Gustaf Ekeberg (1716–1784), who sponsored a botanical expedition to Africa in the 18th century; *capensis:* 'from the Cape'

This large, attractive, fast-growing, evergreen tree has been used to line the streets of many South African cities and towns. It also makes for a popular garden tree. This species grows in various habitats and occurs from sea level to altitudes of about 1,500m.

Cape-ash has a roundish crown and can reach about 15m in height. The rough bark is grey to almost black, especially in older specimens, and often mottled, sometimes flaking in small circles or squares. Its trunk measures up to 9m in height and is swollen at the base. In forests, the trunk may be tall and fluted, but in open areas it is usually much shorter and unfluted. It is buttressed in some specimens.

The glossy green leaves are often tinged with a pinkish patch and are consumed by various browsers and livestock. The small, sweetly scented flowers are white, but may occasionally also have a pink tinge. Being dioecious, only female plants bear fruit. The fleshy, bright pink to red berries are almost spherical and are eaten by birds, including Knysna and purple-crested turacos, bulbuls, barbets, mousebirds and hornbills. Birds, along with primates, are the main distributors of Cape-ash seeds. Bushbuck and nyala also eat fallen fruits, and the plant hosts various moths and butterflies.

The straw-coloured wood is light, soft and easy to work, and has been used to make furniture.

Family Meliaceae

# FOREST NATAL-MAHOGANY

*Trichilia dregeana*

A: bosrooiessenhout  NS: mmaba  V: muṱuhu
X: umkhuhlu  Z: umkhuhlu, umathunzini

*Trichilia:* 'three-lipped', from Greek *kheilos* ('lip') referring to the three-lobed fruit; *dregeana:* named after Johan Drège (1794–1881), a German botanist who collected plants in South Africa

Beautiful dark foliage and a large, dense, rounded crown are characteristic of forest Natal-mahogany. This evergreen dioecious tree occurs in forests from the Eastern Cape through to KwaZulu-Natal, Eswatini, Mpumalanga and Limpopo.

This species is able to reach an impressive 35m in height, sometimes more. The cylindrical trunk is often slightly buttressed. The creamy white flowers, with their large petals, appear in early summer in short, densely packed heads.

The fruit is a creamy brown, green or off-purple capsule that splits into three or four valves in autumn to reveal up to six red seeds, each with a black patch.

This multi-purpose tree is harvested from the wild for its fruit and medicinal properties. The oil in the seeds can be used to make soaps, candles and cosmetics. The smooth and pale grey bark is toxic and is used to poison fish.

The sapwood is whitish and the heartwood pale brown to pink. When oiled, the wood darkens, leaving little difference between sapwood and heartwood. It works easily and polishes well, but is not durable and is subject to borer attack. The wood is used for carvings, furniture, household utensils, construction, shelving and canoes, and also for fuel and making charcoal.

Several butterfly species use the forest Natal-mahogany as a breeding tree, and various bird species nest in the dense foliage. The seeds also attract birds and baboons.

Forest Natal-mahogany is fast-growing and tolerant of fire. Although it is frost-sensitive, it is often able to recover from frost damage. It does not handle prolonged drought well.

## Family Meliaceae

# BUSHVELD NATAL-MAHOGANY

*Trichilia emetica* subsp. *emetica*

A: rooiessenhout  NS: mamba  SW: umkhuhlu
TG: nkuhlu  V: mutshikili  Z: umkhuhlu

*emetica:* 'causing vomiting'

This particularly attractive, fast-growing tree can reach over 20m in height. It is evergreen or semi-deciduous, with a large, dense, rounded crown and dark green foliage. It is an excellent shade tree, occurring in woodland and riverine forest and is widespread on alluvial soils in the higher rainfall areas (600mm and more) of KwaZulu-Natal.

The fragrant, creamy green flowers are borne in dense sprays. The fruit is a velvety, pale green, spherical, woody capsule with black seeds that are largely hidden by a bright red fleshy covering. The seeds and flowers attract various birds and insects; the leaves and shoots are browsed by herbivores such as kudu and nyala; and the fruit is eaten by monkeys and baboons. The seeds are reportedly poisonous, but are nevertheless eaten without ill effect by glossy starlings and turacos. Natal-mahogany is one of the country's 'rain trees', as it is home to spittlebug nymphs that feed on sap and generate foam, which drips from the tree. Several other insects are also associated with the Natal-mahogany: the leaves are eaten by the caterpillars of the leaf emperor moth (*Pselaphelia flavivitta*) and the seeds provide a home for the weevil *Acatus rhombicus*.

The light brown to pinkish wood is soft, light and evenly grained, takes a good polish and darkens with age. Even though the wood is susceptible to borer attack, it has been used for furniture, dugout canoes and household utensils, and is sought after for carvings for the curio industry. The seed oil can be used for making soap. A pinkish dye can be obtained from the bark.

# MOUNTAIN MAHOGANY
## *Entandrophragma caudatum*
A: bergmahonie  TS: mophumêna  V: munzhounzhou

*Entandrophragma:* From Greek *en-* ('in'), *andros* ('male, stamen') and *phragma* ('partition'), which refers to the tube formed by the stamens; *caudatum:* 'having a tail', referring to the long tips of the leaflets

This lovely, drought-tolerant but frost-sensitive deciduous tree has a straight trunk, which usually branches relatively high up and is sometimes fluted. This tree can reach up to 30m in height, growing in open woodland, dry bushveld on rocky hillsides and sandy soil. It is often associated with Zambezi teak (*Baikiaea plurijuga*) on Kalahari sands.

The alternative English name 'wooden banana' is derived from the fruit: a woody capsule that splits into five backward-curving valves, resembling a peeled banana. The fruit is not edible, however. The seeds are large and winged, spinning as they fall, and are dispersed by wind.

The wood is red-brown and highly rated for making furniture, but the trees are not common. In addition, living trees are attacked by borers, resulting in a great deal of damage. A large amount of deep-red sap appears from between the wood and the bark when the tree is cut, and is used for tanning and as a dye. The value of this species as a source of browse is uncertain.

# FLATCROWN

*Albizia adianthifolia* var. *adianthifolia*

**A:** platkroon  **SW:** ligowane  **V:** muelela
**X:** umhlandlothi  **Z:** usolu

*Albizia:* named after Filippo Degli Albizzi, an Italian naturalist who brought seeds from Constantinople to Florence in 1749; *adianthifolia:* refers to the resemblance of the leaves to those of the maidenhair fern *Adiantum*

*Albizia* shrubs or trees look like species of *Vachellia* or *Senegalia* (thorn trees previously grouped in the genus *Acacia*) but have no thorns.

This fabulous tree has a flat crown, which – along with its rectangular leaflets – makes the species easily recognisable. This is a fast-growing, deciduous tree with a tall, straight trunk, and reaches close to 40m in height under ideal conditions. It occurs in the moister eastern parts of South Africa, in low-altitude, open forests, forest margins and ravines.

Scented pincushion-like flowers appear, often in profusion, in early summer and attract a variety of butterflies that feed on the nectar. The flowers are white and arranged in hemispherical heads. The stamens form a tube with reddish pink or green tips. Papery, pale brown pods bulge over the seeds and hang in profusion from the branches well into summer. Blue duiker are known to eat these seedpods, while elephant feed on the leaves and twigs. The bark is believed to be poisonous.

This species has a symbiotic relationship with certain soil bacteria, which form nodules on the roots and fix atmospheric nitrogen. Some of this nitrogen is utilised by the growing plant, but some can also be used by other plants growing nearby.

The sapwood is white and the heartwood light brown to golden-yellow. This straight-grained, soft and light wood is a popular general-purpose timber, and has been used for flooring, as it works easily and is not inclined to warp.

The tree is a natural pioneer species and grows reasonably fast, but does not handle drought and frost well. It is an excellent shade tree for large gardens in suitable habitat, but can be messy near swimming pools.

Flatcrown also has a number of medicinal uses.

# WORM-BARK FALSE-THORN

## *Albizia anthelmintica*

**A:** wurmbasvalsdoring, deurmekaarvalsdoring  **TS:** mmola, monoga
**V:** mukuvhavhadinda  **Z:** umnala

*anthelmintica:* 'for the treatment of intestinal worm infestation', referring to the use of the bark as a cure against parasitic worms

This multi-stemmed deciduous tree reaches up to 10m in height and is often quite untidy in appearance. It occurs in semi-arid areas, from the bushveld in South Africa to Namibia. It prefers clay but can fare well in deep red sand.

The grey to brown bark is typically longitudinally fissured. Young branchlets are mostly smooth and often spine-tipped. The creamy white inflorescences are borne on short branchlets and appear in spring, before the new leaves, attracting a variety of insects and birds. Typical of the false-thorn trees, the flowers are borne in profusion and are powderpuff-like with long stamens.

This tree is browsed by kudu, eland and impala. Elephant strip the bark, which porcupines are also known to eat. Having deep roots, this tree plays an important role in soil protection. It is a fixer of atmospheric nitrogen owing to a symbiotic relationship with certain soil bacteria, which form nodules on the roots. The nitrogen released by the bacteria is used by the growing tree, as well as by other nearby trees.

The heartwood is an attractive, light red-brown colour and can be used for furniture, implement handles, spoons, carvings and turnery. Twigs can be used as toothbrushes.

This is quite an attractive tree when in bloom and is suitable for ornamental purposes. It is hardy and slow-growing. It prefers full sun and can withstand both drought and frost.

# ROCK FALSE-THORN

*Albizia brevifolia*

**A:** bergvalsdoring, klipvalsdoring  **NS:** mošalakgwale
**TS:** mmola, molalakgaka  **V:** mutsilari

*brevifolia:* refers to the short structure of the leaves

This deciduous species grows into a shrub or small tree of up to 15m in height and has a sparse crown. It is found on dry, rocky hillsides – often basalt, but also sandstone.

The bark is grey to almost black, smooth or shallowly fissured, and the pale brown pods are borne singly or in pairs. Branchlets can be spine-tipped, and the blue-green, doubly compound leaves are typically as broad as they are long, with leaflets arranged into 6–10 groups. This species is easily confused with bushveld false-thorn (*A. harveyi*), but the latter has sickle-shaped hairy leaflets arranged in 12–28 groups.

Striking, creamy white to yellowish fluffy flowers appear in spring and attract insects and insect-eating birds, such as green woodhoopoes and mountain wheatears. This species is not well studied, but believed to be browsed by kudu, klipspringer, giraffe and elephant, among others.

The wood is whitish, hard and heavy, but susceptible to wood borers. It is mostly used for implement handles.

# BUSHVELD FALSE-THORN

## Albizia harveyi

**A:** bleekblaarboom, basterwag-'n-bietjie, bosveldvalsdoring
**NS:** mohlalakgakga **TG:** molela **TS:** mmola **V:** muvhola

*harveyi:* named after Irish botanist William Harvey (1811–1866), who spent several years collecting plants in the Cape Colony

This slender, deciduous tree usually has a rounded or narrowly rounded crown (occasionally flat) and does not exceed 12m in height. It occurs in mixed woodland and dry bushveld in the northern and eastern parts of the South African bushveld. It is particularly prevalent around termite mounds in loamy soil. Fast-growing and drought resistant, it seemingly handles hot environments very well.

The grey-brown bark is fissured and reticulate. Fluffy, creamy white flowers appear in hemispherical heads in summer and attract numerous insects and insect-eating birds, such as crimson-breasted shrikes, white-fronted bee-eaters, magpie shrikes, white-crested helmetshrikes and fork-tailed drongos. The tree is pollinated by bees and other insects.

Like other *Albizia* species, the bushveld false-thorn has a symbiotic relationship with ants, which are attracted to the nectar secreted by glands on the leaf stalks and rachis. The ants seem to protect the tree from other leaf-eating insects. As is the case with the rest of the genus, this species is an atmospheric nitrogen fixer.

Though this tree does not seem useful at first glance, it is browsed by a number of herbivores, and elephant sometimes strip the bark. It is occasionally used as fodder for livestock.

# MANY-STEMMED FALSE-THORN

*Albizia petersiana* subsp. *evansii*

A: meerstamvalsdoring  Z: umnala, umnalaqho

*petersiana:* Named after Wilhelm Peters (1815–1863), a German naturalist who collected plants in Mozambique

This deciduous tree reaches up to 20m in height, branching freely from the base at a sharp angle to assume a funnel-like shape. In winter, the V-shape of this tree's multiple bare branches is conspicuous. The crown can be flat or rounded.

The distribution range of this subspecies is restricted to Maputaland, the lowveld of Limpopo, southern Mozambique and Eswatini. It is found in sandy soils in open woodland and bushveld.

The rough, grey bark splits irregularly in longitudinal fissures and peels in thin strips. The leaves, which have rough hairs on the under-surface, have relatively few leaflets. The leaves may resemble those of worm-bark false-thorn (*A. anthelmintica*), but the almost hairless leaves of this species distinguishes it from many-stemmed false-thorn. In spring, the leaves are a beautiful coppery red. In autumn, the leaves turn yellow before being shed. The flowers are produced in small heads with the new leaves from October to December.

The woody pods are narrow and brown to deep reddish purple. Young pods are browsed by giraffe, while the leaves are eaten by elephant and antelope. Leaves and young pods are also used as fodder for livestock.

# PAPERBARK FALSE-THORN

*Albizia tanganyicensis* subsp. *tanganyicencis*

A: papierbasvalsdoring  V: mulelu

*tanganyicensis:* 'from Tanganyika', the former name
of Tanzania

Arguably the most attractive and distinctive of the *Albizia* species, paperbark false-thorn is a deciduous tree with a straight, tall trunk and a sparse, somewhat spreading or flattened crown. It is found throughout southern Africa, mostly on koppies or rocky hill slopes in dry bushveld, and grows up to 20m in height. It is quite a common species in the Waterberg region of Limpopo. In winter, when the leaves have dropped, the bare, almost white trees stand out against the slopes of the dry koppies.

This tree is known for its smooth, creamy white bark, which peels into large, papery sheets – hence the name paperbark false-thorn. One can write on these brittle sheets with a soft pencil.

This species is one of the first to sprout in spring, the flowers appearing before the leaves. The hairy, yellow flowers provide a striking sight in a time when the rest of the bush is still dull and grey. The leaves are initially red-brown, then turn pale green. Mature leaves are grey-green. They are doubly compound and the leaflets are large for an *Albizia* species.

Elephant eat the leaves and young branches, and browsing antelope, such as kudu, may eat the flowers and leaves. Seeds and pods are poisonous – unripe pods especially so – though brown-headed parrots are known to enjoy green seeds. Larvae of the satyr charaxes (*Charaxes ethalion ethalion*) also feed on the leaves.

The light-brown heartwood is fairly hard and of a good texture, but rarely used, other than for carvings. Sawdust from the wood irritates the throat and nose.

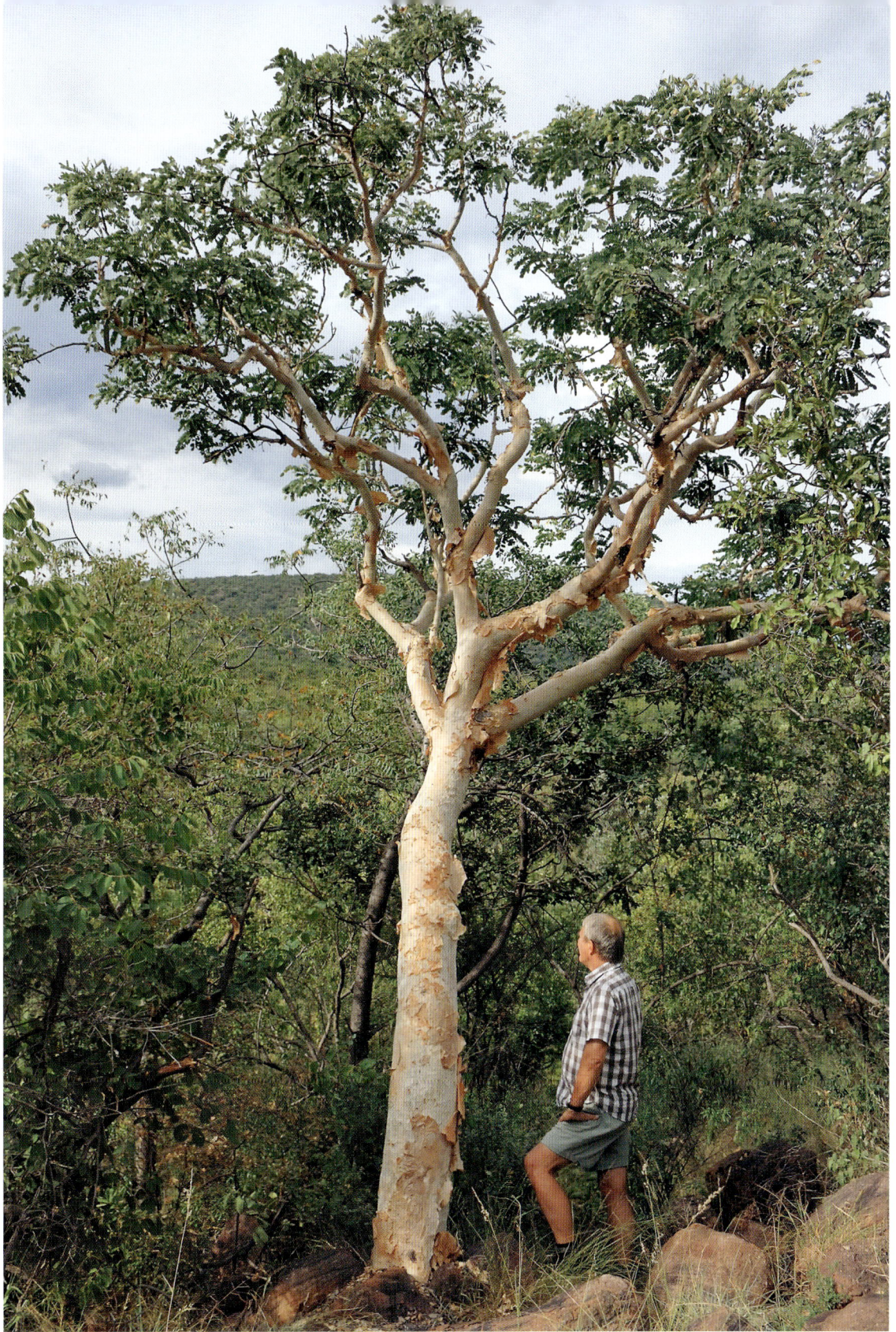

# LARGE-LEAVED FALSE-THORN

## *Albizia versicolor*

**A:** grootblaarvalsdoring  **ND:** umnonjwana  **NS:** mohlalabata
**SW:** sivangatane, umvangatana  **TG:** mbhesu  **TS:** mmola  **V:** muṱamba-pfunda

*versicolor:* Latin, 'variously coloured', referring to the variety of colours displayed by the fresh spring leaves and young pods

This strikingly beautiful, hardy, deciduous tree can sometimes reach 20m in height and has a spreading but somewhat sparse crown. Its presence is considered an indication of groundwater. As the common name indicates, the leaflets of the doubly compound, opposite leaves are quite large. In early summer, the flowers appear in fluffy, creamy white, hemispherical heads, with characteristically long stamens (up to 7cm). The flowers attract pollinating insects. The fruit is a large pod, reddish brown when young but pale brown when mature, and thinly textured, with thickened margins. Pods contain a toxin, tetramethoxypyridoxine, which causes a deadly neurological condition known as albiziosis. Young pods are the most toxic, although animals are more likely to be poisoned by eating fallen ripe pods.

Owing to its toxicity, this tree is not much utilised by game, although elephant and browsing antelope feed on the leaves and brown-headed parrots eat the seeds.

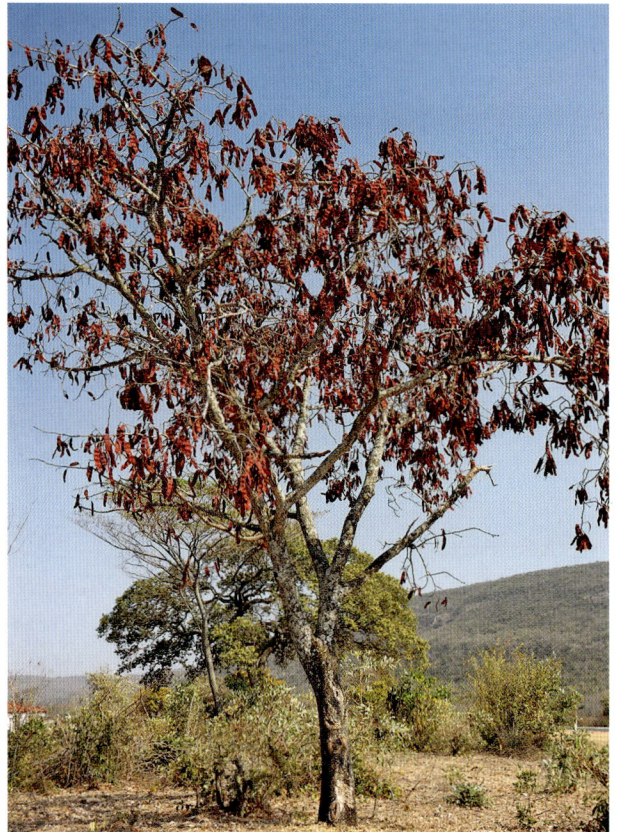

Large-leaved false-thorn is a useful tree: it improves the soil by fixing nitrogen; reduces erosion with its robust rooting system; and provides mulch when its leaves fall. Its light canopy shields crops such as sorghum and maize from too much sunlight, without depriving them completely.

The heartwood is light brown to purplish brown, often with dark (sometimes almost black) stripes, which create a sharp contrast with the white sapwood. It saws and works well, but the sawdust can cause serious irritation to the nose and throat. The wood is susceptible to attack by borers and termites, but has nevertheless been used for light construction, flooring, furniture, containers, musical instruments, implement handles, casks, mortars and kitchen tools. It is also good for making charcoal and is used as firewood.

# SMALL-LEAVED SICKLEBUSH

*Dichrostachys cinerea* subsp. *africana*

**A:** sekelbos **NS:** morêtšê **SH:** mupangara **SW:** lusekwane
**TG:** ndzenga **TS:** mosêlêsêlê **V:** murenzhe **Z:** ugagane

*Dichrostachys:* from Greek *di-* ('two'), *khroma* ('colour'), and *stakhus* ('ear of grain'); *cinerea:* 'ash-coloured', referring to the colour of the hairs on the subspecies from India; *africana:* 'from Africa'

*Charaxes ethalion ethalion*

Small-leaved sicklebush may either grow to be a shrub or a small tree of up to 6m in height, and may be single- or multi-stemmed. It is known for forming secondary bush in overgrazed areas and can become an impenetrable thicket. It is common on a variety of soils in the northern provinces of South Africa. It is armed with long, hard, single spines, which are not true thorns, but side-branches that often bear leaves and have sharp points. These spines are notorious for damaging vehicle tyres – take care to avoid them when driving in the bush.

The bark is dark grey-brown and becomes deeply fissured with age. The fragrant, fluffy flowers are pendulous spikes, borne in spring in the leaf axils, either singly or in bundles. They are lilac in the upper half and yellow in the lower, hence the alternative name 'Chinese lantern'.

The distinctive twisted pods are nutritious, as are the leaves. Both leaves and pods are eagerly eaten by cattle and various other animals, including impala, kudu, nyala, grysbok, giraffe, rhino, bushpigs, monkeys and baboons. Although buffalo are almost exclusively grazers, they have been observed eating small-leaved sicklebush when grass is parched. The larvae of the satyr charaxes (*Charaxes ethalion ethalion*) feed on the leaves.

Small-leaved sicklebush is a nitrogen-fixing legume and enriches the soil by improving its nitrogen content.

The heartwood is red to dark purple with darker streaks, while the sapwood is yellowish brown with dark streaks. The grain is straight or slightly interlocked and the texture rather fine and even. While the wood is extremely hard, durable and resistant to termites, its uses are limited owing to the small size of the tree. It has been used as fencing material and tool handles, and is popular as firewood.

# ELEPHANTROOT
## *Elephantorrhiza burkei*
**A:** basboontjie **NS:** lešitšane **TS:** mositsane, mosidi **V:** tshisese-thavha

*Elephantorrhiza:* from Greek *elephas* ('elephant') and *rhiza* ('root'), referring to the enormous rootstock; *burkei:* named after Joseph Burke (1812–1873), a botanist who collected plants in the then Transvaal

This hardy, deciduous tree has a dense, rounded crown. It may grow as a small tree, reaching 6m under ideal conditions, or a shrub, growing to no more than a metre tall. It is found in the northern regions of South Africa, occurring on rocky ridges and slopes in woodland and grassland.

The feathery foliage makes this an attractive tree. Its fragrant, spiky, creamy white flowers become yellow with age, and are borne in the axils of the leaves. They appear in early summer, attracting insects and birds, including the African honey bee (*Apis mellifera*), the main pollinator of elephantroot. As such, this tree is popular with beekeepers. The fruit is a flat, brown to reddish-brown pod, the centre of which peels out, leaving the persistent woody rims.

Dyes are extracted from the roots, bark and pods. This tree is also a traditional remedy for numerous human and animal diseases and ailments.

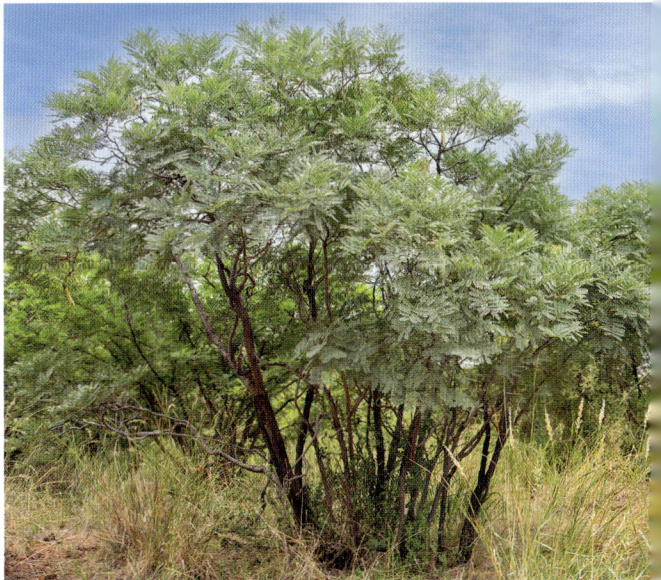

# ANATREE
## *Faidherbia albida*
**A:** anaboom **NS:** mogohlo **TS:** mogôkatau **V:** muhoto **Z:** umhlalankwazi

**PROTECTED IN SOUTH AFRICA**

*Faidherbia:* named after Louis Leon Cesar Faidherbe (1818–1889), a geographer, archaeologist and writer, who was also the governor of French Senegal; *albida:* 'white', referring to the whitish trunk

The anatree is an icon of the bushveld, occurring along full and dry river courses and swamps, and on floodplains. According to folklore, the tree is named after one Anna Hennop, who gave birth under such a tree on a farm in the Gobabis district in Namibia, sometime during the early to mid-19th century. The farm was dubbed 'Anaboom', from which the species' common name is derived.

This species is attractive, fast-growing and deciduous, and reaches up to 30m in height. It is easily recognised by its roundish crown and spreading branches, pale green leaves, conspicuously twisted reddish-brown pods, and the zigzagging appearance of the young branches. The scented pale cream flowers are borne in elongated spikes, and the straight, whitish thorns are situated in pairs. The long taproot makes it a reasonably drought-resistant tree.

The anatree differs from typical thorn trees in that it loses its leaves at the end of summer, but new leaves appear during the drier early winter. Unlike most other trees, it flowers through winter, from May to September. It typically attracts bees during this time. The pods ripen and fall to the ground in late winter. Consequently, the tree is also known as the 'winter thorn'.

The leaves and ripe pods are nutritious and excellent fodder. The seeds are rich in protein and the pods high in starch. Hoofed animals play a role in seed dispersal and germination, and it is common to find seeds in the dung of giraffe, kudu and impala. Elephant are partial to the bark and many anatrees die after being stripped of bark.

Like *Vachellia* and *Senegalia*, the anatree is a legume and improves the quality of the soil by enriching its nitrogen content. The wood is not durable and has no known uses.

# BLACK MONKEY THORN

### Senegalia burkei

A: swartapiesdoring  SW: umkhaya  TS: mokgwa  Z: umkhaya wehlalahlathi

*Senegalia:* referring to Senegal; *burkei:* refers to the naturalist Joseph Burke (1812–1873), who first catalogued this tree in the 1840s after collecting specimens near the Magaliesberg

This spreading, deciduous tree has a rounded, flattened or open crown and is frost tolerant and relatively fast-growing. It occurs on a variety of soil types and can be found in open mixed woodland or thornveld, in dry river valley scrub and on rocky slopes. Under optimal conditions it can become a truly magnificent single-stemmed tree, reaching a height of close to 30m with a crown diameter of 20m.

The short thorns are curved backwards and sharply hooked and are situated in pairs just below the nodes. The creamy flowers and bright green new leaves are conspicuous in early summer. Although the tree is mainly pollinated by bees, many insects and birds visit the flowers too, as they produce abundant nectar.

The flat, bean-like pods hang in drooping clusters. They have pointed tips, are conspicuously veined (especially when young), turn red-brown to dark brown as they ripen and split open on the tree.

The fresh leaves, dry leaves and pods are eaten by a variety of game such as giraffe, kudu, nyala and impala.

The strong and heavy heartwood is light to dark brown, has a fine grain and is termite resistant. Although the wood is difficult to work, it is hard enough to make good-quality furniture. Traditionally is was used for furniture (especially *riempie* chairs) and today it is still used for fencing posts. It is also excellent wood for rifle stocks.

# COMMON HOOK THORN

## Senegalia caffra

A: wag-'n-bietjiedoring, gewone haakdoring  NS: motholo
TG: mbvhinya-xihloka  TS: morutlhare  Z: umtholo

*caffra:* refers to the former colonial region of Kaffraria, now part of the Eastern Cape

Except for two small isolated populations in Zimbabwe, the deciduous common hook thorn does not occur north of the Limpopo River. This fire-, drought- and frost-resistant tree grows up to 10m in height and has an irregular, somewhat rounded crown with drooping, feathery foliage. For a hardwood tree, the common hook thorn grows quite rapidly. It is found on rocky ridges, in wooded grassland and bushveld and along rivers and streams.

The leaves and pods are relished by various game animals, including black rhino and giraffe. In some parts it is considered a valuable fodder tree, as cattle eat the leaves. The wood is a lovely dark brown and is heavy, hard and durable, making it suitable for quality furniture. It is also popular as fencing material as it is resistant to both termites and borers. Owing to the twisted trunks of these trees, it is not possible to get long planks. Although it has an aggressive root system, it is such a striking tree that it is often planted in large gardens where it attracts insects and birds. It is one of the first trees to flower in spring and is visited by butterflies and bees. Van Son's playboy (*Deudorix vansoni*) and Pennington's playboy (*D. penningtoni*) butterflies breed in growths on the branches of this tree.

The common hook thorn also makes an excellent bonsai tree. Xhosa women use the roots to make their characteristic long smoking pipes.

# BLUE THORN

*Senegalia erubescens*

A: blouhaak  TS: moloto  V: mulondo, tshihaka-phele

*erubescens:* 'reddening' or 'blushing', which may refer to the young flowers

Blue thorn is a shrub or small deciduous tree of up to 10m in height. While the shrubs are mostly multi-stemmed, the trees are single-stemmed and branch quite low down. This species has a rounded crown, the spread of which may exceed the height of the tree. It occurs on various soil types in arid bushveld, often forming dominant stands.

The bark is yellowish brown and covered by a peeling papery layer. The tree bursts into bloom just before the new leaves appear, and the scented flowering spikes are cream coloured. The flat, more or less oblong pods are borne in bunches near the ends of branches. They have conspicuous veins and a characteristic dark reddish colour, although sometimes apparent only on one side. The leaves turn mustard-yellow in autumn. Game animals eat the leaves, flowers and pods.

The tree's sweet gum is popular with children.

The sapwood is yellow or off-white and the heartwood is dark brown. Although the wood is hard and heavy, it is prone to borer attack. Moreover, it is difficult to obtain decent planks and equally difficult to saw and plane. As such, the timber is useful only for small items such as handles for knives.

Subfamily Mimosoideae

# BLADE THORN

*Senegalia fleckii*

**A:** bladdoring **NS:** mooka **TS:** mophoka, mfafu

*fleckii:* named after Dr E. Fleck, a geologist who collected plants in Namibia in the 19th century

This relatively little-known deciduous species is either a multi-stemmed shrub or a small single-stemmed tree reaching up to 6m in height. It grows in the sandy soils of the far western arid savannahs in North West and Limpopo. The crown is either round or flat, and its spread may exceed the height of the tree.

Blade thorn can form impenetrable thickets. The numerous paired, vicious thorns are situated below the nodes and are sharply hooked and brown to blackish. The flowering spikes are a light cream colour and are scented.

Dry trees resemble the blue thorn (*S. erubescens*), but the leaflets of the blade thorn are usually smaller and more numerous. Additionally, there is always a ±2mm long gland on the leafstalk, but no glands on the rachis. The leaf stalk is also shorter than that of the blue thorn. While blue thorn flowers before the new leaves appear, blade thorn flowers when the tree is already full of new leaves.

Black rhino and elephant are known to eat the branches, while many other game species will take the leaves, flowers and pods.

# MONKEY THORN
## *Senegalia galpinii*
**A:** apiesdoring  **NS:** mooka-leselo

*galpinii:* named after the plant collector Ernest Galpin (1854–1941)

This impressive semi-deciduous tree can easily exceed 30m in height, making it one of the tallest thorn trees in the region. It is usually single-stemmed, with a roundish crown. In young trees, the bark is yellowish, flaking and corky. Over time, it changes to brown or blackish, with longitudinal furrows when mature. Monkeys are often seen taking cover in the wide branches, and may also eat the pods and seeds, hence the common name.

Monkey thorn almost always occurs on well-drained soils along riverbanks in sweetveld areas of open woodland. The short, broad and hooked thorns are borne in opposite pairs. During spring, when the tree is in full bloom, it is conspicuous and provides a stunning sight. The flowers attract a variety of insects such as bees and wasps. The leaves and flowers are browsed by giraffe and kudu. The latter also pick up fallen pods.

The roots host the bacteria *Rhizobium* and *Bradyrhizobium*, which fix atmospheric nitrogen. This benefits the tree, the bacteria and, eventually, the surrounding vegetation.

The sapwood is light brown and the heartwood much darker. It is hard, heavy and difficult to work, but can be used for good-quality furniture, joinery, fences, flooring, ship building, implements, railway sleepers and as mining timber.

This tree is suitable for larger gardens and grows relatively fast. It handles drought quite well, but not frost.

# BLACK THORN

*Senegalia mellifera* subsp. *detinens*

A: swarthaak  NS: mongangatau  TS: mongana  V: munembedzi

*mellifera:* 'honey-bearing', referring to the sweetly scented flowers; *detinens:* 'detaining, delaying', referring to the many paired, vicious, curved thorns

Black thorn is a single- or multi-stemmed deciduous tree with a roundish or spreading crown. Since it tends to branch low down, it is not unusual for the spread of the crown to exceed the height of the tree, which is typically under 10m. It occurs in bushveld and semi-arid areas, often on Kalahari sand, and prefers deep sandy or gravelly soil. By developing a very deep taproot, this tree can survive harsh conditions away from water.

Black thorn can form dense thickets, which may become impenetrable, owing to the presence of well-developed sharp thorns. These hooked, blackish thorns occur in pairs at the nodes, which are relatively closely spaced, resulting in more thorns per unit length of branch than in any other *Senegalia* species. Despite this formidable defence, black thorn makes for valuable fodder on game ranches, as the nutritional leaves, twigs, flowers and pods have a high protein content. A range of animals feed on this tree, including giraffe, black rhino, kudu, eland, gemsbok, blue wildebeest, impala, springbok, grey duiker and steenbok.

While the flowers of *Senegalia* species are typically borne in long spikes, black thorn flowers form round heads, similar to those of *Vachellia* species. These scented, cream-coloured flowers bud in profusion before the new leaves emerge and are an excellent source of nectar for honey bees and moths. They turn brownish when fading.

The heartwood is dark brown to almost black. Being resistant to termites and borers, the wood makes excellent fencing posts. It is also used for axe and pick handles and is a very good firewood.

# KNOB THORN

## *Senegalia nigrescens*

**A:** knoppiesdoring  **NS:** moritidi  **TG:** nkaya
**TS:** mokoba  **V:** munanga  **Z:** umkhaya

*nigrescens:* 'becoming black', which is thought to refer to the colour of the thorns and pods

This beautiful, single-stemmed deciduous tree has a cylindrical shape and a rounded crown. Its branches and trunk are covered in prominent knobs, though these disappear with age.

Knob thorn is tall, usually growing up to 20m in height, with some exceptional specimens reaching 30m. It is rather common in the region and is found on well-drained soil in low-altitude hot and dry woodland throughout most of the savannah regions. It may form dominant stands – such vegetation is commonly known as knob-thorn veld.

The strongly hooked thorns are borne in pairs. Creamy flowering spikes appear in early spring and the trees can then be quite conspicuous, especially if the preceding rainy season was good.

Many species of game utilise the knob thorn. Giraffe, in particular, are partial to the flowers and green leaves. Leaves and pods are also eaten by steenbok, duiker, impala, kudu and elephant. The tree is pollinated by insects. The larvae of the demon charaxes (*Charaxes phaeus*) feed on the leaves.

The sapwood is light yellow and the heartwood is dark brown with lighter and darker streaks. The grain is irregular but has an even texture. While the wood is hard, heavy and durable, it is also prone to borer attack and is difficult to work. Nevertheless, it has been used for fence posts, railway sleepers, mining props and furniture.

Knob thorn is drought and termite resistant, but sensitive to frost.

# CAMEL THORN

*Vachellia erioloba*

**A:** kameeldoring  **ND:** umfola  **NS:** mogohlo  **V:** musivhiṱha

**PROTECTED IN SOUTH AFRICA**

*Vachellia:* named after George H. Vachell (1789–1839), chaplain and plant collector in China; *erioloba:* from the Greek *erion* ('wool') and *lobos* ('pod'), referring to the ear-shaped pods

Camel thorn is synonymous with the Kalahari, though there are also spectacular specimens in South Africa's western bushveld. It is a beautiful, single-stemmed, evergreen tree with a large spreading crown, found in deep sand and sandy loams and along dry riverbeds in dry woodland. This slow-growing tree is well adapted to arid areas and has an impressively large root system – in fact, the tree is usually much bigger under the ground than above it.

The whitish thorns are straight and stout, paired at the nodes and often swollen at the base. The flowers are borne in golden-yellow balls and are a good source of nectar for honey bees. The grey, woody pods are kidney-shaped and have a velvety texture.

Camel thorn is well used by game animals. The Afrikaans name *kameeldoring* ('giraffe thorn') refers to the giraffes that feed eagerly on the leaves. Not surprisingly, the tree was at one time known as *Acacia giraffae.* The pods are very nutritious, being rich in protein and phosphorus. Some game ranchers collect the pods and use them as fodder during the dry winter months.

The tree produces excellent gum, enjoyed by humans, animals and birds. As the gum is a significant component of bushbabies' diets, these little mammals are closely associated with camel thorn. The Afrikaans name for kori bustard is *gompou* ('gum peacock') – a name derived from the bustard's partiality to camel thorn gum.

The roasted seeds can be used as a substitute for coffee. Good rope can be made from the fibrous inner bark, while the outer bark yields tannins for tanning leather. The heartwood has a rich reddish colour, is hard and durable and has been used for making furniture, among other things.

## Subfamily Mimosoideae

# SWEET THORN

*Vachellia karroo*

**A:** soetdoring  **NS:** mooka  **TS:** munga
**V:** muunga  **Z:** umunga

*karroo:* refers to the Karoo, where this species is the most conspicuous tree

Sweet thorn is the best known and most widespread of all thorn trees in South Africa – for these reasons alone it could have been a strong contender for the title of national tree. This species is typically under 10m in height, though it can reach up to 20m under ideal conditions. The trunk branches low down and the crown is dense and rounded. It is evergreen, but may lose its leaves during severe droughts or cold spells.

The flowers appear in December and produce large quantities of pollen and attract numerous insects. Sweet thorn makes for an excellent 'bee tree' and plays an important role in the honey industry. Insect-eating birds and birds that feed on flowers visit this tree, making it a popular species for a 'bird garden'. The flowers are also relished by monkeys.

Sweet thorn is a good source of fodder – the leaves, flowers and pods are eagerly eaten by game animals such as giraffe, black rhino, kudu, nyala, sable, gemsbok, impala and eland. This tree is also regarded as an indicator of sweetveld and good grazing.

The caterpillars of a number of butterflies, such as club-tailed charaxes (*Charaxes zoolina zoolina*) and topaz-spotted blue (*Azanus jesous*), are dependent on the young shoots and thorns for survival.

Sweet thorn gum is edible and sweet (hence the common name) and quite popular with children. The inner bark can be used to make good quality rope. The bark is rich in tannins used in the tanning industry.

The timber is off-white to pale brown. It is hard and heavy, yet pliable. Though it has a fine grain and is easy to work, the wood is prone to borer attack, and is therefore not a popular timber. It has occasionally been used in construction and to make furniture. It is a good firewood.

# SCENTED-POD

*Vachellia nilotica* subsp. *kraussiana*

**A:** lekkerruikpeul, snuifpeul  **NS:** mogohlo  **SW:** inshakwe
**TS:** motša  **Z:** umnqawe

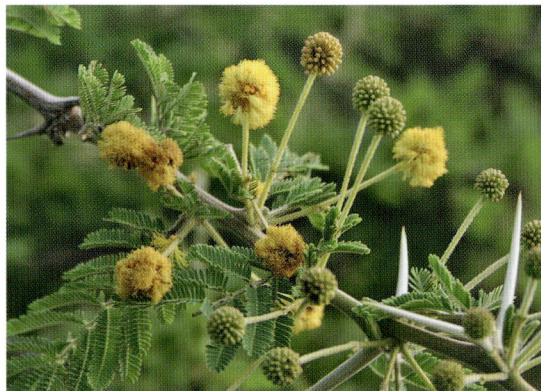

*nilotica:* refers to the trees found along the Nile River;
*kraussiana:* refers to Dr Christian Ferdinand Friedrich von Krauss (1812–1890), a German biologist and professor at the University of Stuttgart who travelled and collected plants in South Africa

Scented-pod has a straight trunk and, when mature, deeply fissured bark. It is semi-deciduous, with a rounded or somewhat flattened crown, and reaches up to 10m in height under ideal conditions. As the seeds can be dispersed by cattle, the species has become widely naturalised outside of its native range, and is found throughout the drier parts of Africa.

Scented-pod is easily recognised by its distinctive thorns and pods. The long, vicious thorns slant slightly backwards. The seed pods are 12–18cm long and hang from the tree like strings of beads. They open only after they have fallen to the ground, where they break into individual segments. The ripe pods are very dark, almost black, and have a strong sweet smell, hence the name 'scented-pod'.

This is a pioneer species and is useful for the reclamation of wastelands and in reforestation projects, especially on alkaline soils. On dry land the tree develops a deep and extensive root system, but on flooded sites, the root system is mostly lateral.

Although the pods and bark are high in tannins, which are typically unpalatable, many browsers, such as black rhino, kudu and impala, utilise these trees, albeit selectively.

The wood is reddish in colour and hard, but is not used for much more than tool handles, fencing poles and firewood. The twigs can be used as toothbrushes. The Voortrekkers made ink and dyes from the pods.

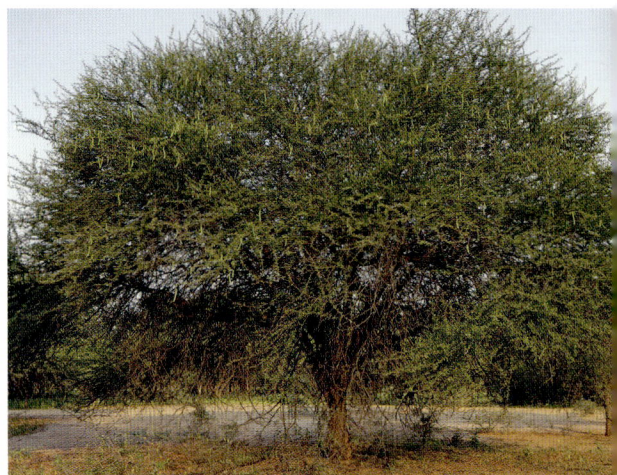

# BROAD-POD ROBUST THORN

## Vachellia robusta subsp. robusta

A: enkeldoring, Engelse doring, aapkop, oudoring  NS: mooka
TG: mvumbangwenya  TS: mokhu  V: muvumba-ngweṇa  Z: umngamanzi

*robusta:* refers to the robust, thick branches and shoots

This fast-growing tree is usually single-stemmed and branches almost vertically. The narrow crown has distinctive dark green foliage. The tree grows up to 10m in height, and occurs in warm and dry savannahs and wooded grassland. Large specimens are often found near streams. This species is resistant to frost and drought and is regarded as an indicator of sourveld, characterised by coarse seasonal perennial grasses, offering an inferior type of winter grazing.

This species has a symbiotic relationship with nitrogen-fixing *Rhizobium* bacteria, which form nodules on the roots.

The leaves and seed pods are eaten by herbivores such as kudu and giraffe, and the strongly scented flowers attract bees, butterflies and many other insects. This tree is the larval host to a number of butterfly species.

The heartwood is pinkish brown to reddish brown, making it quite distinct from the whitish sapwood. It has a moderately coarse texture. Although heavy, the wood has no known uses, since it is brittle and susceptible to borer and termite attack. Furthermore, the sapwood is susceptible to sap-stain, which is caused by a fungus and discolours the wood.

Folklore has it that when the first Voortrekkers arrived from the Cape Colony in what later became the Transvaal, they soon realised that the tree had very few uses. As a result, they named it *Engelse doring* ('English thorn'), a likely reference to British colonial interference in the Cape Colony. With the passing of time the name was corrupted to *enkeldoring*. Another possibility is that the name *enkeldoring* ('single thorn') is based on the fact that these trees usually occur singly, seldom growing in stands.

# PAPERBARK THORN

## *Vachellia sieberiana var. woodii*

A: papierbasdoring  NS: mphoka  SW: umkhambane  TG: nkowankowa
TS: mokha  V: musaunga  Z: umkhamba

*sieberiana:* named after Franz Sieber (1789–1844), a traveller, botanist and plant collector from Prague, Bohemia; *woodii:* after John Medley Wood (1827–1915), the curator of the Durban Botanic Gardens from 1882 to 1913

Paperbark thorn is considered to be a true symbol of the African savannah. With its straight trunk, corky and papery bark, and large, sparse, flat-topped or rounded spreading crown, it is one of the region's most striking thorn trees. The width of the crown often exceeds the height of the tree, which can be up to 18m.

This widespread species occurs in woodland, wooded grassland and along riverbanks. It prefers loamy soils, but also grows in sandy soils.

The thorns are paired at the nodes and are long, strong, straight and white. In mature trees, they are often small and inconspicuous.

Balls of cream-coloured scented flowers are borne in spring and summer and lure beetles, bees, butterflies and thrips, which in turn attract insect-eating birds. The flowers are thought to be an excellent source of nectar for bees.

The brown, woody, slightly curved pods are eaten by various antelope, buffalo and elephant, as well as livestock,

but unripe pods are believed to be poisonous. The leaves are browsed by a variety of game, including the small grysbok, which feeds on young plants. However, the leaves commonly produce toxic chemical compounds when the tree has been heavily browsed. Some of these compounds release hydrogen cyanide when ingested, which may be lethal to livestock such as cattle.

Paperbark thorn is a legume and hosts *Rhizobium* bacteria in its roots. This bacteria convert nitrogen from the air into forms that can be used by plants. Since surrounding plants also benefit from the increase in available nitrogen, *Vachellia* species are of particular ecological importance.

The off-white timber has no heartwood. It is light and soft with large pores and has a coarse texture. It is difficult to saw, owing to gum exudations when green. It is also prone to insect infestation and is not durable. Not surprisingly, the timber has no specific uses.

Paperbark thorn is, however, an attractive garden tree, providing good shade. The gum is edible and a good adhesive. Buffalo weavers seem to favour these trees when building their nests.

# UMBRELLA THORN
## *Vachellia tortilis* subsp. *heteracantha*

**A:** haak-en-steek, fynhaak **ND:** singa **NS:** mošu **SW:** umsasane
**TG:** sasani **TS:** mosu **V:** muunga-khanga **Z:** umsasane

*tortilis:* 'twisted, coiled', referring to the shape of the pods; *heteracantha:* from Greek *heteros* ('different') and *akantha* ('thorn'), referring to the two types of thorn on the same tree

Umbrella thorn is a typical bushveld tree and almost as common as sweet thorn (*Vachellia karroo*). This hardy tree is resistant to drought, wind and heat, and is widely distributed, occuring in deciduous woodland, wooded grassland, thornveld and bushveld. Many people consider umbrella thorn the quintessential African thorn tree.

The dense crown is often distinctively flat. In the arid western parts of southern Africa, where the average rainfall is much lower, these trees often have a rounded crown rather than the more common umbrella-shaped crown.

This species is usually single-stemmed but branches quite low down. The thorns are in pairs at nodes. Straight and hooked thorn pairs usually alternate at consecutive nodes, but a pair may also comprise one hooked and one straight thorn. The Afrikaans name *haak-en-steek* ('hook and stab') refers to the combination of one hooked thorn and one straight thorn.

There are up to four spherical, creamy, scented flowerheads per node, appearing in mid- to late summer. The contorted, flat pods are distinctive and cannot be confused with those of any other *Vachellia* or *Senegalia* species. They are rolled up in a tight helix of three or four turns. The pods are longitudinally veined, somewhat woody, and dry out to a light khaki colour. They occur in bunches and do not open when ripe. A pod contains up to 14 seeds, some of which do not mature. The seeds are rounded and greenish brown with a dark brown horseshoe-shaped area.

The pods are excellent fodder and the nutritional value is relatively high. Most game species, as well as livestock, utilise the fallen pods, which are mostly taken off the ground. The foliage is also palatable. The presence of these trees is an indicator of sweetveld, which is high in nutrients and valued by cattle and game farmers.

The heartwood is an attractive reddish brown but is not very durable and does not have practical uses other than as firewood. It is nevertheless thought that wood from *Vachellia* trees was used by the Israelites to build the Tabernacle and the Ark of the Covenant, as described in the book of Exodus.

# FEVERTREE

## *Vachellia xanthophloea*

**A:** koorsboom  **NS:** mosehla  **TG:** nkelenga
**V:** muunga-gwena  **Z:** umhlosinga

*xanthophloea:* from Greek *xanthos* ('yellow') and *phloios* ('bark')

This is one of the most distinctive thorn trees in South Africa: a striking species with a single trunk and an open, sparse, unevenly rounded crown. It grows up to 30m tall and can be either deciduous or semi-deciduous. Branching commences fairly high up on the straight trunk. Photosynthesis takes place in the bark, which is a distinctive yellowish green.

Fevertrees grow in depressions where there is a high groundwater table, or where surface water collects in pans after summer rains. It is also found in low-lying swampy areas, along the edges of lakes and riverbanks. It often forms pure, dense stands of closed woodland on alluvial soils in seasonally flooded areas. Good places to see fevertree forests are the Pafuri area of the Kruger National Park and Ndumu Game Reserve in Maputaland. This species has become a landscape tree of note, planted throughout the country.

Elephant eat the young branches and leaves, and often push the trees over to get at the roots, making the fallen trees more accessible to other browsers. Vervet monkeys eat both leaves and flowers. Giraffe eat the pods and leaves, and baboons feed on green seeds.

The wood is pale brown with a reddish tinge. It is hard and heavy, with conspicuous annual rings. Though it is a useful general-purpose timber, it should be seasoned before use as it is likely to crack. Borers attack this species, cutting distinctive, large oval holes in the wood.

Early pioneers associated the tree with an illness generally referred to as 'the fever'. Although its cause was unknown, they noted that people were particularly susceptible to the disease when they camped near the large yellow thorn trees, which they then dubbed 'fevertrees'. It was only later that the truth emerged: fevertrees grow in wet habitats, which are also home to the mosquitos that spread malaria. The name 'fevertree' stuck, however.

This tree is easily grown from seed; it grows quite fast and tolerates light frost.

# LEMONWOOD
## *Xymalos monospora*

**A:** lemoenhout **NS:** motshekga **V:** tshipengo
**X:** uvethe **Z:** umhlwehlwe

*Xymalos:* anagram of *Xylosma*, the genus in which these trees were originally placed, from *xulon* ('wood') and *osme* ('scent'); *monospora*: from Greek *mono* ('alone') and *spora* ('seed')

This attractive evergreen tree is typically single-stemmed, with a dense, rounded and spreading crown. It is found from the Eastern Cape northwards, occurring in montane, scarp and coastal forests, grasslands associated with forests, or moist areas near watercourses.

It grows up to 25m tall, and the trunk is usually branchless for up to 9m. The rough, lightly fissured, silvery grey bark flakes off in large scales, leaving conspicuous concentric ridged markings. The leaves have a strong lemon scent when crushed (hence the common name) and have a 'quilted' appearance because of the lateral veins, which are sunken above and prominent below.

This species is dioecious and pollinated by the wind and insects. The small, yellow-green flowers are in short axillary spikes near the ends of branches. The fruit is an egg-shaped, fleshy drupe and takes about a year to ripen, with its colour changing from green to orange or red. It is eaten by primates and birds, which disperse the seeds.

The heartwood is lemon-yellow to pale brown and is not clearly demarcated from the paler sapwood. The grain is straight, with a fine, even texture. It works easily and is durable, but is difficult to air dry. It is used for furniture, light construction, flooring, joinery, door frames, railway sleepers, beehives, carvings, turnery, boxes, crates, plywood and pulp and paper products. The bark, roots and leaves are used in traditional medicine.

Lemonwood is a food plant for the larvae of the mocker swallowtail butterfly (*Papilio dardanus*).

# LARGE-LEAVED ROCK FIG

## *Ficus abutilifolia*

**A:** grootblaarrotsvy  **NS:** monokane  **TG:** nkuwamaribye
**TS:** momelantsweng  **V:** tshikululu  **Z:** impayi

*Ficus:* from Latin, 'fig tree' or 'fig'; *abutilifolia:* refers to the resemblance of the leaves to those of *Abutilon,* a popular ornamental genus

The genus *Ficus* is one of 37 in the family Moraceae, whose members all have non-toxic milky sap and simple or lobed leaves. There are about 750 *Ficus* species, 24 of which occur in South Africa.

Large-leaved rock fig is deciduous to semi-deciduous, reaching up to 15m in height, and has a spreading, sparse crown. It is widespread in the northern and eastern parts of the country, growing on or near rocky outcrops. It has an aggressive root system and is able to reach great depths in search of underground water. Known as rock-splitters, the trees of this species can cause rocks to break up as the roots find their way into cracks and exert pressure on their hosts.

The trunk is usually short, crooked and contorted and branches low down. The whitish bark is generally smooth and typically powdery or slightly flaking. This fig is also easily recognised by its large, almost round leaves. They are usually smooth on both surfaces, but may have velvety hairs underneath.

Fig tree pollination is rather unusual and is described in more detail in the introductory section on symbiotic relationships (page 53). The fruits are borne singly or in pairs in leaf axils on branchlets, and are smooth to slightly hairy. Birds and primates eat the figs off the tree, while fallen figs are eagerly picked up by nyala, bushbuck and duiker.

The wood has no known uses, but the tree has a few traditional medicinal uses.

Family Moraceae

# COMMON WILD FIG

### Ficus burkei

A: gewone wildevy  ND: intenjane  NS: moumo  TS: moumo
V: muumo  X: umthombe  Z: umthombe

*burkei*: named after Joseph Burke (1812–1873), a British naturalist and plant collector who collected the first specimen of this species in 1841, while on expedition with Carl Zeyher in the Magaliesberg

This striking tree is up to 18m tall, with a dense, spreading crown. It is not unusual for the width of the crown to exceed the height of the tree, making it an excellent shade tree. This species occurs in wooded grassland, on hill slopes or in mountainous areas, and in ravines. It seems to favour deep loamy soils. It is typically evergreen, but may be deciduous for a short period, before the onset of the summer rains. Common wild fig does not occur in evergreen forests – that is the domain of the forest fig (*F. craterostoma*).

The masses of aerial roots and fluted trunks are distinguishing features.

This fig sometimes starts life as a strangler of other trees. The seed often germinates in a hollow or forked branch of another tree, sending aerial roots down the trunk to take root in the soil, eventually strangling and killing the host tree.

This tree is utilised by a variety of birds, insects, reptiles and mammals. The leaves are eaten by bushbuck, kudu, nyala, giraffe and elephant. The fruits are eaten off the tree by bats, pigeons, turacos, parrots, bulbuls, barbets, starlings, baboons and monkeys, while dassies, mongooses, civets and porcupines eat the fallen fruits. It is an excellent tree to attract fruit-eating birds.

The light-coloured wood is relatively hard and can be used as a general-purpose timber, although it is not resistant to termite and borer attack. A good-quality rope can be made from the bark.

Family Moraceae

# FOREST FIG

*Ficus craterostoma*

**A:** bosvy, wurgvy, basternatalvy  **NS:** moumo  **TG:** nhlulawumbe
**V:** muumo  **X:** umthombe  **Z:** umthombe

*craterostoma:* from Greek *krater* ('bowl') and the Greek *stoma* ('mouth'), referring to the shape of the opening, or mouth, of the figs

This fig is usually evergreen, with glossy, dark foliage. It may reach a height of up to 20m, and has a dense, rounded, spreading crown. It occurs from the Great Kei River northwards, through the Eastern Cape, KwaZulu-Natal, Mpumalanga and Limpopo, and is found in moist Afromontane and coastal forests, evergreen forest, riverine and swamp forests and wooded mountain ravines. It does not occur in the dry bushveld or miombo woodlands, where it is replaced by the common wild fig (*Ficus burkei*).

Typically, and like the common wild fig, the forest fig is a strangler of other forest trees. Should a seed settle in a little hollow where it can germinate in another tree, it sends long aerial roots down to the ground. The young fig sapling grows roots and stems that branch and fuse, and in time they may strangle and kill the host tree. The aerial roots eventually develop into a large, buttressed trunk.

This fig can also be a rock-splitter, which happens when a seed settles and germinates in a rock cranny and sends aerial roots down through a crack, or over the rock surface, until they find soil. Rocks may crack and split as the tree grows.

The fruit of this species is palatable but not suitable for human consumption as it is usually full of insects. Monkeys, baboons and birds, however, eagerly feed on the fruit.

The timber is light and soft, without heartwood; it is not durable and has no practical use.

Family Moraceae

# HAIRY ROCK FIG

## *Ficus glumosa*

A: bergvy, harige rotsvy  ND: inkiwane  NS: mphaya
SW: inkokhokho  V: tshikululu  X: umthombe  Z: inkokhokho

*glumosa:* 'glume-like', referring to the bracts on the fruits – a glume is a small, dry scale found around the flowers of grasses and sedges

This tree is deciduous in areas of high rainfall and semi-deciduous in arid areas. It has a roundish, spreading crown. The widely spreading, low-growing branches form a dense canopy, giving the tree a striking, distinctive shape. It seldom exceeds 12m in height, and is found mostly in mountainous terrain or on rocky outcrops, growing in shallow rocky soils unsuitable for most other trees. It also occurs along watercourses and in open bushveld.

Several traits make this species easy to distinguish: the greyish-cream bark, which often flakes off; the short, distorted trunk; the conspicuous hairs on the branchlets; the oblong to elliptic, leathery leaves with silky hairs on both surfaces; and the fruit, which is borne singly or in pairs in the axils of the leaves, turning red when ripe.

It often splits rocks or grows over them in the same fashion as the large-leaved rock fig (*F. abutilifolia*). It may be confused with Stuhlmann's fig (*F. stuhlmannii*), but the latter is less hairy and has grey bark and narrower and more rectangular leaves.

The fruit is edible, but not particularly tasty, and is eaten by fruit bats, birds, monkeys, baboons, klipspringer, duiker and bushbuck. The wood is light in weight and has no known uses. The latex can be used to make bird lime.

Like most other figs, this species is easy to propagate from cuttings. It is drought resistant, and makes a fine garden tree in the warmer areas, and is a good tree for birds.

Family Moraceae

# RED-LEAVED FIG

## *Ficus ingens*

**A:** rooiblaarrotsvy  **NS:** monokane  **TS:** motlhatsa
**V:** tshikululu  **X:** umthombe  **Z:** umgonswane

> *ingens:* 'enormous' or 'huge', but the allusion is unclear as this species is of average size, nor are its leaves exceptionally large

This semi-deciduous tree grows up to 15m tall, but its width usually exceeds its height by a considerable margin. It is mostly found on rocky hillsides and in woodlands, but also occurs in riverine thickets and savannah. Characterised by an aggressive root system, this fig may grow in a flattened form against cliff faces, its roots pushing into the rock cracks. However, it is better known as a shade tree, due to its lovely spreading crown.

The most distinctive feature of this species is the fresh coppery red leaves that appear in spring.

The almost spherical figs are produced year-round, but are especially abundant in summer. They are borne on short stalks, in pairs, in the axils of leaves and are eaten by a variety of birds and mammals.

The best-known specimen of this species in South Africa is probably the enormous fig tree known as the 'Inhabited Tree' or 'Moffat's Tree' near Boshoek in the Rustenburg area. In 1829, on his way to see the Matabele chief Mzilikazi, the missionary Robert Moffat came across this unique specimen. Up in the spreading branches, locals had built 17 conical thatch huts to protect themselves against lions.

This species is fairly hardy and drought resistant and has an aggressive root system. The wood is not durable and is hardly used.

# KNOBBLY FIG
## *Ficus sansibarica*
A: knoppiesvy  SW: inkhokhokho  V: muṱamvu

*sansibarica:* refers to the island of Zanzibar, where this species was first collected in 1889 by the German naturalist Franz Ludwig Stuhlmann (1863–1928)

This magnificent tree has a spreading crown and is capable of reaching 30m in height. It grows in deep, sandy soil in low-altitude riverine forest, bushveld and along the base of the eastern lowveld escarpment. It is usually evergreen, but during drought it may become deciduous. It is often a strangler, germinating in a host tree and sending out aerial roots that will eventually kill the host.

The mature tree, however, is usually without aerial roots. The trunk is short and branches low down with numerous fruit-bearing spurs on the branches. The fruits are borne singly or in clusters of four and are dark purple with yellow-green dots when ripe.

The figs attract a wide range of fruit-eating birds, fruit bats, baboons, monkeys and insects. Insect-eating birds feed upon the wasps that pollinate the figs. Elephant, giraffe, kudu and nyala also browse on the leaves of this tree.

The wood is pale brown, soft and has no known uses.

# WONDERBOOM FIG

## *Ficus salicifolia*

**A:** wonderboomvy  **ND:** inkiwane  **NS:** mohlatša  **SW:** umkhiwane
**TS:** motlhatsa  **V:** muumo  **Z:** isisantu

*salicifolia:* from Latin *salix* ('willow tree'), and *folia* ('leaf') thus 'willow-leaved'

Wonderboom fig is normally about 9m tall and grows along watercourses in open woodland and rocky areas. The bark of young trees is grey and smooth, becoming dark grey and rough with age.

The figs are small and massed in the leaf axils along the branchlets, turning pinkish or red with white dots as they ripen. They attract fruit-eating birds such as African green pigeons and barbets. Fruits on the ground are often picked up by game animals such as kudu, impala and bushpigs.

The most famous specimen in the region is the unusually large tree growing at the base of the northern slope of the Magaliesberg in Pretoria. It is believed that this particular tree is about 1,000 years old. Its growth pattern is unusual: the branches drooped down to the ground and took root, forming a circle of new trunks or 'daughter trees' around the original tree. Today, there are thirteen trunks and the massive tree covers an area with a diameter of 55m. The diameter of the main trunk is 5.5m and the tree's height is 25m. This specimen used to be much larger, in fact, but its size was drastically reduced by fire in 1870 and, more recently, by a parasite infestation. When the Voortrekkers of the Potgieter Trek saw this remarkable tree in 1836, they named it *wonderboom* ('wonder tree'). In the years that followed, many Voortrekkers used the tree as an *outspan* or rest stop.

Another well-known wonderboom fig specimen can be found in the middle of the Gauteng highway (N4), about 10km outside Mbombela in Mpumalanga. It is estimated to be about 200 years old. In 2011, the highway had to be upgraded and the initial plan was to transplant this special tree to another site. However, it was not certain that the tree would survive the replanting. Local residents protested successfully and the authorities agreed to change their plans and build one set of lanes around the tree. Today this wonderboom fig stands defiantly in the middle of the highway, with traffic rushing past on both sides.

*A fine wonderboom fig specimen grows in the middle of the N4.*

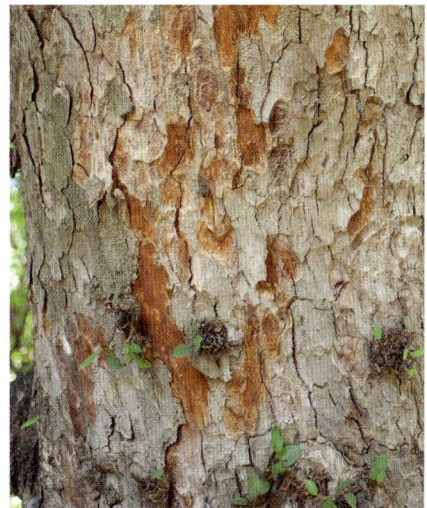

# SYCAMORE FIG

## *Ficus sycomorus* subsp. *sycomorus*

**A:** gewone trosvy, geelriviervy  **ND:** umkhiwa  **NS:** mogobôya
**TS:** motšhaba  **V:** muhuyu-lukuse  **Z:** umncongo

*sycomorus:* from Greek *sukon* ('fig'), and *moron* ('mulberry')

This evergreen or deciduous tree is also known as the sycamore fig. It can grow up to 30m tall and 30m wide, typically with a short, thick trunk and yellowish bark. The rounded crown is wide and dense. This tree is found in bushveld woodlands, especially seasonally flooded areas, and riverine forest.

The fruit is borne on clusters of leafless branchlets and is heavily utilised by wildlife. Birds such as pigeons, turacos, barbets, hornbills and parrots eagerly feed on the fruit. Monkeys, baboons, bushbabies and fruit bats find the fruit irresistible, and fallen figs are also eaten by bushbuck, nyala, bushpigs, duiker, impala and even elephant. The fluted trunk usually forms flattened buttresses that strengthen the tree, making it difficult for elephant to uproot.

Humans also enjoy the fruit, either fresh, before it becomes infested with insects, or dried.

The wood is light and soft and works easily, but the quality is poor and it has little commercial value. It was traditionally used, especially by San people, to start fire by friction. The ancient Egyptians reportedly used wood from this species to build coffins for the embalmed remains of their royalty.

Family Moraceae

# BROOM CLUSTER FIG
### *Ficus sur*

**A:** besemtrosvy  **NS:** mogo-tshetlo  **X:** umkhiwane  **Z:** umkhiwane

*sur:* refers to the Sur region in Ethiopia

Occurring in riverine bush and woodland, this is one of South Africa's most striking species: a tall, fast-growing, evergreen tree with a rounded crown. In open woodland it is usually a stocky tree, but in forests it often grows up to 25m or more, with a smallish crown. It is seldom found among rocks and is not a strangler.

Like all fig trees, it produces copious amounts of milky latex. The large fruits are borne on large branched trusses. As they ripen, they become red, mottled with pink or cream. They are quite palatable and are sought after by fruit-eating birds and mammals. Humans also eat and make jam from the figs.

Broom cluster fig and sycamore fig (*F. sycomorus*) can be confused as both species bear fruit on large clusters of branchlets on the main branches and trunk. The leaves of sycamore fig, however, are rounder and have more uniform margins, whereas broom cluster fig leaves are usually irregularly toothed. The bark of the sycamore fig is also more yellow.

The wood is soft and light but is of little practical use. In the past, it was used to make brake blocks for ox wagons, and San people used it to kindle fire. The inner bark can be made into rope. The broom cluster fig is an excellent and popular shade tree for the large garden, and has also been grown as a shade tree in coffee plantations. The root system, however, is quite aggressive.

# SMALL-LEAVED ROCK FIG
## *Ficus tettensis*
A: kleinblaarrotsvy   ND: umkululu   V: tshikululu

*tettensis:* refers to the Tete region in Mozambique, where Sir John Kirk collected the first specimen

This small, sturdy deciduous tree grows as a rock-splitter, usually reaching no more than 7m or 8m in height. It occurs in and on rocks and boulders in dry savannah bushveld, the roots often growing in spectacular fashion among rocks and across cliff faces. The trunk is whitish and may sometimes form small buttresses.

The broadly oval to kidney-shaped leaves are distinctive: they are as wide as they are long, are very velvety and have a wavy margin.

The fruits are borne in pairs in leaf axils or on bare branches below the leaves. They are covered in small warts and become red when ripe.

The wood is light and soft, but difficult to saw as the latex becomes sticky when exposed to the air. The timber has no known uses.

Family Myrtaceae

# UMDONI
## Syzygium cordatum

**A:** waterbessie **NS:** montlho **TG:** muthwa
**V:** muṭu **X:** umswi **Z:** umdoni

*Syzygium:* from Greek *suzugia* ('union, yoke, pair'), referring to the paired leaves; *cordatum:* from Latin *cordatus* ('heart-shaped'), referring to the base of the leaf

This evergreen tree grows up to 15m in height and has a dense, rounded, spreading crown and corky bark. It usually occurs along rivers and in forests. The trunk is typically somewhat crooked. The flowers appear in August, are rich in nectar and attract large numbers of insects. The fruits are fleshy and, though edible, have an unpleasant taste; they are put to better use by making an alcoholic beverage. Ripe fruits are eaten off the tree by monkeys, baboons, bushbabies, tambourine doves and turacos, while the fallen fruits are picked up by various game species.

The leaves are often browsed by kudu.

Umdoni is a host for the emperor moth *Micragone cana* and is also a food plant for the larvae of a number of butterflies. These caterpillars attract insect-eating birds such as the crowned hornbill, and are also collected for food by humans.

The wood is reddish brown to grey. It is heavy and has a fine grain, but should be properly seasoned in water to make it durable. It is easy to work, produces a smooth surface and has been used in construction and for building boats. The pulverised bark is sometimes used as a fish poison.

Umdoni is an excellent shade or ornamental tree, but the root system is extensive and aggressive. This tree may become invasive and may form groves. It is resistant to fire but not frost.

Family Myrtaceae

# FOREST WATERBERRY

*Syzygium gerrardii*

A: boswaterbessie, boswaterhout  V: mupone

*gerrardii:* named after William Gerrard, a 19th-century English plant collector in Natal and Madagascar

This evergreen tree is found in mistbelt montane forests and some coastal forests. It grows up to 30m tall. The strong, upright trunk is sometimes buttressed near the base. Its diameter can measure 2.5m, with the first branches appearing quite high up. The bark is silvery white. This tree has a dense crown and its twigs are almost square. Young leaves are deep red to yellow-green. Mature leaves are dark and shiny green above and pale green below. The strongly scented, nectar-rich white flowers are borne in dense heads at the ends of branches throughout the whole summer. They have masses of protruding stamens.

This tree is pollinated by bees and other insects. The fruit is a red to purplish-black oval berry. It is eaten by humans, birds and primates. The timber, which is pale brown, often with a darker brown grain, is not very hard and saws easily. It has been used for furniture and flooring, as it is durable and also takes a fine polish.

# WOODLAND WATERBERRY

## *Syzygium guineense* subsp. *guineense*

**A:** waterpeer, bosveldwaterbessie **ND:** umdoni

*guineense:* 'of Guinea', where the tree was first collected

Forest waterberry is an evergreen tree with a rounded yet upright crown. It grows in sandy soils in open woodland or near water – sometimes even in water. The trunk is broad and fluted and the bark is smooth and pale grey when young, becoming rough and black with age. The young leaves are purple-red in colour, changing to dark green as they mature. The leaves are typically shiny and smooth on both surfaces.

Browsers do not appear to feed on this tree's leaves, but the dark purple fruit is eaten by animals such as fruit bats, bushbabies and birds. The larvae of the orange-coloured apricot playboy butterfly (*Virachola dinochares*) and the brown playboy (*V. antalus*) feed on the fruit too. Beer can also be made from the fruit.

The flowers of the forest waterberry have showy white stamens, are borne in dense branched heads and release a honey-sweet smell that attracts many insects.

Forest waterberry is a useful tree: it has been planted to provide shade in Ethiopia's coffee plantations, it is considered an indicator of relatively shallow underground water, and the flowers are a good source of nectar for honey bees. It easily hybridises with umdoni (*S. cordatum*).

The wood is brown with a reddish tinge. It is tough, strong and durable and is suitable as a general-purpose timber and for furniture. It saws and works easily, but is liable to splitting. The bark can be toxic and has been reported to cause human deaths.

# PEELING PLANE

*Ochna pulchra* subsp. *pulchra*

**A:** lekkerbreek  **NS:** monamane  **TG:** nzololo  **TS:** monyêlênyêlê  **V:** tshiṭhoṭhonya

*Ochna:* from Greek *ochne* ('wild pear'); *pulchra:* 'beautiful'

Peeling plane is one of 12 *Ochna* species found in South Africa, and is one of the commonest. It is a small but beautiful deciduous tree occurring in mixed bushveld and open woodland, usually in sandy areas or on rocky sandstone slopes and often in sourveld.

The bark is distinctive: grey and flaking, scaly at the base, and peeling lightly to reveal the creamy underbark. It is also known as the 'mermaid tree' because the stem is often scaly at the bottom but smooth higher up. The branches are brittle and the wood cracks easily, hence the Afrikaans name *lekkerbreek* ('breaking nicely').

The spring foliage comes in shades of light green to bronze or bright red, eventually turning to a fresh, shiny green when mature. In autumn, the leaf colour changes to coppery red-brown. The yellowish, sweetly scented flowers appear in abundance in spring, at the same time as the new leaves. The fruit, a kidney-shaped drupe, is initially green, turning black when ripe, and is surrounded by pink to reddish enlarged sepals, giving it a striking flower-like appearance. The seeds yield a foul-smelling oil, which can nevertheless be used to make soap. Game animals are not known to utilise this species. Some birds eat the fruit, but the seeds are thought to be poisonous.

The timber has no differentiation between sapwood and heartwood, is light and brittle and cracks easily – it is therefore seldom used.

# SOURPLUM
## *Ximenia caffra* var. *caffra*
**A:** suurpruim  **NS:** motšhidi  **Z:** umthunduluka-obomvu

*Ximenia:* named after a 17th-century Spanish monk, Francisco Ximenez, who wrote about the plants of Mexico; *caffra:* refers to the former colonial region of Kaffraria, now part of the Eastern Cape

Sourplum is a typical bushveld tree: thorny, low-branching, and with an untidy open crown. It grows up to 6m tall. This frost- and drought-tolerant tree occurs in a variety of habitats and can be found in mixed bushveld and grassland, on rocky hillsides and sometimes on termite mounds. While deciduous, it sheds its leaves so gradually and so late in winter that the new leaves appear before all the old ones have fallen.

The fruit is bright red when ripe, and is edible. The outer layer of the flesh is sweet, but the rest is extremely sour.

Baboons are particularly partial to sourplum fruit, but it is also eaten by monkeys, warthogs, duiker, eland and kudu, as well as various birds. It is high in vitamin C and can also be used to cook jam and jellies. Non-drying oil can be extracted from the seeds, and was traditionally used to soften bow strings and leather.

The leaves are eaten by giraffe and some antelope, as well as the larvae of a number of butterflies, such as the silvery silverline (*Cigaritis phanes*) and Bowker's marbled sapphire (*Stugeta bowkeri*). It is a good tree for the bird and butterfly garden.

The sapwood is white, but the heartwood is reddish brown, hard and fairly heavy, with a fine grain. It is used as a general-purpose timber and for firewood. It saws and works well, but the sawdust may cause severe sneezing.

# BUSHVELD IRONWOOD

## *Olea capensis* subsp. *enervis*

**A:** bosveldysterhout  **NS:** morašane  **SW:** sinhletje  **V:** musiri  **Z:** umsishane

*Olea:* Latin, 'olive', related to Greek *elaia*; *capensis:* 'from the Cape'

Bushveld ironwood is a slow-growing, long-lived evergreen tree with a rounded crown. Under ideal conditions, it may reach a height in excess of 30m, but is usually only about 12m tall. This species occurs on rocky outcrops in dry bushveld.

The bark is pale grey, becoming longitudinally fissured with age. The leaves are broadly elliptic and are glossy, light to dark green above and paler below. The tip is tapering, usually with a sharp point. The leaf stalk is relatively short. White, sweetly scented, bisexual flowers are borne at the ends of the branches. Like those of other *Olea* species, the flowers are quite small. The edible fruit is fleshy, turning black as it ripens.

The wood of bushveld ironwood is one of the world's hardest, strongest and heaviest timbers. It is brown with a straight grain, somewhat oily, and exceptionally durable. Although it is an attractive wood for turning and ornamental work, is is difficult to work and therefore not often used.

# IRONWOOD

## *Olea capensis* subsp. *macrocarpa*

**A:** ysterhout, swartysterhout  **V:** musiri
**X:** umhlebe  **Z:** umzimane

*capensis:* 'of the Cape'; *macrocarpa:* from the Greek
*makros* ('long') and *karpos* ('fruit'), the fruit being about
double the size of that of other subspecies

The slow-growing evergreen ironwood is probably second
in size only to the yellowwoods (*Afrocarpus falcatus* and
*Podocarpus latifolius*) of the southern Cape forests, and is
equally long-lived. This hardy tree may reach up to 40m in
height under ideal conditions. It has a straight trunk and a
dense but narrow crown. The bark is light grey, becoming
darker and vertically fissured with age.

*Olea capensis* subsp. *macrocarpa* occurs in the
evergreen forests of the south and east coasts, where it is
one of the canopy trees. Its distribution range overlaps with
that of the subspecies *O. capensis* subsp. *capensis*, which
occurs in the Knysna forest and possibly in other forests
in the southern Cape. *O. capensis* subsp. *macrocarpa*
is tall, with wavy leaf margins and oval fruit, while
*O. capensis* subsp. *capensis* only grows to about 12m
and has rolled-under leaf margins and round fruit.

Ironwood exudes a characteristic blackish gum from
wounds in its bark. The opposite pairs of glossy dark green
leaves are paler green below. They are oblong or elliptic in
shape, with a pointed tip and a prominent midrib. The leaf
stalk is often purplish. The small, sweetly scented, white or
cream flowers appear mostly in terminal heads. Ironwood
is said to be a good 'bee tree'.

The heartwood is pale brown with black and yellow
streaks, has an attractive grain and takes a fine polish.
The timber is heavy and hard (as can be deduced from the
name ironwood) and is becoming increasingly popular for
furniture. Other uses include carving, handicraft, turning,
flooring, panelling, railway sleepers and veneer.

This species is a natural pioneer and drought resistant.

# WILD OLIVE

## *Olea europaea* subsp. *cuspidata*

A: olienhout  NS, SS: mohlware  SW, X, Z:
umnquma  TS: motlhware  V: mutlhwari

*europaea:* 'from Europe'

This beautifully shaped evergreen tree has a dense, spreading crown. It is slow-growing and can reach 18m under ideal conditions. The wild olive is drought and frost resistant and occurs in woodland throughout South Africa, except in the northern parts of the lowveld and the northern and western parts of the bushveld. It is often found near water and on rocky hillsides. Since this species commonly grows on chalky soils, it is regarded as an indicator of this soil type.

The leaves are shiny grey-green to dark green above and silvery underneath. The fruits are eaten by birds, including starlings, pigeons, parrots, mousebirds, bulbuls and turacos, as well as vervet monkeys, baboons, bushpigs and warthogs. The leaves are browsed by kudu and grey and blue duikers, as well as livestock. It is a valuable fodder tree in the drier parts of the region. It also attracts a number of butterflies and bees.

The sapwood is whitish to light brown, but the heartwood is golden brown with beautiful dark flames. It is fine-grained, strong, very hard and durable. It works well, takes a fine polish and is very popular for quality furniture, turning, ornaments, spoons, knife handles, walking sticks and carvings. Since the wood is resistant to termite and borer attack, it is also used for fencing posts.

The wild olive is regarded as a small-fruited subspecies of the European olive. As it is resistant to most of the diseases that attack commercial olives, it can be used as a rootstock for grafting the commercial trees. It is also a popular bonsai species.

# HARDPEAR

## *Olinia ventosa*

**A:** hardepeer **X:** umngenalahla, ingobamakhosi, inqudu, umnonono

*Olinia:* named after Johan Hendrik Olin (1769–1824), a Swedish botanist and author; ***ventosa:*** 'windy'

This attractive endemic can be found along forest margins and in the coastal scrub of the eastern and southern coastal regions of South Africa, from the Cape Peninsula to southern KwaZulu-Natal. It is a fast-growing, hardy, evergreen tree with a spreading crown and is typically 5m in height, though it can reach 25m in the evergreen forests of the southern Cape. When growing on dunes, it may be no more than a shrub.

The bark is smooth and pale grey, becoming dark and fissured, with small rectangles lifting at the lower ends to reveal the red-brown, flaky underbark. Mature trunks are often fluted and gnarled. The leaves are in opposite pairs, and are glossy dark green above and dull pale green below. The tip is tapering to rounded, and the base tapers to a very short leaf stalk, which is often red. The leaf margin is smooth-edged, wavy and slightly rolled under. When crushed, the leaves smell strongly of almonds, as does the freshly cut wood. This tree is breathtaking in spring when it is in full flower. The very small, sweetly scented, whitish flowers are borne in dense clusters, each consisting of three groups of three flowers each.

The nectar attracts various birds and insects that act as pollinators. The fruit is thinly fleshy and turns from pink to bright red when ripe. It is eaten by bird species such as African olive pigeons, turacos and mousebirds. The seeds are encased in a hard shell and take a long time to germinate. However, under optimal conditions the tree grows more than a metre per year.

The yellowish-brown wood is hard, heavy, durable and strong. There is no difference between the heartwood and the sapwood, but the heartwood may have darker streaks. The wavy grain gives the wood a fine finish, but makes it difficult to work with. The wood may also chip in areas where the grain is very wavy. In the past, the wood of this tree was used for wagon building and telegraph poles. Today, it is popular for furniture, cabinetry, carving, turnery and panelling.

# TREE-WISTERIA

*Bolusanthus speciosus*

**A:** Vanwykshout **NS:** kgomo-nahlabana **Z:** umhohlo

**PROTECTED IN SOUTH AFRICA**

*Bolusanthus:* a combination of Bolus and Greek *anthos* ('flower'), in honour of Harry Bolus (1834–1911), founder of the Cape Town Bolus Herbarium; *speciosus:* 'beautiful'

Tree-wisteria is named for its flowers resembling those of *Wisteria* creeper from Japan and China. This slender, decorative, deciduous tree has a narrow crown and drooping branches. It grows 5–10m in height and is found in woodland, where it prefers clay soils.

Tree-wisteria is easily recognised by its shape, deeply grooved bark and long, drooping, scented clusters of dark bluish-mauve flowers, which appear in early summer.

This tree retains its foliage during winter and is bare for only a short while in early spring. Mammals such as grey duiker, kudu, gemsbok, giraffe and vervet monkeys utilise this species by eating the flower buds, pods and leaves. The flowers also attract bees.

The sapwood is yellow and the heartwood brown. The wood is heavy, strong and borer and termite resistant, making it an excellent wood for fencing poles and fine furniture. Tree-wisteria is also suitable for planting along urban streets as the crown is narrow, the flower display spectacular and the root system non-invasive. It is hardy and drought resistant.

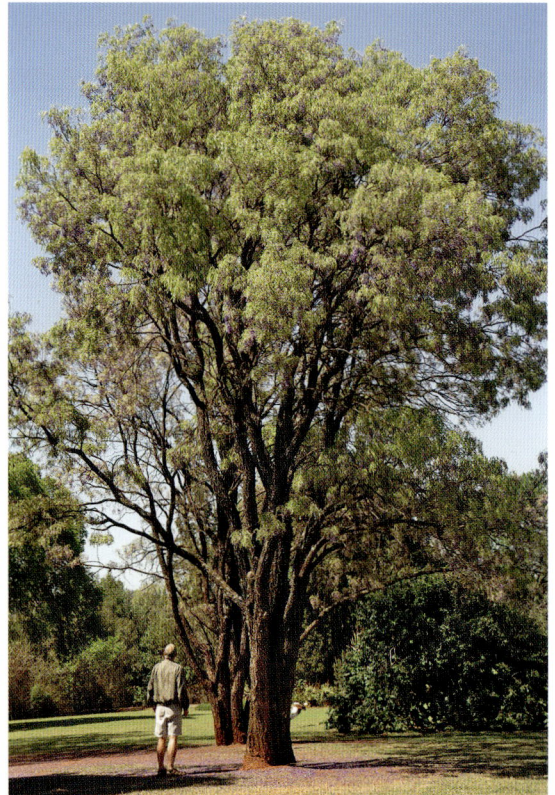

# WILD-MANGO

## Cordyla africana

A: wildemango  SW: thunzikhulu, vovovo
TG: xivuvule  Z: igowane-lehlati

*Cordyla:* from Greek *kordule* ('club'), referring to the club-shaped fruit and fruit-stalk; *africana:* 'from Africa'

Wild-mango is a spectacular, fast-growing deciduous tree with a large, much-branched, spreading crown. It reaches up to 25m in height. The straight trunk can be free of branches for up to 15m and is also free of buttresses.

This species is found on sandy soils in miombo woodland, large river valleys and swampy evergreen forest in the eastern parts of South Africa.

The long compound leaves are a shiny bottle-green. This tree is a splendid sight when the flowers appear alongside the new leaves in spring. The flowers are without petals and display rich yellow stamens in axillary clusters. They face upward, like those of *Schotia* species, and attract a large variety of birds. The fruit is initially an ellipsoid to nearly globose berry-like pod, but develops into a golden-yellow and glossy oval drupe that is slightly depressed on one side. The fruit drops from the tree before it is ripe and ripens fully on the ground. One or two pale brown seeds are embedded in the pulp and they often germinate while still in the fruit. Various mammals, including elephant, eagerly eat the fruit, as do humans. The fruit is rich in vitamin C and can be enjoyed either fresh or cooked.

The sapwood is pale yellow and the heartwood yellowish brown with darker bands. The wood is light, somewhat durable and resistant to termite attack but vulnerable to borer attack. It has been used for construction, flooring, mine props, railway sleepers, beehives, household utensils, joinery, drums and canoes. It also makes for good firewood.

# APPLE-LEAF

*Philenoptera violacea*

**A:** appelblaar  **NS:** mphata  **SW:** umhomuhomu  **TG:** mbhandzu
**TS:** mohata  **V:** mufhanda  **Z:** isihomohomo

*Coeliades forestan*

**PROTECTED IN SOUTH AFRICA**

*Philenoptera:* from Greek *philenos* ('tractable' or 'manageable') and *pteros* ('wing'), referring to the winged pods of some species in this genus; *violacea:* 'violet', a reference to the flowers

This attractive deciduous to semi-deciduous tree has an open, rounded crown and sparse, drooping foliage. The main trunk is usually tall and bare, though often bent and twisted. The sweetly scented flowers appear before or with the new leaves in September and are scattered at the tips of the branches. They vary in colour from white and pink to bluish-pink, mauve or deep violet. The copious nectar attracts many birds and insects that also feed on the nutritious fallen flowers.

The fruit is a flat, hairless, non-splitting pod that stays on the tree during winter. The dull green leaves are browsed by a variety of game animals, including eland, kudu, giraffe, impala and nyala, as well as livestock.

The larvae of the striped policeman butterfly (*Coeliades forestan*) and the large blue emperor (*Charaxes bohemani*) feed on the leaves. The bark and roots are believed to be poisonous.

The wood is light brown, heavy and hard, but is susceptible to borer attack. It is nevertheless sometimes used for household utensils, such as grain mortars and tool handles, and also for carvings. It burns too fast to be useful as firewood. Apple-leaf can be grown from seed. It is an attractive, drought-resistant tree for parks and larger gardens, but is not frost resistant.

The apple-leaf is one of the region's 'rain trees'. The 'rain' is caused by the nymph of the spittlebug *Ptyelus grossus*, which covers itself with a frothy substance commonly known as 'cuckoo-spit'. The insect feeds on the sap of the tree by piercing the bark. It releases liquid at an almost equal rate, which drips from the tree, giving rise to the name 'rain tree'.

# KIAAT

## *Pterocarpus angolensis*

**A:** kiaat, dolfhout **NS:** morôtô **TS:** mokwa **Z:** umvangazi

**PROTECTED IN SOUTH AFRICA**

*Pterocarpus:* from Greek *pteros* ('wing') and *karpos* ('fruit') referring to the unusual seed pods; *angolensis:* 'from Angola'

Kiaat is a deciduous tree with an open, rounded crown and a bare, straight trunk. Under ideal conditions, it can reach a height of more than 20m. The shiny, compound leaves characteristically hang downwards.

This is a relatively common species in the woodlands of northeastern South Africa. It prefers deep sandy soil or rocky slopes where the rainfall is more than 500mm per year and where there are contrasting dry and wet seasons. It is regarded as an indicator of well-drained soils and favours areas free of frost. This species may form stands.

The deep yellow flowers appear before the new leaves in spring and early summer and are a good source of pollen, making the trees popular with beekeepers. The larvae of the bushveld charaxes butterfly (*Charaxes achaemenes achaemenes*) also feed on the leaves.

The seed pod of this lovely tree looks like a brown and papery fried egg with sharp bristles in the centre. The pods remain on the tree long after the leaves have been discarded, making it easy to identify the species. Squirrels,

monkeys and baboons feed eagerly on the pods despite the somewhat sharp bristles. Elephant and kudu eat the leaves.

The brilliant red sap gave rise to the alternate common name 'bloodwood'. The traditional Afrikaans name *dolfhout* refers to one of the Dorsland trekkers of the 1870s, Roedolf (Dolf) Holtzhausen, who is believed to have worked extensively with this wood. *Kiaat* is a corruption of the Dutch word *kajaten*, the name given to a teak species (*Tectona grandis*) occuring in Southeast Asia.

The rich brown wood is sought after for making high-quality furniture, as it is easy to work and takes a fine polish. In fact, many consider it second only to stinkwood for making furniture. It is also an excellent wood for building canoes, as it does not contract or expand much. It can also be used for making drums, bowls, ornaments, door and window frames, and household items. The heartwood is durable and resistant to termites and wood-borers. The red sap has traditionally been used as a dye.

Kiaat is a key timber species throughout its range and is certainly one of the most popular and most valuable trees for the people of the region. Over-utilisation of the species in the absence of control over the rate of harvesting has caused the tree to be classified as Near Threatened on the IUCN Red List of Threatened Species.

# ROUND-LEAVED BLOODWOOD

### *Pterocarpus rotundifolius* subsp. *rotundifolius*

**A:** dopperkiaat, wildekweper, rondeblaarkiaat **NS:** mohwahlapa
**SW:** lidlebe-lendlovu **TG:** muyataha **V:** muaṱaha **Z:** indlandlovu

*rotundifolius:* refers to the round shape of the leaf

This deciduous tree is 10–20m in height and can be either single- or multi-stemmed. It occurs throughout much of the region, preferring stony hills and grassy slopes in mixed bushveld, wooded grassland, *Brachystegia* woodland and open forest. It differs from kiaat (*Pterocarpus angolensis*) in a number of ways: the crown is more upright; the fruit is smaller and lacks the hairy centre; and the compound leaf has fewer leaflets, each with a rounded rather than pointed tip.

The yellow, pea-shaped flowers with their crinkly petals are a gorgeous sight during spring and early summer. These honey-scented flowers last only a day or two, but the tree flowers intermittently over a period of weeks, providing a spectacular ongoing display. The flowers attract many pollinating insects. Being a good source of nectar and pollen for honey bees, this species is popular with beekeepers.

Elephant feed on the foliage, and the young leaves are also eaten by cattle and browsers such as kudu and impala. Larvae of the bushveld charaxes butterfly (*Charaxes achaemenes achaemenes*) feed on the leaves.

The wood has an attractive grain and works quite well, but is not durable. It has been used on a limited scale as a general-purpose timber. These trees burn easily and may show signs of veld fire damage.

# NYALATREE

## *Xanthocercis zambesiaca*

A: njalaboom  ND: umhlati  TG: nhlarhu  TS: mhota  V: mutshato

*Xanthocercis:* from the Greek *xanthos* ('yellow'), and referring to the genus *Cercis*, a non-indigenous member of the Fabaceae family; *zambesiaca:* refers to the Zambezi region

This spectacular evergreen or semi-deciduous legume grows up to 30m tall and usually has an elegant, rounded crown. An indicator of the presence of groundwater, it occurs on the rich alluvial soils of river valleys and floodplains, often on termite mounds. It is prolific along the northern stretch of the Limpopo River and along the Shashe River, where it is regionally known as the *mashatu tree*.

The trunk is massive and branches quite low down, making it look like a collection of stems twisted together. The leaves turn a distinctive bright yellow when shed.

In November or December, white or creamy flowers appear at or near the ends of twigs. They have a pleasant scent and are visited in large numbers by a variety of insect pollinators. The fruit is a berry that turns dark brown from March and stays on the tree for a long time. When it falls to the ground, elephant are quick to pick it up. Primates, fruit bats, birds and antelope also feed on the fruit. Humans either eat the fruit fresh or grind it into a meal when dry. Various browsers feed on nyalatree leaves.

The wood is very dark, durable and works well, making it suitable for furniture. The sawdust, however, may irritate the nose and throat.

Although it grows slowly, this is an excellent and beautiful shade tree for large gardens in hot, frost-free areas.

# WINGPOD
## *Xeroderris stuhlmannii*
**A:** vlerkboon  **V:** mudzungu

*Xeroderris:* from Greek *xeros* ('dry') and *derma* ('skin' or 'hide'), referring to the rough seed pods; *stuhlmannii:* named after Franz Ernst Stuhlmann (1863–1928), acting governor of Tanganyika (now Tanzania) and an avid plant collector

Wingpod is a drought-resistant, deciduous legume with a rounded crown that is half-spreading and quite sparse. This tree is usually about 10m in height, though some specimens are larger. It has a limited distribution range in South Africa, and is found in the far north and northeast of the country, occurring in deciduous woodland, savannah and bushveld, particularly on well-drained soils.

This species is easily recognised by its pendulous, flattened pods, which have a distinct 'wing' or ridge around the edge. The branches are ascending, the straight cylindrical trunk often being free of branches for several metres. Leaves are spirally arranged and crowded at the ends of branches. Snow-white, waxy flowers are borne in conspicuous sprays and the pods hang in large, dense, pendent clusters. Livestock and game often eat the pods and leaves. It is said the seeds are toxic if eaten raw, but safe if cooked.

When damaged, the bark exudes a dark red sap. Extracts from the bark are sometimes used as a dye and for tanning.

The heartwood is not distinctly demarcated from the sapwood and is cream to dark yellow, sometimes with reddish streaks. The grain is straight and the texture moderately fine and even. Wingpod wood is heavy, fairly hard and moderately durable. It is susceptible to beetle attack, but not particularly vulnerable to termites and borers. It is used for furniture, railway sleepers, canoes, flooring, sporting goods, joinery, poles, carvings, toys, turnery, veneer, plywood and utensils. It is also used in heavy construction and makes for excellent firewood.

# SESAMEBUSH

## *Sesamothamnus lugardii*

A: sesambos  TS: moboana  V: tshiṋonzhe

*Sesamothamnus:* from Greek *sesamon* ('oily plant') and *thamnos* ('bush'); *lugardii:* named after Major Edward James Lugard (1865–1957), a British-born naturalist who collected plants in southern Africa

This strange-looking, multi-stemmed, spiny tree or shrub somewhat resembles a small baobab. The succulent-like swollen lower trunk is fairly thick and can reach a metre in diameter, but the tree itself seldom exceeds 4m in height.

It occurs mainly in the hot, dry country north of the Soutpansberg, where it grows singly or in scattered, small groups, usually on chalky soils or in mopane veld. it also occurs between rocks in shrublands.

Straight or slightly curved spines grow on the twigs and branches. These spines are typically 5–15mm long and become hard and sharp with age.

Sesamebush produces only a small number of flowers. These beautiful white flowers are trumpet-shaped, with a long, thin, red-brown floral tube, which is elongated into a 'spur' at the base where it joins the twig.

The tree is not utilised by browsers and the timber has no known use.

# MITZEERI

## *Bridelia micrantha*

A: mitserie, bruinstinkhout  NS: motsêrê  SW: umhlala-magcwababa
TG: ndzerhe  V: munzere  X: umhlahla-makhwaba  Z: umhlalamgwababa

*Bridelia:* named by German botanist Carl Ludwig Willdenow in honour of Samuel Elisée Bridel-Brideri; *micrantha:* 'with small flowers'

This impressive deciduous or evergreen tree is fast-growing and reaches up to 20m in height. It has a single, straight trunk and a dense, rounded or domeshaped crown, usually with some scattered bright red leaves.

Mitzeeri occurs in riverine forest or open woodland, preferring moist places. It is not found west of the Drakensberg escarpment.

This species is a larval food plant for various butterflies. The sweet fruit is adequate for human consumption and is also popular with fruit-eating birds, making this tree a must for the 'bird garden'.

The dark brown wood has a fine grain and is durable and termite resistant. Cabinet makers regard this wood to be as good as stinkwood (*Ocotea bullata*) for making high-quality furniture. It is also used for construction, poles, flooring, joinery, mine props, boat building, crates, carvings, turnery, wood veneers and plywood.

This lovely shade tree is easily propagated from seed, and should make an excellent street tree in places where the extensive root system can be accommodated. It can withstand light frost, but not drought.

# VELVET SWEETBERRY

*Bridelia mollis*

A: fluweelsoetbessie  TG: swatima  TS: mokokonala
V: mukumba-kumbane

*mollis:* 'soft', referring to the velvety, hairy leaves

This typical bushveld tree is relatively small, with a height of no more than 15m – usually significantly less. It occurs in sandy soils among rocks or on granite koppies. In contrast to mitzeeri (*B. micrantha*), it prefers dry, stony soils. Good places to see this species include the Magaliesberg, Waterberg and Strydpoortberg rangcs.

The bark is grey to dark brown with rough longitudinal grooves. The leaves of this deciduous tree turn golden-yellow to dark brown in winter.

Velvet sweetberry blooms only after good rains. Male and female flowers occur on separate trees and are borne in small groups in the leaf axils. They are yellow-green, tiny and unobtrusive.

The fruit is an edible, fleshy berry, which is black or blue-black when ripe. Kudu are known to browse this tree, and the larvae of several butterfly and moth species make use of *Bridelia* species as food plants.

The wood has a very fine texture, conspicuous annual rings and many small pores. It is easy to work, takes a fine polish and is suitable for the manufacture of ornaments and curios.

*The fruit turns blue-black as it ripens.*

Family Phyllanthaceae

# FALSE-TAMBOTI

*Cleistanthus schlechteri* var. *schlechteri*

A: valstambotie  TG: nxiri  Z: umzithi

**PROTECTED IN SOUTH AFRICA**

*Cleistanthus:* from Greek *kleistos* ('closed') and *anthos* ('flower'), a reference to the partially closed flowers; *schlechteri:* named after Friedrich Schlechter (1872–1925), a German botanist, taxonomist and traveller

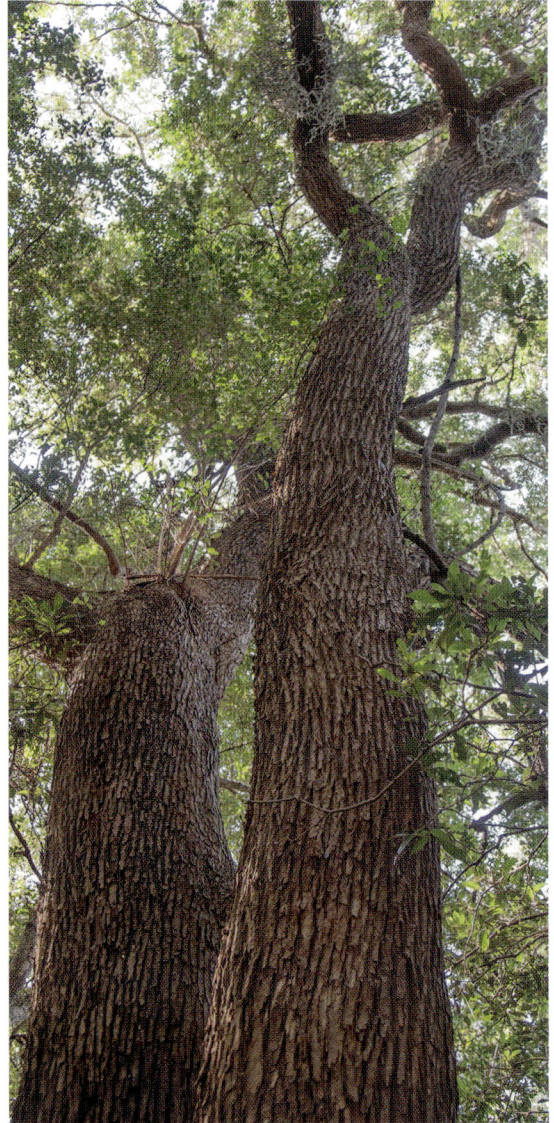

In South Africa, this species has a limited distribution in the Limpopo and Mpumalanga lowveld and the sand forests of northern Zululand and Maputaland. It is usually a large, slow-growing, upright, deciduous tree with a narrow crown. Forest specimens are tall, growing up to 15m in height, typically with a single straight trunk. Woodland specimens can be either single- or multi-stemmed and usually do not exceed a height of 8m.

The bark is grey to dark brown and cracks into small, flat, more or less rectangular blocks. The simple, alternate leaves are borne on short, gnarled lateral twigs and are dark green and glossy above. Minute domatia (small cavities that house arthropods) are present in the axils of prominent lateral veins on the lower surface of the leaves. The foliage is dense and bright green, turning red-brown in autumn.

The yellow-green to pale green unisexual flowers appear in October and November and are borne in small bunches. The fruit is a small, smooth, glossy, three-lobed capsule that ripens from yellow-green to brown. It is similar to that of tamboti (*Spirostachys africana*). Fallen leaves are eaten by game, especially suni and red duiker, and the seeds are eaten by various bird species, such as crested francolin, emerald-spotted wood doves and crested guineafowl. Elephant also seem to favour this tree.

The golden-brown to reddish wood is very hard, termite resistant and very attractive. It is used for carving, hut building and fuel.

Family Pittosporaceae

# CHEESEWOOD

*Pittosporum viridiflorum*

A: kasuur  NS: kgalagangwe  SW: umvusamvu  TG: mpatakhamelo
V: mulondwane  X: umkhwenkwe  Z: umfusamvu

### PROTECTED IN SOUTH AFRICA

*Pittosporum:* from Greek *pitta* ('pitch') and *sporos,* ('seed'), a reference to the sticky seeds; *viridiflorum:* 'with green flowers'

A perfect garden tree, cheesewood grows reasonably fast, has evergreen foliage and non-invasive roots, and attracts a variety of wildlife. This hardy tree is usually 9–10m in height, with a dense, rounded crown and shiny green foliage. Under ideal conditions, it can reach up to 15m in height. It is found in drier types of forest, riverine and swamp forest, humid woodland and evergreen bushland, but not above an altitude of about 1,800m.

The trunk is typically light grey with characteristic bands of darker lenticels. The leaves have a resinous smell when crushed. Small, sweetly scented, greenish-white flowers are borne in terminal clusters in early summer and are followed by masses of yellow to brown capsules. These split open to expose bright red, sticky seeds. The flowers attract numerous insects and bees, and the fruits are eaten by birds such as doves, barbets, starlings, turacos and parrots. Fallen fruits are picked up by Natal francolins, Swainson's spurfowl and guineafowl. Kudu, nyala, bushbuck, duiker, klipspringer and goats feed on the leaves.

Cheesewood can withstand mild frost and some drought, but flourishes in areas with good rainfall and well-drained soils. A red dye is made from the bark and the root fibres are used in basketry.

Cheesewood's common name is derived from its light and fairly soft wood. The wood is white in colour. Although generally of little use, it has been utilised for shelving, tool handles and kitchen utensils. The tree is also a key species in traditional African medicine.

# OUTENIQUA YELLOWWOOD

*Afrocarpus falcatus*

A: outeniekwageelhout, kalander  NS: mogôbagôba
SW: umsonti  V: mufhanza  X: umkhoba  Z: umsonti

**PROTECTED IN SOUTH AFRICA**

*Afrocarpus:* from Latin *afer* ('African') and Greek *karpos* ('fruit'); *falcatus:* from Latin 'sickle-shaped', a reference to the leaves

*The endemic Cape parrot nests in this tree and feeds on its fruit.*

The majestic Outeniqua yellowwood is a hardy, evergreen tree with a long, straight, cylindrical trunk and a slender crown. It occurs in moist forests, wooded ravines, mountain forest and coastal swamp forest. Historically, its range stretched from Swellendam in the south to northern Zululand, the Drakensberg escarpment, Blouberg and the western Soutpansberg, as well as Eswatini and Mozambique, but recently the species has also been introduced into the Cape Peninsula and surrounds.

Outeniqua yellowwood is the fastest growing species of the region's yellowwoods. Under ideal conditions, this giant can reach up to 60m in height, but in exposed habitat it rarely exceeds 25m. Tall specimens can be branchless for up to 25m. Some of the largest specimens occur in the Knysna–Amatole montane forests, where certain individuals are estimated to be as old as 1,000 years.

A characteristic feature of this tree is the bark, which starts off smooth and later flakes off in large curly pieces, which vary from round to almost rectangular. As a dominant canopy species, this tree is often festooned with an epiphytic lichen known as 'old man's beard' (*Usnea barbata*).

The narrow, leathery leaves are spirally arranged and are blue-green when young, becoming dark green with age.

Outeniqua yellowwood is dioecious and belongs to the primeval clade Gymnospermae, meaning that it produces cones rather than flowers and fruit. Dry cones on the forest floor are indicative of male trees. In female trees, the cones develop round yellow seeds. These can take up to a year to ripen, and are eaten by bushpigs, bats, monkeys and fruit-eating birds, including parrots, pigeons, hornbills and turacos.

Many different birds favour this tree for nesting, but the threatened Cape parrot (*Poicephalus robustus*) is particularly relevant. This species is South Africa's only endemic parrot and it is believed that fewer than 2,000 birds survive. It is a forest bird with a strong preference for these yellowwoods when it comes to nesting. It also eagerly eats the seeds of this tree.

The pale yellow wood is sought after for furniture, ship building, door and window frames, and roof beams. The younger trees were once used as topmasts for ships because the trunks are tall and straight.

Owing to the popularity of the wood, the species was over-utilised in the past and many large, ancient specimens have been lost.

Family Podocarpaceae

# REAL YELLOWWOOD
## *Podocarpus latifolius*
**A:** opregte geelhout, Kaapse geelhout  **NS:** mogôbagôba
**V:** muhovho-hovho  **X:** umcheya  **Z:** umkhoba

### PROTECTED IN SOUTH AFRICA

*Podocarpus:* from Greek *pous* ('foot') and *karpos* ('fruit'), referring to the fruit-like structure formed by the seed-bearing cone; *latifolius:* refers to broad leaves

*Knysna turaco*

Real yellowwood, with its dense, narrow-branched crown, is the national tree of South Africa. This slow-growing, long-lived, evergreen tree reaches up to 35m in height.

This species is found in evergreen and mountain forests in the southern, eastern and northern parts of the country. It also occurs on open, rocky hillsides and mountain slopes, but is then low-growing, seldom exceeding 2m in height. It is most common in the mistbelt forests, where it reaches maximum size. Epiphytic lichen known as 'old man's beard' (*Usnea barbata*) often hangs from the branches.

The main trunk is usually tall, straight and cylindrical, and can be very impressive – the largest specimens have a trunk diameter of up to 3m. The trunk is occasionally buttressed at the base. The yellowish to greyish-brown bark peels in thin, longitudinal strips.

Real yellowwood has the broadest leaves of the yellowwoods in South Africa (in Zimbabwe, its common name is 'broad-leaved yellowwood'). The leaves are tough, rubbery and a lush dark green. New leaves are pale green and situated in clusters at the ends of branches.

These trees are wind pollinated. Yellowwoods are conifers, like pine trees, and pollen and seeds are produced by cones, not flowers. In pine trees, the scales of the seed cones are separate. In many yellowwood trees, the scales of seed cones fuse to form a fleshy, fruitlike structure called a receptacle. The seeds are blue or blue-green and become purplish. The receptacle can be bright pink, red or purple. One or two round seeds are borne on the receptacle. When the berry-like receptacles ripen, they are eagerly eaten by birds such as pigeons and turacos, and also by monkeys and bushpigs.

Yellowwood timber is extremely popular, especially in the furniture industry. The soft yellow colour of the wood contrasts spectacularly with the dark wood of stinkwood (*Ocotea bullata*) and, when available, these two timbers are still used together to make beautiful traditional Cape furniture. Many of the floorboards in the early Cape Dutch homes were made from this lovely wood. Due to over-utilisation in the past, real yellowwood has become almost extinct in parts of its distribution range.

This species can handle light frost, but not drought.

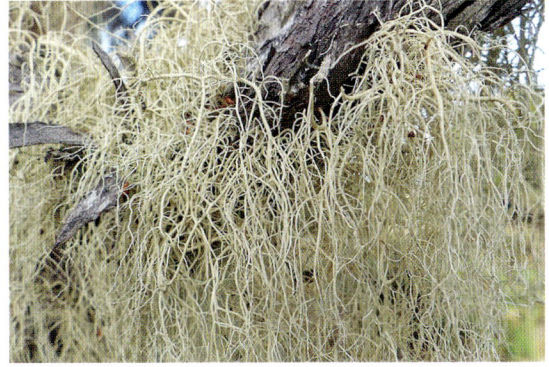

*Old man's beard lichen* (Usnea barbata).

# SNEEZEWOOD
## Ptaeroxylon obliquum
**A:** nieshout **SW:** umtsatse **TG:** ndzari
**TS:** thate **V:** munari **X:** umthathi **Z:** umthathe

**PROTECTED IN SOUTH AFRICA**

*Papilio demodocus*

*Ptaeroxylon:* from Greek for 'to sneeze' and 'wood';
*obliquum:* Latin for 'oblique, slanting', referring to the
asymmetrical shape of the leaflets

Sneezewood is a decorative tree, occuring in diverse, widespread habitats, including bushveld and forests, from the Eastern Cape northwards. This hardy, fast-growing, drought-resistant tree has a rounded crown and reaches up to 15m in height. In mistbelt forests, it can become huge. Sneezewood can be single- or multi-stemmed; in forests the trunk is tall, straight and cylindrical, sometimes fluted. Its whitish-grey bark becomes fissured with age.

Sneezewood can be deciduous or evergreen. The compound leaves are opposite, with 3–8 pairs of dark green leaflets. The leaflets are characteristically obliquely rectangular and have a very asymmetrical base. In autumn, they turn mustard-yellow, and later dark brown, before being shed. Although the leaves have an unpleasant smell and a very bitter taste, browsers such as kudu, giraffe and impala eat them. The citrus swallowtail butterfly (*Papilio demodocus*) is known to breed on this tree.

This tree is dioecious, although the male and female flowers appear similar to the naked eye at first glance. The fragrant creamy yellow flowers have four petals and an orange centre. The fruit is an oblong capsule that splits open to release winged seeds.

Sneezewood gets its common name from the peppery oils in the wood, which cause violent sneezing when the wood is sawn or sanded. While not toxic, sneezewood is known to have caused respiratory complications.

The tree is highly valued for its exceptionally beautiful timber. The golden heartwood turns golden-brown or brown over time, and has attractive light orange 'flames'. The wood is extremely hard, dense and durable. It was used extensively for railway sleepers, fences and telephone poles, as well as for furniture, carving, turnery, vats, handles and implements. The high demand for this wood led to the destruction of most of the huge specimens.

*Young stems are smooth with pale, blotched bark, but become fissured with age.*

# BOEKENHOUT
## *Faurea saligna*

A: bosveldboekenhout, boekenhout, rooiboekenhout  ND: isidwadwa, umonyeli  NS: mohlakô  TS: monyena  V: muṱango  Z: isefu

*Faurea:* in honour of W.C. Faure (1822–1844), a soldier who was passionate about botany; *saligna:* 'Salix-like', referring to the drooping leaves and flower spikes, which resemble those of a willow tree (*Salix*)

Boekenhout is also known as willow beechwood, and is named for its wood, which resembles that of the European beech (*Fagus sylvatica*), and for its drooping, willow-like leaves. This slender, graceful tree grows up to 10m tall and is associated with mountain sourveld. It is common in the Magaliesberg and Waterberg ranges. The leaves are yellowish green, but may turn red in the winter months. A large boekenhout tree can have a spreading, albeit fairly sparse, crown. The trunk is usually straight, but may be twisted. The flowers, which are present from August to February, have a sweet smell and are rich in nectar. They attract bees, which pollinate the tree.

The beautifully figured reddish wood is highly valued as furniture timber as it works and polishes well. Being resistant to termite and borer attack, it can be used for poles, posts, panelling, joinery, flooring, railway sleepers, tool handles and carving.

This species is a slow grower and susceptible to severe cold and fierce fires, but may survive moderate fire.

# FOREST BOEKENHOUT

## *Faurea galpinii*

**A:** bosboekenhout, platorandboekenhout, rooiboekenhout
**NS:** mohlakô **SW:** sisefo **V:** muṱango

*galpinii:* named after Ernest Edward Galpin (1858–1941), a banker and amateur plant collector who discovered half a dozen genera and hundreds of new species

This small evergreen species is either an upright tree or much-branched shrub with an upright crown. It grows up to 10m high. Forest boekenhout, also known as 'escarpment beechwood', is a southern African endemic, occurring in the high-altitude mistbelt areas, along the forest margins of the Drakensberg escarpment in Mpumalanga and Limpopo and in Eswatini. While its distribution range is limited, the species is common within its range.

When growing in a forest, the tree has smooth, grey bark. In exposed positions, the bark is much rougher and darker.

The dark green leaves are arranged alternatively and have a wavy margin. The leaf stalk is about 10mm long.

New leaves are typically red. The midrib and stalk are often also reddish in colour.

The greenish-white spikes of bisexual flowers appear from October to February. They are about 10cm long and finely velvety. The erect spikes of this species distinguishes it from other species in the genus, which have drooping flower spikes. The spike may sometimes become horizontal, with only the end portion angled upright. The fruit appears from November to April. It is small, dry and single-seeded, and is covered in whitish hairs and does not split open.

The wood is termite resistant and has occasionally been used for furniture and poles.

This species has lost some habitat to timber plantations, but, fortunately, commercial plantations no longer seem to be expanding. Forest boekenhout is nevertheless vulnerable to invasive plants such a pine seedlings escaping from plantations.

Established trees are resistant to frost and drought.

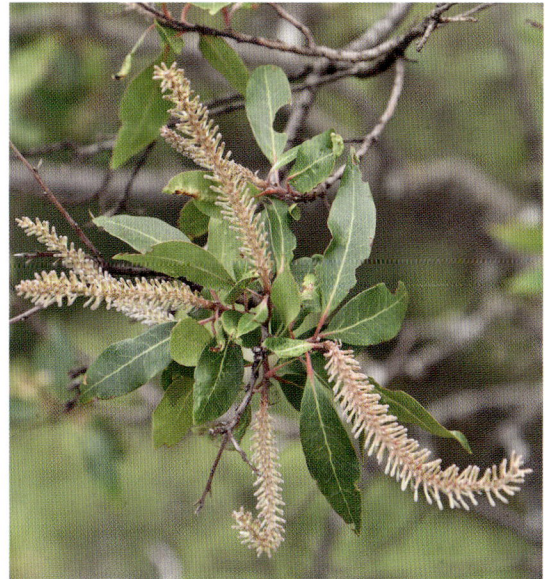

# COMMON SUGARBUSH
## *Protea caffra* subsp. *caffra*
A: gewone suikerbos  NS: segwapi  V: tshiḓzungu  X: isadlunge  Z: isiqalaba

*Protea:* named after the Greek god Proteus, who was believed to be capable of changing his shape, an allusion to the great variability of this genus; *caffra:* refers to the former colonial region of Kaffraria

Common sugarbush is the most widely distributed *Protea* species in South Africa, and is associated with mountain slopes and mountain grassland.

This evergreen tree reaches up to 8m in height and has a somewhat rounded crown. It can be single- or multi-stemmed. The grey to black bark is thick, rough, deeply fissured and corky, protecting the tree against the veld fires that are so common in the mountain grasslands. The seed of this species requires fire to germinate.

The grey-green, leathery and hairless leaves are crowded towards the branch tips. Young leaves are red.

Common sugarbush flowers from November to March. Many small, single flowers are clustered together in flowerheads, which are situated at the ends of branches. The outer leaf-like bracts of the flowerheads vary in colour, from red to pink to cream. Old, dead flowerheads can remain on the tree for a long time, giving it an untidy appearance.

The common name derives from the tree's copious nectar, which attracts pollinators such as birds (especially sunbirds) and insects, including butterflies. The caterpillars of some butterflies feed on the flowers. After pollination, densely hairy nuts develop, then fall to the ground, releasing seeds that are dispersed by the wind.

If common sugarbush were not such a difficult tree to grow, more specimens of this striking, frost-tolerant tree might be seen in gardens and parks.

# SILVER SUGARBUSH

*Protea roupelliae* subsp. *roupelliae*

**A:** silwersuikerbos  **NS:** segwapi  **V:** tshiḓiḓiri  **X:** isiqalaba  **Z:** isiqalaba

*Malachite sunbird*

*roupelliae:* named after Arabella Elizabeth Roupell (1817–1914), who spent a few years in the Cape and painted the local flowers

Silver sugarbush has two subspecies. *Protea roupelliae* subsp. *hamiltonii* is a small shrublet that grows up to 0.3m tall, while *Protea roupelliae* subsp. *roupelliae* (the subspecies featured here), may reach up to 8m in height. It is a fast-growing, single-stemmed, low-branching, upright evergreen tree with somewhat spreading branches and a neat crown. It is found in mountain grassland and on rocky slopes.

The thick, grey to black bark is deeply fissured and cracked. The leathery leaves are bluish green and curve

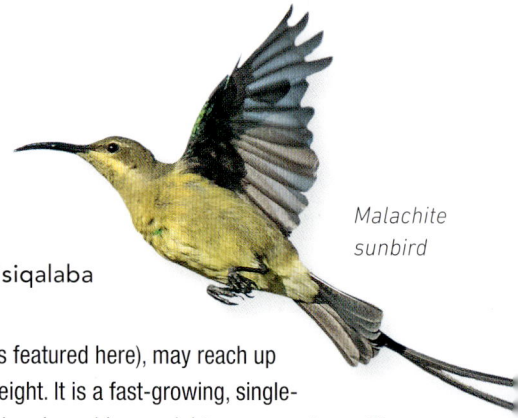

upwards in rosettes at the ends of branches. The common name refers to the silvery hairs found on young leaves.

Silver sugarbush flowers thoughout the year, peaking between February and April. The large, goblet-shaped flowerheads vary in colour throughout its distribution range in the eastern parts of South Africa, but are usually pink to ruddy brown, with the leaf-like bracts covered in silvery, silky hairs. Each thread in the central cone is an individual flower. The flowerheads are often largely hidden by the leaves. As with the common sugarbush (*P. caffra*), the fruit is a hairy nut.

A variety of beetles, bees and sunbirds pollinate this species. Gurney's sugarbird and the malachite sunbird, in particular, seem to have a close relationship with this tree.

Silver sugarbush is sensitive to fire damage and, as such, favours rocky habitats with low fire intensity. It does, however, require some fire for the seeds to germinate. If the fire interval is shorter than 10 years, the seed banks will not be able to accumulate sufficiently for the propagation of the species. The presence of silver sugarbushes in grassland could be regarded as an indicator that the veld is in a good condition.

This hardy and relatively frost-tolerant tree can be grown from seed and will attract many birds to the garden.

# BUFFALO-THORN

## *Ziziphus mucronata*

**A:** blinkblaar-wag-'n-bietjie  **NS:** mokgalwa  **SW:** umlahlabantfu
**TG:** mphasamhala  **TS:** mokgalo  **V:** mutshetshete  **X:** umphafa  **Z:** umphafa

*Ziziphus:* the Latinised form of the Arabic name *zizouf* for the common jujube, *Z. jujuba*; *mucronata:* 'pointed', referring to either the thorns or the leaf tips

Buffalo-thorn is one of the most common trees in southern Africa. It occurs in a variety of habitats throughout the summer-rainfall areas, such as mixed bushveld and open woodland. It is typically found in sandy areas and alluvial soils along rivers, and often on termite mounds. It grows up to 10m tall. The shiny leaves and thorns are distinctive, with both hooked and straight thorns on the same tree.

The leaves and fallen fruit are eaten by game such as impala, klipspringer, kudu, nyala, sable, eland, Sharpe's grysbok and warthogs, as well as livestock. It is a useful fodder tree in times of drought. Giraffe are known to be particularly fond of the leaves. The fruit is utilised by a variety of birds, including Burchell's coucals, grey go-away-birds, guineafowl, francolins and turacos.

The flowers are green to yellow and very small, but yield abundant nectar. Bees attending this tree produce good honey.

*Bristle fly* (Chromatophania picta)

During the Anglo–Boer War (1899–1902), buffalo-thorn seeds were used by some Boers to make coffee.

The timber has no definite heartwood and its colour varies considerably, probably depending on climate and soil type. The wood is heavy and hard and has a fine texture, but many small pores are present. The annual rings are conspicuous. The grain is twisted and the wood warps badly. The timber is used only when better material is not available.

This species grows quite fast in various soil types and is resistant to both drought and frost.

It is believed that the crown of thorns of Jesus Christ was most probably made form *Z. spina-christii*, a species from North Africa that resembles our buffalo-thorn.

Family Rhamnaceae

# BROWN IVORY

## *Phyllogeiton discolor*

**A:** bruinivoor, wilde-amandel  **ND:** umzinzila  **NS:** mogokgomo
**TS:** motsintsila  **V:** munie  **Z:** nmumu

*Phyllogeiton:* derived from Greek *phullon* ('leaf') and *geiton* ('neighbour'), though the allusion of the latter term is unclear; *discolor:* 'not of the same colour', a reference to the tree's leaves, which are dark green above and pale green below

This attractive, well-shaped tree is also known as 'bird plum'. It has a dense, round crown and grows up to 20m in height. It occurs in the northern and northeastern parts of South Africa, where it favours well-drained soils in woodlands and also grows along drainage lines.

Brown ivory and red ivory (*P. zeyheri*) are very similar. Both species are large and evergreen or semi-deciduous. Their leaves, however, differ slightly: the tip of brown ivory leaves is more rounded than the more pointed leaves of red ivory. In both species, the side veins end at the leaf margins and are prominently raised on the lower surface. However, the leaf blade of brown ivory bulges between the side veins, giving the leaf a 'bubbled' appearance.

The solitary flowers of brown ivory are small and greenish yellow. The fruit is shaped like a date, and the skin turns yellow during the ripening phase.

The leaves are browsed by elephant, giraffe, kudu, bushbuck and impala, and the fruits are eaten by primates and birds, as well as humans.

The sapwood is off-white and the heartwood yellowish to brownish with a red tinge. It is a hard and heavy wood, with a fine texture and conspicuous annual rings. It is easy to work and is suitable as a general-purpose timber.

Family Rhamnaceae

# RED IVORY

## *Phyllogeiton zeyheri*

A: rooi-ivoor  ND: umnaga  X: umnini  Z: umncaka

*zeyheri:* in honour of C.L.P. Zeyher (1799–1858), a well-known German botanist

Red ivory has a wider distribution range than brown ivory (*P. discolor*), reaching KwaZulu-Natal and North West. It is an evergreen or semi-deciduous tree with a dense, round crown, and reaches up to 15m in height. It occurs in open woodland, on rocky ridges and along watercourses.

The star-like flowers are yellowish or greenish white and appear in clusters on stalks between September and December. The edible fruit is yellow to brownish red. The sweet-tasting fruits are collected by the local people and are sometimes sold at markets.

The leaves are browsed by game species, including giraffe, kudu, eland, bushbuck and black rhino. The fruits are eaten by primates and fruit-eating birds. It is an excellent garden tree for attracting birds.

The freshly cut heartwood is an unusual bright pink-red, but fades to deep red over time. The wood is hard and strong, with a particularly fine texture, and is excellent for furniture, household items and curios. Being termite resistant, it also makes for good fencing poles.

The tree is drought resistant but not frost resistant.

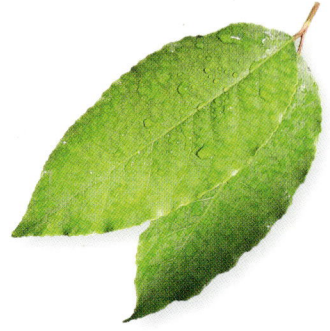

Family Rosaceae

# RED-STINKWOOD

*Prunus africana*

**A:** rooistinkhout, bitteramandel  **NS:** mogohloro  **V:** mulala-maanga
**X:** umkhakhase  **Z:** umdumezulu

### PROTECTED IN SOUTH AFRICA

*Prunus:* from Latin *prunum* ('plum'); *africana:* 'of Africa'

This frost-sensitive forest species has a wide distribution range: from the high-rainfall evergreen forests of the Eastern Cape, northwards to the montane tropics of central Africa. It is the tallest member of the *Prunus* genus and can reach up to 40m in height, with an impressive, spreading crown of up to 20m in large specimens.

This fast-growing, much-branched, evergreen tree has a straight trunk and dark brown bark that cracks in a characteristic oblong pattern. The leaves are dark green and have an almond scent when crushed. The leaf stalks are either red or pink. Small, scented, white flowers are borne in the axils of the leaves during the summer months.

The spherical, purplish-brown fruit appears in spring and early summer. Primates and various bird species feed on the fruit and distribute the seeds.

Red-stinkwood presents an interesting case of symbiosis: extrafloral nectaries (glands that produce nectar) along the leaf margin provide nutrients to anti-herbivore insects. The presence of these insects deters herbivores and thus protects the foliage.

The heartwood is reddish brown, tough and close-grained, and takes a fine polish. It is prone to twisting and splitting, however. Red-stinkwood has been used for furniture, carving, chopping blocks and tool handles. It is also good for flooring and heavy construction.

This species is an excellent addition to parks and large gardens, and is suitable for lining streets. It is becoming increasingly popular as an agroforestry tree, being planted as a shade tree in coffee plantations.

As the bark is highly regarded for its medicinal properties, including the treatment of prostate disorders, this species has been over-exploited and is becoming scarce in many areas. It is classified as Vulnerable on the Red List of South African Plants and the IUCN Red List of Threatened Species.

# MATUMI

*Breonadia salicina*

A: mingerhout, waterboekenhout   NS: mohlomê
V: mutulume   Z: umfula

African olive pigeon

**PROTECTED IN SOUTH AFRICA**

*Breonadia:* honours Jean Nicolas Brèon (1785–1864), a French horticulturist; *salicina:* willow-like, resembling *Salix*

Matumi is a tropical species occurring in KwaZulu-Natal, Mpumalanga and Limpopo. It is found in riverine forests, often right on the edge of permanent streams. This evergreen tree has a straight trunk, a tall upright crown and invasive roots. It can grow up to 40m in height.

The whitish, bisexual flowers are borne in compact spherical heads. The small seeds are mainly dispersed by wind, but fruit-eating birds, such as African olive pigeons, also contribute to seed dispersal. Since this tree often grows near or in large rivers, it has fallen victim to the destructive floods of recent years and many fine specimens have been lost.

Matumi wood is of exceptional quality and is sought after for furniture, parquet flooring, mine props, boat building and general construction. This tree was once extensively harvested for railway sleepers. In Malawi, it is still the most sought-after wood for making canoes.

This lovely tree is a fast grower but cannot handle drought or frost.

# CRYSTALBARK
## *Crossopteryx febrifuga*
**A:** sandkroonbessie **TG:** nkombekwa **V:** mukhobigwa

*Crossopteryx:* from Greek *krossos* ('fringe') and *pteron* ('wing'), alluding to the fringed, wing-like seed; *febrifuga:* from Latin *febris* ('fever') and *fugare* ('drive away'), referring to a medicine used to reduce fever

Crystalbark has a very limited distribution in South Africa and is much more common further north. It occurs on sandy soils in dry mixed woodland in the northeastern corner of Limpopo. It is a deciduous tree with a rounded crown and drooping branches. It can reach a height of 15m, but such large specimens are rare – usually it grows to no more than 6m, and sometimes it is just a shrub. The trunk is often crooked, gnarled and low-branching.

Small flowers are borne in dense, conspicuous sprays at the ends of twigs, attracting birds, bees and insects. The fruits are borne in dense clusters and are inedible. Leaves and young shoots are occasionally eaten by elephant, kudu and bushbuck.

The bark is used in traditional medicine for the treatment of dysentery, diarrhoea and fever. The seeds can be used to fumigate clothes. The wood has a pale pink tinge and is very hard and durable, with a fine texture. It can be used for building, domestic utensils, sculptures and tool handles. It also makes for excellent firewood. Green wood is not attacked by borers, but dry logs are.

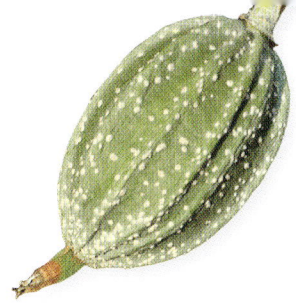

# BUSHVELD GARDENIA

*Gardenia volkensii* subsp. *volkensii* var. *volkensii*

**A:** bosveldkatjiepiering, koedoeklapper **TS:** morala **TG:** ntsalala

*Gardenia:* named after Alexander Garden (1730–1791), an American doctor and plant collector; *volkensii:* named after German plant collector G.L.A. Volkens (1855–1917)

Bushveld gardenia is a common tree in the bushveld regions of Limpopo, Mpumalanga and KwaZulu-Natal. This hardy, multi-stemmed tree is semi-deciduous or evergreen, and reaches a height of 10m. It has a roundish, dense, much-branched crown, the spread of which is often wider than the tree's height.

Shiny, spoon-shaped leaves are clustered at the ends of knobbly branchlets. They are eaten by a variety of browsers, such as eland, kudu, impala and giraffe, making this a much-appreciated tree on any game farm. The fruits are taken by nyala, kudu, baboons and vervet monkeys, while elephant eat all parts of the tree. The larvae of the apricot playboy (*Deudorix dinochares*) also feed on the leaves.

With its shiny leaves, non-aggressive root system and masses of large, fragrant flowers, this is a popular garden tree. The flowers open at night and fade the next day, changing from white to creamy yellow. Only a few open at a time, extending the flowering season.

The fruit is almost round and is greyish green to white, with slightly raised white dots. It is shallowly to strongly ribbed longitudinally and contains numerous seeds.

The yellowish wood is hard and heavy, with a fine grain. It is used for household items and for carving ornaments.

In well-drained soil, this tree is relatively fast-growing. It is drought resistant, but does not handle cold well. It grows well in containers or as a bonsai tree.

# SCENTED-BELLS

*Rothmannia capensis*

**A:** valskatjiepiering, wildekatjiepiering, aapkos, witklokke
**NS:** monkgobo **V:** muratha-mapfene **X:** umzukuza **Z:** isiqathankobe

*Rothmannia:* named in honour of Georg Rothman (1739–1778), a pupil of Carl Linnaeus and friend of Swedish botanist Carl Peter Thunberg (1743–1828); *capensis:* 'from the Cape'

This hardy evergreen tree typically grows 10m in height, though forest specimens may reach up to 20m. It occurs on rocky hillsides in forests and wooded ravines throughout much of the country, except the Free State and Northern Cape.

The trunk is usually straight and the branches erect. The roundish crown is dense, and the glossy, deep green leaves are typically bunched together at the branch ends. There are conspicuous domatia (small cavities that house arthropods) in the axils of the veins.

The large, creamy white, bell-shaped flowers are strongly scented and very eye-catching and have maroon markings in the throat of the corolla tube. The fruit is green, ribbed, leathery and almost spherical. Initially hard and shiny, the fruit becomes soft when mature, with many smooth, flat seeds embedded in its solid mass of pulpy tissue. Baboons and monkeys pick fruit from the trees – hence the Afrikaans name *aapkos* ('monkey food'). Bushpigs, bushbuck and bush duiker are quick to pick up fallen fruit.

The wood is strong and hard, yet pliable, and has been used for implement handles, household items, wagon building and hut poles. This decorative tree is an excellent garden tree as it attracts birds, lacks an aggressive root system, grows relatively fast, and is to some degree resistant to frost and drought.

The Afrikaans name *katjiepiering* is derived from *katsjapirand*, the Malay name for a Chinese ornamental cultivated in Dutch East India and introduced to the Cape.

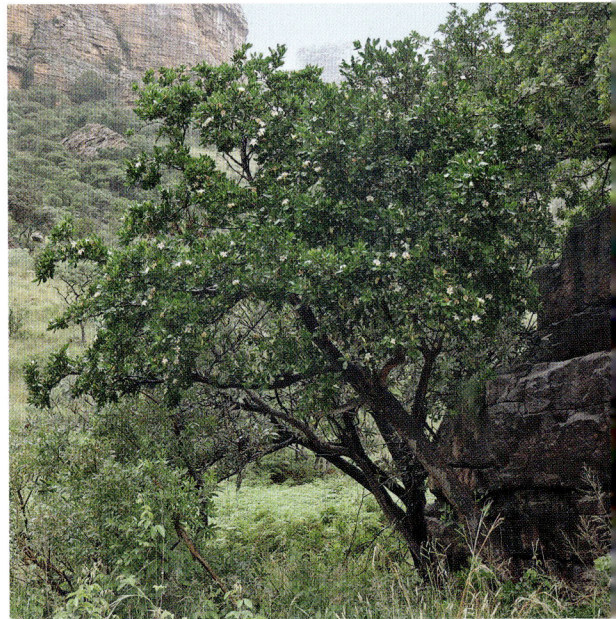

# WILD-MEDLAR

*Vangueria infausta* subsp. *infausta*

A: wildemispel  ND: umthofu  NS: mmilo  SW: umntulwa
TG: mpfilwa  TS: mmilo  V: muzwilu  X: umvilo  Z: umviyo

*Vangueria:* derived from *voa vanguer*, the Madagascan name for *Vangueria edulis*; *infausta:* 'unlucky', referring to the magical properties locals believed the tree possessed

Wild-medlar is a deciduous tree of up to 8m in height. It occurs throughout the northern half of the country, favouring open woodland and grassland, where it usually grows among rocks or on rocky hillsides. This tree is known for its delicious sweet-sour fruit. The fruit is almost spherical and has a leathery skin, which turns yellowish to brown as it ripens. The soft, fleshy ripe fruit is rich in vitamin C and popular with humans, fruit-eating birds, monkeys, baboons, bushbabies, squirrels and bushpigs. It also makes an excellent *mampoer* (home-distilled brandy) and the pulp can be made into a sauce for meat. It is surprising that this species has not been cultivated for commercial purposes.

Various animals, including elephant, giraffe and kudu, browse the leaves. There are often elongated growths on the leaves, which are caused by insects. The flowers attract many insects, including butterflies, as well as insect-eating birds.

The wood is hard, strong and relatively heavy, with a fine texture, but has no known popular uses.

This hardy, slow-growing tree is drought resistant and fairly frost tolerant. It is propagated from seeds or cuttings.

Family Sapindaceae

# JACKETPLUM

*Pappea capensis*

A: doppruim  NS: mopsinyugane  SW: liletsa  TG: xikwakwaxu
X: ilitye  Z: umgqogqo

*Pappea:* named after the German physician and plant collector, Karl Wilhelm Ludwig Pappe (1803–1862); *capensis:* 'from the Cape'

Jacketplum is known for its longevity, with some suggesting that it can live for more than 1,000 years. It is an evergreen or deciduous tree that grows up to 10m in height, with a dense, rounded spreading crown.

A tough plant, this typical bushveld tree occurs throughout much of South Africa. It grows in open woodland, scrub veld and on rocky outcrops, often on termite mounds. It can survive in arid conditions and is not sensitive to frost.

The fruit is a roundish green capsule that splits open to reveal a single black seed with an orange-red, fleshy covering. The fruit can be used to make jam, jelly, vinegar and alcoholic beverages. The tree also attracts fruit-eating birds such as starlings, barbets and mousebirds, which distribute the seeds in their droppings. *Charaxes* and other butterfly species attend the tree as well. The leaves are browsed by giraffe, elephant, kudu, nyala, bushbuck, steenbok, bush duiker and impala.

The wood is light brown with a reddish tinge. It is heavy, tough and hard, with a twisted grain, but owing to the small size of the trunk it is difficult to find large pieces of timber.

The roasted seeds yield an edible golden-brown oil. It can be used as a purgative or lubricant, and to make soap.

*Black-collared barbet*

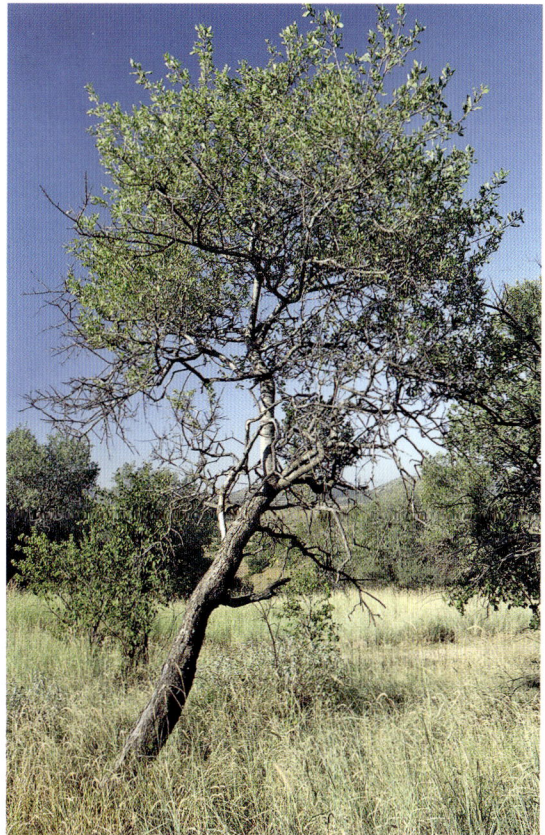

# BUSHVELD RED-BALLOON
## *Erythrophysa transvaalensis*
**A:** bosveldrooiklapperbos  **TS:** mofalatsane

**PROTECTED IN SOUTH AFRICA**

*Erythrophysa:* from Greek *erythros* ('red'), and *phusallis* ('bladder'), referring to the red, balloon-like fruit; *transvaalensis:* 'of the Transvaal', referring to a former province of South Africa

This rare, semi-deciduous species can be a sparsely-branched tree or a multi-stemmed shrub, growing up to 5m in height. It is hardy and drought resistant, occurring among rocks and boulders on mountains and koppies. The distribution range is small and disjointed – it is restricted to the western Waterberg in Limpopo, Pilanesberg Game Reserve and Bospoort near Rustenburg in North West, and a few places in western Gauteng.

The tree usually branches low down and the stems are slender and brittle with smooth, shiny bark. The silvery green foliage glistens beautifully in the sun. The compound leaves, with about seven pairs of opposite leaflets and a terminal unpaired leaflet, are crowded together at the ends of branches. The leaf stalks can be up to 2.5cm long.

The striking green flowers are suffused with red and appear in erect branched clusters before the new leaves in September and October. They are especially attractive to sunbirds and butterflies.

The fruit is unusual: a large, inflated, bladder-like, three-angled capsule with three chambers, which can be either red or green flushed with red. There are one or two black seeds in each chamber. The seeds are dispersed by wind and rain. The fruit may remain on the tree into winter.

The seeds have reportedly been used to make beads, but the tree has no other known uses. It is, however, a lovely garden tree that can be propagated easily from seeds. It is sensitive to frost.

Family Sapotaceae

# STEMFRUIT

*Englerophytum magalismontanum*

A: stamvrug NS: mohlatswa SW: umnumbela TS: motlhatswa
V: munombelo Z: umnumbela

*Englerophytum:* named after Gustav Heinrich Adolf Engler (1834–1930), a famous German botanist; *magalismontanum:* 'from the Magaliesberg', where the tree was first collected and described

Stemfruit is named for its distinctive, bright red fruit, which are borne on its trunk, branches and branchlets.

This hardy, drought-resistant, evergreen tree typically reaches 10m in height, though it may grow taller in evergreen forests. It occurs on mountains, hills and rocky outcrops, as well as in wooded ravines and forest – almost always among rocks. It is a common tree throughout South Africa, particularly in the kloofs and on the slopes of the Magaliesberg and Waterberg ranges.

This somewhat fast-growing species has a dense crown and grey-green leaves. The small flowers bud directly from the branches and trunk and may occur in dense groups. They are strongly (and rather unpleasantly) scented. The fruit is high in vitamin C, sweet and best eaten fresh. It is also used to make *mampoer* (home-distilled brandy), syrup, jelly and the tastiest of jams.

The tree is a food source for the larvae of Boisduval's false acraea (*Pseudacraea boisduvalii trimenii*). Bushpigs eat the roots, while monkeys and baboons are keen on the fruit. The wood is hard and heavy and is used for small items such as tool handles and spoons.

Family Sapotaceae

# MOEPEL

## *Mimusops zeyheri*

A: moepel  NS: mmupudu  TG: nhlantswa
V: mubululu  Z: umphushane

*Mimusops:* from Greek *mimos* ('actor, imitator'), and *ops* ('face, resembling'); the allusion is unclear; *zeyheri:* named in honour of C.L.P. Zeyher (1799–1858), a German botanist who collected plants in southern Africa

This gorgeous evergreen tree has glossy, dark green leaves and casts deep shade. Although it is usually medium-sized, reaching up to 15m in height, it can grow much taller under ideal conditions. The beautiful spreading crown can easily be as wide as the tree is tall.

This species occurs on mountain slopes and rocky hillsides, along the margins of evergreen forest and in open woodland. When it is not in fruit, it looks somewhat like a wild fig (*Ficus*), and the tree also has milky latex. The fissured bark is a giveaway, however.

The leaves are leathery and usually broadest near the centre. They are arranged alternately or spirally. Young leaves are covered in a fine layer of dense red hairs. The white to cream flowers are sweetly scented and occur singly or in groups in the leaf axils. Ripe fruits are bright yellow and fleshy; they are high in vitamin C and quite

tasty, and are eaten by humans, primates and birds such as African olive and green pigeons. Fallen fruits are picked up by bushpigs and smaller antelope, such as bushbuck and duiker. The tree relies on these animals for seed dispersal. The leaves are occasionally eaten by antelope and elephant.

The heartwood is creamy brown to reddish brown, fairly heavy, hard, fine-grained and durable. It works well and is useful as a general-purpose timber. Red milkwoods make lovely garden trees in areas with well-drained soil, good summer rains and mild winters.

Family Sapotaceae

# WHITE-MILKWOOD

*Sideroxylon inerme* subsp. *inerme*

A: witmelkhout, melkbessie  X: ximafana  Z: umakhwelafingqane

## PROTECTED IN SOUTH AFRICA

*Sideroxylon:* from Greek *sideros* ('iron') and *xulon* ('wood'), referring to the hardness of the wood; *inerme:* 'unarmed'

White-milkwood is a leafy, evergreen tree with a sturdy but gnarled, twisted and crooked trunk and the branches have a similar appearance. This species is slow-growing and long-lived, reaching up to 15m in height, and has a large, dense, rounded crown.

It occurs in coastal woodland and forests along the seashore, where it can form forests of its own. In times gone by, dense forests of large milkwood trees grew along the coast and bays of Cape Town, especially at Noordhoek, Macassar and Gordon's Bay. This species is also found inland, mainly along rivers and in open woodland.

The bark is grey to black with rectangular cracks. Young branches are covered in fine hairs. The leaves are spirally arranged, leathery, and shiny dark green above and paler green below. The midrib is ridged on both surfaces. The leaves produce a milky latex. Old leaves turn red before being shed.

The bell-shaped, greenish-white bisexual flowers are borne in the leaf axils. The fruit is a round, fleshy berry on a short stalk, ripening to a purplish-black colour. It is eaten by birds, bats, monkeys and bushpigs.

The most famous white-milkwood specimen is probably the Post Office tree in Mossel Bay. In the 16th century, this tree served as a site where Portuguese seafarers left messages for ships they knew would anchor there to collect fresh water. This tree must be at least 600 years old – likely considerably more, as it must have already been a large tree when it was used as a 'post office'.

There is another impressive white-milkwood near Bredasdorp, with a crown diameter of over 20m. This tree is believed to be well over 1,000 years old and is a proclaimed monument.

The fine-grained, yellowish-brown wood is very hard and heavy, strong and durable. When the first Europeans sailed around the Cape, the wood proved useful for ship repair. These European ships were originally built from oak (*Quercus*), and often sustained damage on the open sea. The gnarled and bent trunks of the white-milkwood yielded the most suitable planks for repair work. White-milkwood was hardly ever used to build an entire vessel, though, since long, straight planks were extremely scarce.

This species is well adapted to salty air, wind and sand. It makes an excellent shade tree or windbreak along the coast. It is also drought resistant.

# WILDPEAR

*Dombeya rotundifolia var. rotundifolia*

**A:** blompeer, drolpeer, bruid-van-die-bosveld  **NS:** mokgoba
**TG:** xiluvarhi  **TS:** mokgofa  **Z:** unhliziyonkulu

*Dombeya:* named in honour of the French botanist Joseph Dombey (1742–1793); *rotundifolia:* refers to the round shape of the leaves

Also known as 'the harbinger of spring', wildpear flowers very early in the season. It is covered in white or pinkish flowers, which are truly spectacular in the otherwise dull, grey landscape of the bushveld.

This common, deciduous tree has a rounded crown. It is fast-growing, reaching up to 15m in height under ideal conditions. It occurs on most soil types in mixed bushveld and woodland throughout South Africa.

The tree bears resemblance to a true pear when in full bloom, but the species are not related at all. The flowers produce large quantities of nectar and attract bees and butterflies. Not surprisingly, it is a popular garden tree, and grows easily under garden conditions. This hardy tree withstands cold weather and drought remarkably well.

Wildpear is the larval host of one butterfly and nine moth species. Livestock and game feed on the leaves.

The wood is grey, heavy, strong, tough, termite resistant and durable, with a fine texture. It has limited potential as a general-purpose timber, however, because the pieces available are usually too small and twisted. Wildpear is often used for fencing posts and for making ornaments and tool handles. The dried flowers are also popular in flower arrangements.

# LOWVELD STAR-CHESTNUT

*Sterculia murex*

**A:** laeveldsterkastaiing  **SW:** umbhaba  **TG:** mbava

*Sterculia:* named after Sterquilinus, the Roman god of manure, alluding to the foul smell of the leaves of *Sterculia foetida*; *murex:* a genus of marine snails with spiny shells, referring to the spiky fruit

This deciduous, fast-growing endemic reaches up to 12m in height and has a spreading crown. It is frost sensitive, preferring a warm climate with good summer rains and long periods of drought in winter. It occurs on well-drained sandy or loamy soils in the southern parts of the South African lowveld and Eswatini, and is mostly found on rocky ridges or koppies. Its distribution range is limited, but there are good viewing opportunities in the Pretoriuskop area in the Kruger National Park, especially towards Numbi Gate.

Lowveld star-chestnut flowers are waxy, yellow and beautifully marked with brown or crimson. Typical of *Sterculia* species, the flowers have no petals.

The large, five-lobed, woody fruits are thickly covered with hard spines. The inside of the fruit contains stinging hairs, which can be irritating to human skin. The tree may produce a large number of fruit, which are shed over a short period in February and March, the wettest time of the lowveld's rainy season. When roasted in a pan, the seeds will 'pop' slightly, showing the flesh of the seed. The oily seeds are edible and are relished by humans, primates and rodents. They have soft, leathery shells that provide little protection against herbivores other than the short, irritating hairs on the inner rim. When the seeds are shed, they dry out rapidly because the shells lack water-retention properties. The seeds germinate quickly and produce storage organs (an enlarged rootstock or succulent caudex) and grow thick, fleshy roots deep into the soil. These remain dormant throughout the winter before finally sending shoots above ground. By getting its seeds underground as fast as possible, this species is able to escape herbivores and to protect itself against fire and drought. It is not known to what extent the leaves are browsed.

Although the timber has been used for fruit boxes, this species is not a popular timber tree. The wood is quite soft, with few uses.

# STAR-CHESTNUT

## *Sterculia rogersii*

A: sterkastaiing  NS: mokgwakgwatha  TS: mokakata

*rogersii:* named in honour of the English missionary and plant collector Archdeacon F.A. Rogers (1876–1944)

This squat deciduous tree is endemic to southern Africa. It has a characteristicly swollen trunk, which branches low down to form a sparse, spreading crown. It seldom exceeds 5m in height. This species is found in low, dry bushveld, usually on rocky outcrops or in rocky gorges.

The bark is smooth and quite thin, flaking to reveal a mottled patchwork of reddish to purple or yellowish under-bark. The leaves fall early in autumn and new leaves appear late in spring. Striking little bell-shaped greenish-yellow flowers with radiating red streaks appear before the leaves. They are normally borne in clusters and the tree flowers for a long time.

The velvety, star-shaped fruit capsules ripen late in summer and turn from green to pale yellow. When ripe, the capsule splits open to release about ten smooth, grey seeds. Game animals and birds relish these seeds. Leaves and young stems are also eaten by various browsers, and the tree seems to be an important source of nourishment for elephant. The timber is soft, light, very fibrous and has no functional use.

# CAPE-CHESTNUT

*Calodendrum capense*

**A:** wildekastaiing, Kaapse kastaiing  **NS:** molalakgwedi
**V:** muvhaha  **X:** umbhaba  **Z:** umbhaba

*Calodendrum:* derived from Greek *kalos* ('beautiful') and *dendron* ('tree'); *capense:* 'from the Cape', where the tree was first studied

Based solely on its beauty, Cape-chestnut could just as well have been named South Africa's national tree. It is slow-growing and typically deciduous, though coastal specimens may be evergreen. The canopy is dense and rounded. Forest trees can reach up to 20m in height, and tend to have straight trunks, which are sometimes buttressed. Elsewhere, trees are usually gnarled and not as tall, and the leaves and flowers may also be somewhat smaller. This species occurs in riverine and high-altitude forests, along evergreen fringe forests and in wooded ravines in the east of the country all the way down to the Western Cape.

Cape-chestnut is cultivated for its prolific flower display in early summer. The striking, large, fragrant, pink flowers are produced in loose clusters at the ends of branchlets and cover the entire tree canopy. Not surprisingly, this is an excellent 'bee tree'. It is also visited by butterflies. Crushed leaves smell of citrus.

The seeds are eaten by samango and vervet monkeys, pigeons, doves and parrots.

There is hardly any difference between the sapwood and heartwood. The wood is light yellow with a straight grain. It is tough, moderately hard and heavy, and works easily. In earlier times wagons were made from this wood; more recently it has been used for planks, furniture and tool handles.

The seeds germinate and transplant well.

# WILD-ELDER

## *Nuxia congesta*

**A:** wildevlier, gewone wildevlier  **X:** umkhobeza  **Z:** umkhobeza

*Nuxia:* named after Jean Baptiste François de Lanux (1702–1772), a French amateur botanist on Réunion Island; *congesta:* 'accumulated', referring to the dense clusters of flowers

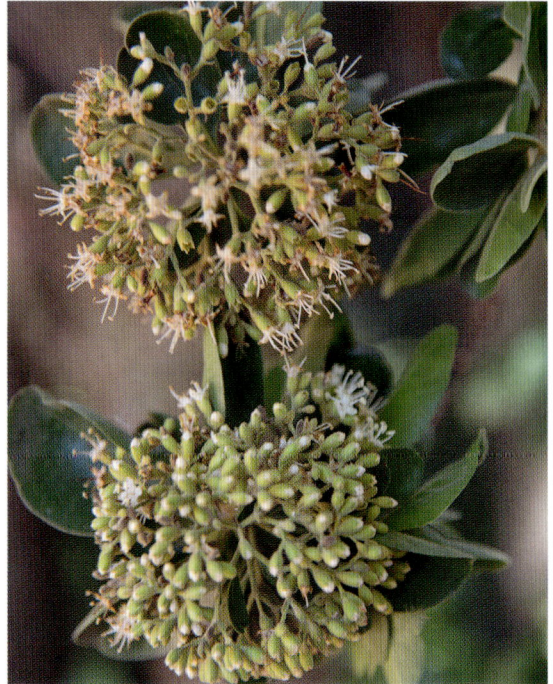

The wild-elder is a hardy, fast-growing evergreen tree. While it can reach up to 20m under ideal conditions, it is usually much smaller. It is found in bushveld and along forest margins, where it prefers rocky ridges and hilltops. The distribution range covers most of the northern parts of South Africa, as well as the Indian Ocean coast.

The tree is usually multi-stemmed and can be gnarled, with pale grey-brown to dark bark, which is fissured and peels in longitudinal strips on the larger branches. The branchlets are usually hairy. The attractive dark green leaves are clustered at the ends of branchlets and whorled in groups of three. They are somewhat leathery, yet hairy, and quite variable in shape and size. In immature trees, the leaf margins are saw-toothed and the branchlets are reddish. In mature trees, the leaf margins are smooth and typically rolled under.

Wild-elder may be confused with rock-elder (*N. glomerulata*), which has a restricted distribution range between Pretoria and Zeerust. The leaves of the latter are more elliptic, leathery and not hairy. Wild-elder differs from forest-elder (*N. floribunda*) in that the latter has longer leaf stalks and larger, looser flowering heads. Dense clusters of small, fragrant, creamy white flowers are produced from March to July. These long-lasting flowers are arranged in congested heads and attract numerous insects, which in turn draw insect-eating birds. The abundant nectar makes this an excellent 'bee tree'. The fruit is a small, hairy capsule that contains fine, inconspicuous seeds.

The whitish-yellow wood is hard and durable and is used for fence posts and as firewood.

Wild-elder is an ideal garden tree or container plant, as it does not have an aggressive root system.

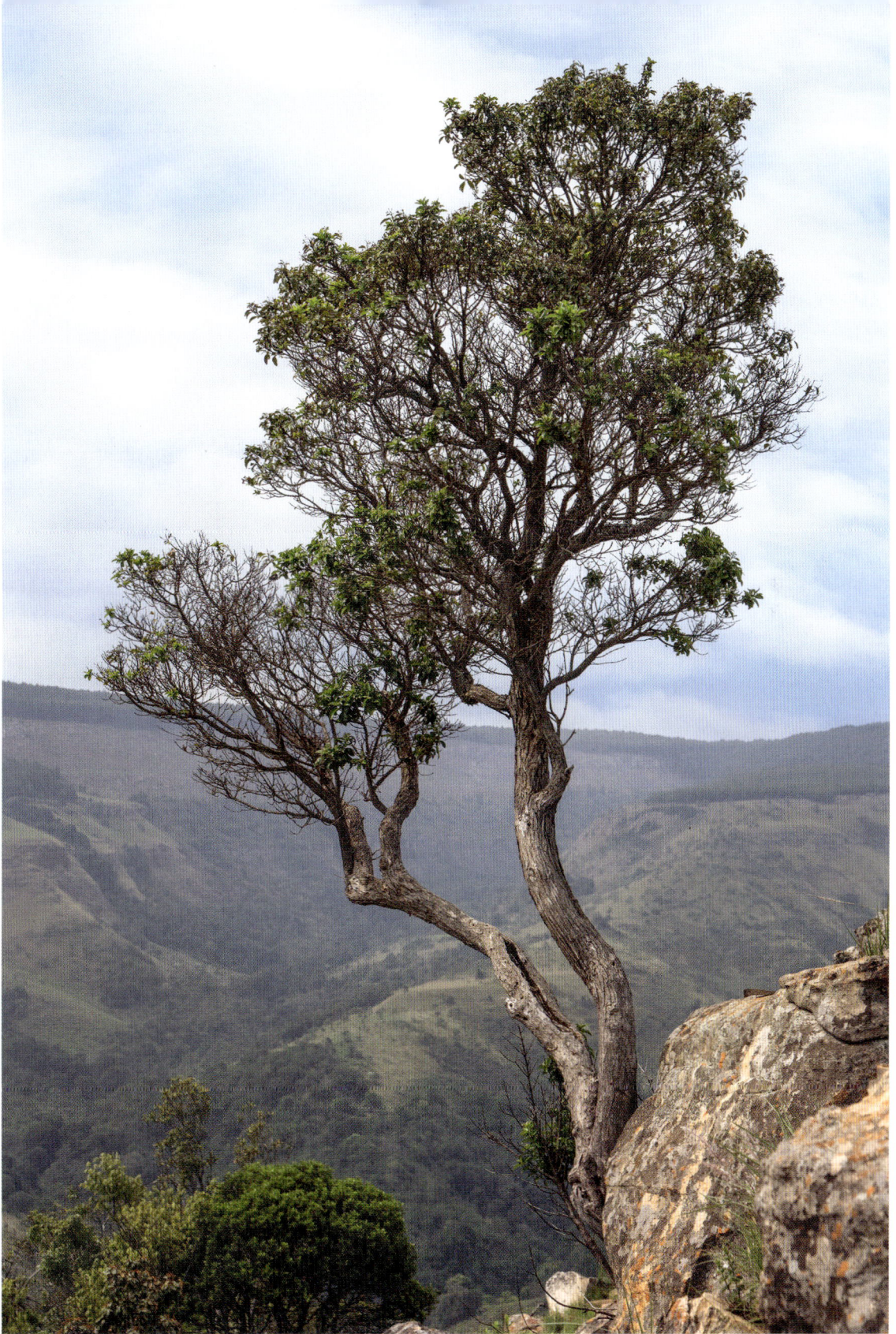

# FOREST-ELDER

*Nuxia floribunda*

A: bosvlier  NS: motlhabare  V: mula-notshi
X: isikhali  Z: umhlambandlazi

*floribunda:* 'many-flowered' or 'flowering profusely'

This tree can be found in evergreen forests, along forest margins and in mountainous terrain. It is a hardy, fast-growing evergreen tree with a dense rounded crown. It grows up to 10m tall, and may reach 25m under ideal conditions. It is sensitive to drought and cold and is absent from the dry western parts of the country and the highveld.

The trunk usually grows in a twisted fashion. The grey to brown bark is smooth and somewhat hairy on younger trees, but rough and flaking on mature trees. The glossy, dark green leaves are simple, oblong to elliptic, with a pointed tip. They can be opposite or in whorls of three. The leaf margin is smooth or finely toothed and the leaf stalks vary in length.

This tree produces an abundance of fragrant, creamy white flowers between May and September. The flower clusters are carried near the ends of branches. While the flowers themselves are very small (measuring only 3mm in diameter), the large, loose sprays are up to 300mm long. This showy flower display attracts bees, moths, butterflies and other insects.

The fruit is a tiny, oval capsule no more than 4mm in diameter, splitting into four lobes and turning brown as it ripens. Fine, inconspicuous seeds are released when the fruit capsule splits open.

The wood is pale yellowish brown and hard, heavy and close-grained. It is a useful general-purpose timber and has been utilised in carpentry, for furniture and fencing, and as firewood.

Manketti

Anatree

# ACKNOWLEDGEMENTS

I could not have put this book together without the support, assistance and encouragement of a number of people. First, I wish to thank my wife, Lorraine, and my son, Flippie, for always being willing to hold the fort on the farm while I wandered off into the blue yonder in search of yet another tree in yet another season. Thanks to Wimpie Frost, too, who was always ready to lend a hand, especially with some of the software intricacies.

Dutch Reformed minister Petrus Kriel of Levubu introduced me to the wonders of the Soutpansberg and we shared some marvellous experiences while exploring the region. My friend Marius Fuls of Lephalale is probably the country's most knowledgeable conservationist when it comes to manketti trees and I will forever treasure the times we spent exploring the lives of these remarkable trees. Various other landowners and ranch managers gave me access to their properties to search for trees and to photograph them. I wish to single out John Burrows of Buffelskloof Nature Reserve, Pieter and the late Nadine Vervoort of Swebeswebe Private Nature Reserve, Joe and Hanni Synjich, Jan Beukes, Piet Wessels, Gary Koen and Gerhard and Elmarie van Emmenis.

I am particularly grateful for what I have learned from the members of the Dendrological Society of South Africa, especially my friends at the Manketti branch and the president of our organisation, Naas Grové. I am also grateful to Dr Francois du Randt of Hluhluwe whose passion, enthusiasm and willingness to share information and knowledge have been a source of inspiration for much of the time that I worked on the manuscript. Professsor Braam van Wyk was extremely helpful with suggestions and guidance. It was a privilege to benefit from his vast experience and phenomenal knowledge.

The initial editors (Marissa Greeff, Ina Engelbrecht and Robert Smith, as well as Izak van der Merwe – all members of the Dendrological Society) have contributed in no small way to my humble efforts and I am grateful not only for the quality of their input but also for their time and effort. Robert and Ina also guided me for a most enjoyable week in the Knysna forests and I will forever be grateful for their assistance.

My publisher at Struik Nature, Pippa Parker, played a major role in creating the published book. Her ideas, suggestions and support all added significant value. Senior editor Heléne Booyens, together with the rest of the publishing team, deserve a special, sincere thanks for a job exceptionally well done.

I am forever indebted to all these contributors.

**WILLEM FROST**
Goedgedacht, Limpopo

# PICTURE CREDITS

AS = stock.adobe.com, **BDP** = Bernard DUPONT from FRANCE, CC BY-SA 2.0, WC, **SAP** = SAplants, CC BY-SA 4.0, WC, **WC** = via Wikimedia Commons
**b** = bottom, **c** = centre, **l** = left, **m** = middle, **r** = right, **t** = top

**Back cover tr:** Stoffel – AS
**Title:** Kobus – AS
**4:** Paul Souders/Danita Delimont – AS
**10:** Paulina – AS
**12:** PACO COMO – AS
**13:** henk bogaard – AS
**15 t:** Curioso.Photography – AS, **b:** Gianfranco Bella
**16:** NatalieJean – AS
**17 bl:** Hans Hillewaert, **br:** William Stein and Christopher Berry
**19:** Michael – AS
**21: t:** Giuma – AS, **b:** Antje – AS
**22 l:** Pedro Bigeriego – SA, **c:** wolfavni – AS, **r:** Dirk M. de Boer
**23 l:** andrewhagen – AS, **c:** estivillml – AS, **r:** 25ehaag6 – AS
**24: l:** sara_winter – AS, **r:** Attie Gerber/iStock.com
**25:** Roger de la Harpe – AS
**26:** Ernst Haeckel, Public domain, WC
**29:** Mit *HPS* auf Reisen – AS
**30:** fotoember – AS
**32 l illustrations:** Anne Stadler
**36:** lovelyday12 – AS
**37 bl:** Maksim Shebeko – AS
**38:** retbool – AS
**39 bl:** nataliya_rodenko – AS, **br:** barbol – AS
**41 bl:** Roger de la Harpe – AS, **br:** Megan Paine – AS
**42 t:** John – AS, **b:** henk bogaard – AS
**43:** Tony Campbell – AS
**44 b:** Hans Hillewaert
**45:** Ezume Images
**50:** Aggi Schmidt – AS
**51 t:** JJ van Ginkel – AS, **b:** Igor Kramar – AS
**52 l:** BDP, CC BY-SA 2.0, WC, **r:** ChrWeiss – AS
**53:** Justlight – AS
**54 tl:** Elenarts – AS, **tr:** wayne – AS, **bl:** forcdan – AS, **br:** Maresol – AS
**56:** sunsinger – AS
**57 bl:** photographer unknown, **br:** Alexey Protasov – AS
**58:** Franz Xaver, CC BY-SA 4.0, WC
**59:** henk bogaard – AS
**60 bl:** KColby Photography – AS, **br:** angeldibilio – AS
**61: tr:** YK – AS, **br:** Búho – AS
**62:** Delia Oosthuizen
**64:** Scott Smith, Corbis Documentary, Getty Images
**65: br:** Karl Brodowsky, CC BY-SA 3.0, WC
**67:** DirkDaniel – AS
**68 t** and **b:** Bilal – AS
**71:** swisshippo – AS
**73:** Petr – AS
**76 t:** Derek Keats from Johannesburg, South Africa, CC BY 2.0, WC
**77 t:** SAP, **b:** Geoff Nichols
**78 l:** SAP, **r:** James Goldfinch – AS
**81 bl:** Bart Wursten, CC BY-SA 3.0, WC

**82 t:** AngelinaNatural – AS, **br:** Karlos Lomsky – AS
**83 t** and **br:** SAP
**84 l:** SAP, **r:** John Burrows
**88 t:** SAP
**89 bl:** SAP
**90 m:** SAP
**91 tr:** SAP
**93 tr:** SAP
**94 tr:** Dinkum, CC0, WC
**96 b:** EcoView – AS
**97:** javarman – AS
**99 mr:** Bev Oscroft, CC BY-SA 3.0, WC, **br:** BDP
**100:** slowmotiongli – AS
**101 tr:** Louis – AS
**104 tr:** wasanajai – AS, **mr:** Kobus – AS, br: jonnysek – AS
**105 b:** Louis – AS
**107 bl:** JMK, CC BY-SA 3.0, WC
**110 tr:** Andrew Hankey, CC BY-SA 4.0, WC
**112 t:** SAP
**113 tr flowers:** Rotational, Public domain, WC, **tr pods:** SAP
**114 tr:** Bart Wursten, CC BY-SA 3.0, WC, **br:** John Burrows
**116 br:** Jeppestown CC BY-SA 2.0, WC
**117 tl:** BDP, **tr:** JMK CC BY-SA 4.0, WC
**118 t** and **mr:** BDP
**119 t:** SAP
**120 t:** SAP
**121 tl:** SAP
**122 t:** Bart Wursten, CC BY-SA 3.0, WC
**123 t:** photographer unknown
**124 t:** Stoffel – AS
**125 t:** Philip Nel, CC BY-SA 4.0, WC
**126 t:** Gideon Cornie Odendaal, CC BY-SA 4.0, WC
**127 t:** Marco Schmidt, CC BY-SA 3.0, WC
**128 br:** photographer unknown
**129 br:** NoahElhardt, CC BY-SA 4.0, WC
**130 mr:** Krzysztof Ziarnek, Kenraiz, CC BY-SA 4.0, WC, **br:** Rotational, public domain, WC
**134 b both:** JMK, CC BY-SA 3.0, WC
**138 mr:** John Burrows
**140 b:** JMK, CC BY-SA 3.0, WC
**141 ml** and **bl:** JMK, CC BY-SA 3.0, WC
**142 br:** JMK, CC BY-SA 3.0, WC
**146 t:** BDP
**147 bl:** BDP
**150 t:** Gilles San Martin from Namur, Belgium, CC BY-SA 2.0, WC, **bl:** S Molteno, CC0, WC
**152 t:** JMK, CC BY-SA 3.0, WC
**153 tr:** Roger de la Harpe – AS, **br:** Marco Schmidt, CC BY-SA 3.0, WC
**154 t** and **bl:** Braam van Wyk, **br:** Paul venter, CC BY-SA 3.0, WC
**156 br:** BDP
**157 t both:** BDP
**158 br:** rudiernst – AS
**160:** Dieter Geppert

**163 butterfly:** Michaelwild at English Wikipedia & Purves, M
**164 tr:** Braam van Wyk, **tr:** John Burrows,
**165 tl:** JMK, CC BY-SA 3.0, WC
**170 mr:** Random Harvest Nursery
**178 bl:** Abu Shawka public domain, WC
**182 bl:** BDP, **br:** JMK, CC BY-SA 3.0, WC
**190 b:** Jinge Norvall Andrews, CC BY-SA 3.0, WC
**196 t:** Steve Woodall
**197 t** and **ml:** SAP
**208 m** and **b:** Rotational, Public domain, WC
**210 t:** BDP
**211 tl:** etfoto – AS, **tr:** SAP
**212 t:** Franz Xaver, CC BY-SA 4.0, WC
**213 bl:** SAP, **br:** JMK, CC BY-SA 3.0, WC
**215 mr:** SAP, **br:** Glenice Ebedes
**217 t:** gdvcom – AS
**218 tr:** SAP, bl: Paul – AS, **br:** Gerrit Rautenbach – AS
**220 tr:** JMK, CC BY-SA 3.0, WC
**222 tr:** sergey – AS
**224 br:** JMK, CC BY-SA 3.0, WC
**228 mr;** JMK, CC BY-SA 3.0, WC, **br:** flowcomm, CC BY-SA 2.0, WC,
**231 t:** BDP
**235 tr:** Geoff Nichols
**238 mr:** photographer unknown
**241 tr:** JMK, CC BY-SA 3.0, WC
**242 t:** Geoff Nichols, **m:** SAP
**246 tr:** Charles J. Sharp, CC BY-SA 4.0, WC
**253 tr:** John Burrows
**255 mr:** JMK, CC BY-SA 3.0, WC
**259 tr:** Dave Brown, Public domain, WC, br: Subatomicscope/Wirestock Creators – AS
**261:** Antje – AS
**262 tr:** Duncan Noakes – AS
**263 tr:** Christian Grenier, Public domain, WC
**264 tr:** Direk Takmatcha – AS, **bl:** JMK, CC BY-SA 3.0, WC
**269 tl:** BDP
**270 tr:** Dewald – AS
**271 tr:** Anton Perekrestov – AS
**272 tr:** BDP, bl: JMK, CC BY-SA 3.0, WC
**273 ml:** Rotational, Public domain, WC, **mr** and **b:** JMK, CC BY-SA 3.0, WC
**276 tr:** Photo by David J. Stang, CC BY-SA 4.0, WC
**278 tr:** wolfavni – AS, **mr:** BDP
**282 tr:** JMK, CC BY-SA 3.0, WC
**284 both:** JMK, CC BY-SA 3.0, WC
**285 tl:** JMK, CC BY-SA 3.0, WC, **tr:** Derek Keats from Johannesburg, South Africa, CC BY 2.0, WC
**286 bl** and **c:** Braam van Wyk
**287 tr:** JMK, CC BY-SA 3.0, WC
**288 tl:** Paul venter, CC BY-SA 3.0, WC
**289 b:** JMK, CC BY-SA 3.0, WC
**290 tr:** Dinkum, CC0, WC
**292 tr:** JMK, CC BY-SA 3.0, WC
**301 tl:** SAP

# BIBLIOGRAPHY

Acocks, J.P.H. 1952. *Veld Types of South Africa*. Botanical Research Institute, Department of Agriculture, Pretoria.

Baluska, F., Gagliano, M. & Witzany, G. (eds). 2018. *Memory and Learning in Plants*. Springer International Publishing, Switzerland.

Brenner, E.D., Stahlberg, R., Mancuso, S., Vivanco, J., Baluška, F. & Van Volkenburgh, E. 2006. Plant neurobiology: An integrated view of plant signalling. *Trends Plant Science*, 11, 413–419.

Bonilla, J.Z. 2016. The not so secret life of plants: The emergence of plant neurobiology. https://mappingignorance.org/2016/06/08/not-secret-life-plants-1-emergence-plant-neurobiology.

Burrows, J. & Burrows, S. 2003. *Figs of Southern and South-central Africa*. Umdaus Press, Pretoria.

Burtt Davy, J. 1922. The suffrutescent habit as an adaptation to environment. *Journal of Ecology* 10(2), 211–219.

Byrne, A.K. & Green, C. 2004. The role of forests in the global carbon cycle and in climate change policy. *Irish Forestry* 61, 7–15.

Calvo, P. 2016. The philosophy of plant neurobiology: A manifesto. *Synthese*, 193(5), 1323–1343.

Conners, D. 2017. *Why Tees Shed their Leaves*. https://earthsky.org/earth.

Delistraty, C. 2019. The intelligence of plants. *The Paris Review,* (26 September).

Dengel, S., Aeby, D. & Grace, J. 2009. A relationship between galactic cosmic radiation and tree rings. *New Phytologist*, 184, 545–551.

Douglas, A.E. 1927. Solar records in tree growth. *Science*, 65, 220–221.

Du Randt, F. 2018. *The Sand Forest of Maputaland*. South African National Biodiversity Institute, Pretoria.

Esterhuyse, N., von Breitenbach, J., Söhnge, H. & Van der Merwe, I. 2016 *Remarkable Trees of South Africa*. Briza Publications, Pretoria.

Finckh, M., Gomes, A. & Zigelski, P. 2019. *Suffrutex dominated ecosystems in Angola in Huntley, B.J., Russo, V., Lages, F. & Ferrand, N. (eds), Biodiversity of Angola – Science & Conservation: A Modern Synthesis:* 109–121. Springer Open, Switzerland.

Funston, M. 1993. *Bushveld Trees, Lifeblood of the Transvaal Lowveld*. Fernwood Press, Cape Town.

Furstenburg, D. & Van Hoven, W. 1994. Condensed tannin as anti-defoliate agent against browsing by giraffe (*Giraffa camelopardalis*) in the Kruger National Park. *Comparative Biochemistry and Physiology* 107(2), 425–431.

Gabbatiss, J. 2019. Massive restoration of world's forests would cancel out a decade of $CO_2$ emissions, analysis suggests. https://www.independent.co.uk/climate-change/news/forests-climate-change-co2-greenhouse-gases-trillion-trees-global-warming-a8782071.html.

Galbenu, J. 2014. Why do some barks peel? *Bang! The Oxford Scientist Magazine* (23 March).

Grace, J. 2004. Understanding and managing the global carbon cycle. *Journal of Ecology*, 92, 189–202.

Jordaan, J.J., Swart, J.S. & Venter, S. 2010. Research note: A preliminary study of the root distribution of *Commiphora pyracanthoides* in the Sweet Bushveld of the Northern Province of South Africa. *African Journal of Range & Forage Science*, 15(1–2), 61–63.

Kirby, J. 2007. Cosmic rays and climate. *Surveys in Geophysics*, 28, 333–375.

Kulmala, M., Hari, P., Riipinen, I. & Kerminen, V. 2009. On the possible links between tree growth and galactic cosmic rays. *New Phytologist*, 184(3), 511–513.

Lagomarsino, V. 2019. Exploring the underground network of trees – The nervous system of the forest. Science in the News, Harvard Graduate School of Arts and Sciences. https://sitn.hms.harvard.edu/flash/2019/exploring-the-underground-network-of-trees-the-nervous-system-of-the-forest (6 May).

Lambers, H., Chapin, F.S. III, & Pons, T.L. 2008. *Plant Physiological Ecology* (2nd edition). Springer, New York.

Lawes, M.J., Eeley, H.A.C., Shackleton, C.M. & Geach, B.G.S. (eds). 2004. *Indigenous Forests and Woodlands in South Africa*. University of KwaZulu-Natal Press, Scottsville.

Lima, M. 2014. *The Book of Trees – Visualizing Branches of Knowledge*. Princeton Architectural Press: New York.

Luntz, S. 2018. It turns out that trees have a 'heartbeat' too. *IFLScience,* www.iflscience.com/it-turns-out-that-trees-have-a-heartbeat-too-47279 (23 April).

Maurin, O., Davies, T.J., Burrows, J.E., Barnabas, H.D., Yessoufou, K., Muasya, A.M., Van der Bank, M. & Bond, W.J. 2014. Savanna fire and the origins of the 'underground forests' of Africa. *New Phytologist*, 204(1), 201–214.

Meerts, P. 2017. Geoxylic suffrutices of African savannas: Short but remarkably similar to trees. *Journal of Tropical Ecology*, 33(4), 1–4.

Morgenthal, T. 2020. Olienhout *africana* vs. *cuspidata*. *Dendron* (December).

Mucina, L. & Rutherford, M.C. (eds). 2011. The Vegetation of South Africa, Lesotho and Swaziland. *Strelitzia* 19, South African National Biodiversity Institute, Pretoria.

Palgrave, K.C. 2002. *Trees of Southern Africa* (3rd edition). Struik Nature, Cape Town.

Palmer, E. & Pitman, N. 1972. *Trees of Southern Africa*. A.A. Balkem, Cape Town.

Pienaar, B. 2015. The biogeography of *Brachystegia* woodland relicts in southern Africa. M.Sc. dissertation, University of the Witwatersrand, Johannesburg.

Roodt, V. 1998. *Trees and Shrubs of the Okavango Delta – Medicinal Uses and Nutritional Value*. Shell Oil Botswana, Gaborone.

Saidi, T.A. & Tshipala-Ramatshimbila, T. 2006. Ecology and management of a remnant *Brachystegia spiciformis* (miombo) woodland in north eastern Soutpansberg, Limpopo province. *South African Geographical Journal*, 88(2), 205–212.

Sankaran, M., Hanan, N., Scholes, R., *et al.* 2005. Determinants of woody cover in African savannas. *Nature*, 438, 846–849.

Schimel, D.S. 1995. Terrestrial ecosystems and the carbon cycle. *Global Change Biology*, 1, 77–91.

Schmidt, E., Lötter, M. & McCleland, W. 2002. *Trees and Shrubs of Mpumalanga and Kruger National Park*. Jacana, Johannesburg.

Scholes, R.J. & Walker, B.H. 1983. *An African Savanna: Synthesis of the Nylsvley Study*. Cambridge University Press, Cambridge, United Kingdom.

Scott, P. 2008. *Physiology and Behaviour of Plants*. John Wiley & Sons Ltd, Chichester, England.

Smit, N. 1999. *Acacias of South Africa*, Briza Publications, Pretoria.

Stephenson, N.L., Das, A.J., Condit, R., Russo, R.E., *et al.* 2014. Rate of tree carbon accumulation increases continuously with tree size. *Nature,* 507, 90–93.

Tainton, N. (ed.). 1999. *Veld Management in South Africa*. University of Natal Press, Pietermaritzburg.

Van Hoven, W. 1984. Bome se geheime wapen teen koedoes. *Custos*, 13(5).

Van Wyk, B. & Van Wyk, P. 1997. *Field Guide to the Trees of Southern Africa*. Struik Nature, Cape Town.

Van Wyk, P. 1972. *Trees of the Kruger National Park* (Vols I & II). Purnel, Cape Town, Johannesburg and London.

Van der Walt, P.T. (ed.). 2010. *Bosveld: Ekologie en Bestuur*. Briza Publications, Pretoria.

Venter, E. 2011. *Trees of the Garden Route*. Briza Publications, Pretoria.

Venter, F. & Venter, J-A. 2005. *Making the Most of Indigenous Trees*. Briza Publications, Pretoria.

Von Breitenbach, F. 1974. *Southern Cape Forests and Trees*. Government Printer, Pretoria.

Von Maltitz, G., Mucina, L., Geldenhuys, C., Lawes, M., *et al.* 2003. *Classification system for South African indigenous forests. An objective classification for the Department of Water Affairs and Forestry*. Environmentek Report ENV-P-C 2003-17. Pretoria: CSIR.

White, F. 1976. The underground forests of Africa: A preliminary review. *The Gardens's Bulletin, Singapore,* 29, 57–71. Available at: www.biodiversitylibrary.org/item/148221#page/11/mode/1up.

Wischik, M. 1998. How and why do plants defend themselves? www.wischik.com/marcus/essay/def.html.

Wohlleben, P. 2016. *The Hidden Life of Trees*. Greystone Books & David Suzuki Institute, Vancouver, Canada.

## USEFUL WEBSITES

Biocyclopedia **www.biocyclopedia.com**

Dendrological Society of South Africa **www.dendro.co.za**

Environment **https://environment.co.za**

Flora of Mozambique **www.mozambiqueflora.com**

Flora of Zimbabwe **www.zimbabweflora.co.zw**

Forestry in South Africa **www.forestry.co.za**

International Laboratory of Plant Neurobiology **www.linv.org**

iSpot **www.ispotnature.org**

Livescience **www.livescience.com**

Northern Woodlands **https://northernwoodlands.org**

Operation Wildflower **www.operationwildflower.org.za**

Plant Resources of the World **www.prota4u.org**

SA Forestry Online **https://saforestryonline.co.za**

Science Focus **https://sciencefocus.com**

South African National Biodiversity Institute **www.sanbi.org**

Thoughtco **www.thoughtco.com**

Trees for life **www.treesforlife.org.uk**

Utah State University Forestry Extension **https://forestry.usu.edu**

Woodland Trust **www.woodlandtrust.org.uk**

Worldview International Foundation **https://wif.foundation**

# GLOSSARY

**alien**   a plant whose presence in a given area is not natural, but due to introduction from elsewhere. Compare **invader**.

**alternate**   applied to leaves placed singly at different heights on a stem. Compare **opposite**, **whorled**.

**anther**   the pollen-producing part of the stamen.

**apex**   the tip of a plant organ.

**armed**   bearing thorns, spines, barbs or prickles.

**axil**   the upper angle between the leaf and the stem on which it is carried.

**axillary**   in, or arising from, an axil.

**bacterial nodule**   a swelling or knob containing bacteria.

**berry**   a many-seeded fleshy fruit with a soft outer portion, with the seeds embedded in the fleshy or pulpy tissue (e.g., the tomato). Compare **drupe**.

**blade**   the flat, expanded part of a leaf.

**bloom**   the flower, or process of flowering.

**bole**   the part of the trunk below the lowermost branches; the unbranched part of the trunk. Compare **trunk**.

**bract**   a small, leaf-like structure, in the axil from which arises a flower or a branch of an inflorescence.

**branchlet**   a twig or small branch.

**bushveld**   used in a general sense to include any vegetation type in which both trees and grasses are conspicuous (= savannah). Compare **forest**, **miombo woodland**, **woodland**, **thicket**.

**calyx**   collective term for all the sepals of a flower; the outer whorl of most flowers.

**capsule**   a dry fruit produced by an ovary comprising two or more united carpels and usually opening by slits or pores. Compare **follicle**, **pod**.

**carpel**   leaflike structures that constitute the innermost whorl of a flower.

**compound**   consisting of several parts; e.g., a compound leaf has two or more separate leaflets.

**cone**   a rounded or elongate structure comprising, on a central axis, many overlapping bracts which bear pollen, spores or seeds; characteristic of many gymnosperms.

**congested**   crowded.

**coppice, coppicing**   vegetative shoots at the base of the stem; sprouts arising from a stump.

**corolla**   term for the petals of a flower; usually coloured.

**deciduous**   shedding leaves at the end of the growing season. Compare **evergreen**.

**domatia**   small structures in the forks of the midrib and the main lateral veins. They take two main forms: either conspicuous tufts of hairs, or small pits. These structures are formed by the plant to act as shelter for mites, who in return help clean the leaf surface and protect it against damage by plant-eating mites (singular: **domatium**).

**doubly compound**   when the first divisions (leaflets) of a leaf are further divided, i.e., with leaflets borne on branches of the rachis.

**drooping**   bending or hanging downwards, but not quite pendulous. Compare **pendulous**.

**drupe**   a fleshy, indehiscent fruit with one or more seeds, each of which is surrounded by a hard stony layer formed by the inner part of the ovary wall (e.g., stone fruit such as peaches, olives). Compare **berry**.

**ellipsoid**   a solid body elliptic in long section and circular in cross section.

**elliptic**   oval and narrowed to rounded ends, widest at or about the middle.

**evergreen**   retaining green leaves throughout the year, even during winter. Compare **deciduous**.

**extrafloral nectaries**   nectar-secreting glands located outside the flower, as in leaves or bracts.

**flower**   the structure concerned with sexual reproduction in flowering plants. Generally interpreted as a short length of stem with modified leaves attached to it. Four sets of modified leaves may be present. The outermost are the **sepals**, usually green, leaf-like, in the bud stage enclosing and protecting the other flower parts, and collectively known as the **calyx**. Within the sepals are the **petals**, usually conspicuous and brightly coloured, collectively known as the **corolla**. Within the petals are the **stamens**, which are the male reproductive organs, each comprising a **filament** (stalk) which bears an **anther**, in which pollen grains are produced. In the centre of the flower is the female reproductive organ, the **pistil(s)**. Each pistil consists of an **ovary** (derived from modified leaves called **carpels**) at its base, a slender, ± elongated projection (more than one in some species) called a **style**, and an often enlarged tip called a **stigma**, which acts as the receptive surface for pollen grains. The ovary contains a varying number of **ovules**, which after fertilisation develop into **seeds**. The male and female parts may be in the same flower (**bisexual**) or in separate flowers (**unisexual**). Compare **ovary**.

**follicle**   a dry fruit which is derived from a single carpel and which splits open along one side only. Compare **capsule**, **pod**.

**forest**   a tree-dominated vegetation type with a continuous canopy cover of mostly evergreen trees, a multi-layered understorey, and almost no ground layer. **Coastal forest** is found at low altitude, under humid, subtropical conditions along the east coast of southern Africa. **(Afro) montane forest** is mostly found inland, at higher altitude under more temperate conditions. **Sand forest** is a rare and distinctive forest type, comprising mainly deciduous to semi-deciduous trees and shrubs; restricted to ancient coastal dunes in the Maputaland Centre.

**fruit**   the ripened ovary (pistil) and its attached parts; the seed-containing structure. Compare **seed**.

**fynbos**   a vegetation type characterised by evergreen shrublets with hard, often needle-shaped leaves. It is exceptionally rich in plant species diversity, especially among the Restionaceae, Ericaceae, Proteaceae and the bulbous plants.

**gall**   a localised abnormal growth on a plant induced by a fungus, insect or other foreign agent.

**glabrous**   smooth; hairless.

**gland**   an appendage, protuberance, or other structure that secretes sticky, oily or sugary liquid; usually found on the surface of, or within, an organ (e.g., leaf, stem or flower).

**globose**   spherical, rounded.

**heartwood**   the innermost, generally harder and slightly darker wood of a woody stem. Compare **sapwood**.

**indehiscent**   remaining closed; not opening when ripe or mature.

**indigenous**   a plant occurring naturally in a given area and not introduced from elsewhere (= native). Compare **alien**, **invader**.

**inflorescence**   any arrangement of more than one flower; the flowering portion of a plant (e.g., spike).

**invader**   naturalised plant that produces reproductive offspring, often in very large numbers, at considerable distances from the parent plants, and thus has the potential to spread over a large area. Compare **alien**, **indigenous**.

**lateral**   borne on or at the side.

**latex**   copious liquid exudate.

**leaf**   an aerial outgrowth from a stem, numbers of which make up the foliage of a plant. Characterised by an axillary bud. A leaf typically consists of a stalk (petiole) and a flattened blade, and is the principal food-manufacturing (photosynthetic) organ of a green plant.

**leaflet**   the individual division of a compound leaf, which is usually leaf-like. It has a stalk of its own, but lacks an axillary bud in the axil with the rachis.

**lenticel**   a slightly raised, somewhat corky, often lens-shaped area on the surface of a young stem; facilitates gaseous exchange between plant tissues and the atmosphere.

**lobe**   a part or a segment of an organ (e.g., leaf, petal) deeply divided from the rest of the organ but not separated; segments are usually rounded.

**midrib**   the central or largest vein or rib of a leaf or other organ.

**miombo woodland**   an attractive, very distinct kind of woodland dominated by species of *Brachystegia*, *Julbernardia* and *Isoberlinia*; common on acid, usually shallow soils. Compare **bushveld**, **woodland**.

**montane forest**   see **forest**.

**nectar**   the sugary liquid produced by the flowers or other floral parts on which insects and birds feed.

**nectary**   any structure that produces nectar, such as glands or special hairs.

**nut**   a dry, single-seeded and indehiscent fruit with a hard outer covering (e.g., acorns, walnuts).

**oblong**   an elongated but relatively wide shape, two to four times longer than broad with nearly parallel sides.

**obovate**   inversely egg-shaped; with the broadest end towards the tip.

**opposite**   applied to two organs (e.g., leaves) growing at the same level on opposite sides of the stem, or opposite each other. Compare **alternate**, **whorl**.

**oval**   broadly elliptic, the width more than half the length.

**ovary**   the hollow basal portion of a pistil which contains the ovules within one or more chambers, and which produces the fruit if pollination and fertilisation take place.

**ovate**   egg-shaped in outline and attached at the broad end (applied to flat surfaces).

**ovule**   the minute roundish structure(s) within the chamber of the ovary. The ovule contains the egg cell and, after fertilisation, develops into the seed.

**parasite**   a plant which obtains its food from another living plant (the host) to which it is attached.

**pedicel**   the stalk of an individual flower.

**pendulous**   hanging downward. Compare **drooping**.

**perennial**   living for three or more years.

**persistent**   remaining attached and not falling off.

**petal**   see **flower**.

**petiole**   the leaf stalk.

**petiolule**   the stalk of a leaflet of a compound leaf.

**phenotype**   an organism's observable traits, as expressed by its genetic code and the influence of its environment.

**pioneer species**   refers to the first plant species which colonise bare or disturbed areas; and the first tree species which start the orderly change in composition of vegetation towards the establishment of a climax forest.

**pistil**   the female reproductive part of a flower.

**pod**   a general term applied to any dry and many-seeded dehiscent fruit, formed from one unit or carpel. Compare **capsule**, **follicle**.

**rachis**   the axis of a compound leaf (plural: **rachides**).

**receptacle**   the expanded uppermost part of the flower stalk, on which the floral parts are inserted.

**sand forest**   see **forest**.

**sapwood**   the outer, newer, usually softer and somewhat lighter wood of a woody stem; the wood that is alive and actively transporting water. Compare **heartwood**.

**savannah**   see **bushveld**.

**secretory cavities**   roundish cavities within the leaf blade that contain secretions, such as resin, mucilage and oil.

**seed**   the ripened ovule containing an embryo. Compare **fruit**.

**sepal**   see **flower**.

**shrub**   a perennial woody plant with, usually, two or more stems arising from or near the ground; differs from a tree in that it is smaller and does not possess a trunk or bole. Compare **tree**.

**simple**   leaf with only a single blade; the opposite of a compound leaf.

**smooth**   with an even and continuous margin; lacking teeth, lobes or indentations. Compare **toothed**.

**spike**   an inflorescence with stalkless flowers arranged along an elongated, unbranched axis.

**spine**   a hard, sharp-pointed structure, often long, narrow.

**spray**   a slender shoot or branch together with its leaves, flowers, or fruit.

**spreading**   extending outwards in all directions.

**stamen**   one of the male reproductive organs of the flower, usually made up of a narrow stalk (filament), and an anther in which the pollen is produced.

**stem**   the main axis of the plant, or a branch of the main axis, that produces leaves and buds at the nodes. Usually above ground, but sometimes modified and underground.

**stigma**   the part of the pistil on which the pollen grains germinate, normally situated at the top of the style and covered with a sticky secretion.

**stone**   the hard, seed-containing pit of a drupe (e.g., the so-called 'seed' of a peach, cherry or olive). Compare **drupe**.

**style**   a more or less elongated projection of the ovary, which bears the stigma.

**taxonomy, taxonomic**   the science of the classification of organisms into groups according to relationships.

**thicket**   a vegetation type characterised by thickly growing (almost impenetrable) deciduous or evergreen shrubs, occasionally with trees rising above, and lacking a conspicuous grassy ground layer; sometimes very thorny, or with many succulents. Compare **bushveld**.

**thorn**   in this book, often used in a generalised sense for any sharp-pointed structure.

**toothed**   used in a generalised sense in this book to refer to leaf margins that are toothed in various ways, including dentate (coarse sharp teeth perpendicular to the margin), serrate (sharp, forward-pointing teeth) and crenate (shallow, rounded teeth).

**tree**   a woody plant, self-supporting, with a stem at breast height greater than 10mm and a height greater than 3m (single-stemmed) and, if multi-stemmed, a height greater than 5m. Compare **shrub**.

**trunk**   the main stem of a tree from the roots to where the crown branches; the bole plus the main axis of the crown. Compare **bole**.

**unarmed**   lacking spines, thorns or prickles.

**whorl**   the arrangement of three or more leaves or flowers at the same axis node, forming an encircling ring. Compare **alternate**, **opposite**. Also, more than two of any other organs (e.g., petals, stamens) arising at the same level.

**wing**   any thin, flat extension of an organ, as in winged fruit or seed. Also, each of the two side (lateral) petals of a Fabaceae flower.

**woodland**   an open, park-like vegetation type with scattered trees at least 8m tall, a canopy cover of 40 percent or more, and a grass-dominated ground layer. Compare **bushveld**.

**woolly**   with long, soft, rather tangled hairs.

*Paperbark corkwood*

# SUBJECT INDEX

This subject index covers Part One only. **Bolded** page numbers refer to photographs.

# INDEX TO SCIENTIFIC NAMES

# INDEX TO COMMON NAMES

## KEY TO LANGUAGE ABBREVIATIONS

**A:** Afrikaans  **H:** Herero  **ND:** isiNdebele  **NS:** Sepedi (Northern Sotho)  **SH:** Shona  **SS:** Sesotho (Southern Sotho)
**SW:** siSwati  **TG:** Xitsonga  **TS:** Setswana  **V:** Tshivenda  **X:** isiXhosa  **Z:** isiZulu

## ENGLISH COMMON NAMES

sesamebush 253
shakama plum 87
shepherd's tree 126
silver clusterleaf 149
silver sugarbush 270
sjambokpod 116
small-leaved rock fig 233
small-leaved sicklebush 196
sneezewood 264
sourplum 238
star-chestnut 296

stemfruit 287
stink shepherd's tree 128
stinkwood 178
sweet thorn 210
sycamore fig 230
tamboti 164
tinderwood 176
toadtree 90
tree-wisteria 244
umbrella thorn 216
umdoni 234

velvet bushwillow 146
velvet sweetberry 255
velvet-leaved corkwood 108
weeping boerbean 124
white-alder 150
white-milkwood 290
white-syringa 174
white-stem corkwood 110
white-stinkwood 134
wild olive 241
wild peach 76

wild plum 78
wild-elder 298
wild-mango 245
wild-medlar 283
wildpear 292
wild-syringa 113
wingpod 252
wonderboom fig 229
woodland waterberry 236
worm-bark false-thorn 188
zebra-barked corkwood 111

## AFRIKAANS COMMON NAMES (A)

aapkop 213
aapkos 282
Afrikageelmelkhout 138
anaboom 198
apiesdoring 204
appelblaar 246
basboontjie 197
basternatalvy 224
basterrooibos 146
bastersuikerappel 87
basterwag-'n-bietjie 190
bergboegoe 154
bergmahonie 184
bergsering 175
bergvalsdoring 189
bergvy 225
besemtrosvy 232
bitteramandel 276
bitterblaar 176
bladdoring 203
bleekblaarboom 190
blinkblaar-wag-'n-bietjie 272
bloedvrugboom 148
blompeer 292
blouhaak 202
bloustamkanniedood 110
boekenhout 266
boerboon 122
boesmanstee 130
bosboekenhout 267
boskoorsboom 168
boslaventelboom 170
bosrooiessenhout 182
bostaaibos 84
bosvaderlandswilg 140
bosveldboekenhout 266
bosveldkandelaarnaboom 158
bosveldkatjiepiering 281
bosveldrooiklapperbos 286
bosveldsaffraan 132
bosveldvalsdoring 190
bosveldwaterbessie 236
bosveldysterhout 239
bosvlier 300
bosvy 224
boswaterbessie 235

boswaterhout 235
bruid-van-die-bosveld 292
bruinivoor 274
bruinstinkhout 254
buffelbal 90
deurmekaarvalsdoring 188
dikbas 80
dolfhout 248
dopperkiaat 250
doppruim 284
drolpeer 292
Engelse doring 213
enkeldoring 213
essenhout 180
fluweelboswilg 146
fluweelkanniedood 108
fluweelsoetbessie 255
fynhaak 216
geelriviervy 230
gewone haakdoring 201
gewone naboom 160
gewone suikerbos 268
gewone trosvy 230
gewone wildevlier 298
gewone wildevy 222
groendoring 98
grootblaarboom 168
grootblaarrotsvy 221
grootblaarvalsdoring 194
grootkoorsbessie 156
grysappel 136
haak-en-steek 216
hardekool 144
hardepeer 242
harige rotsvy 225
harpuisboom 83
horingpeultjieboom 88
huilboerboon 124
huilboom 122
jakkalsbessie 152
Kaapse geelhout 262
Kaapse kastaiing 297
kalander 259
kameeldoring 208
karee 86
kasuur 258

kiaat 248
kiepersol 94
kierieklapper 143
kinaboom 92
kleinblaarrotsvy 233
klipvalsdoring 189
knoppiesboontjie 129
knoppiesdoring 207
knoppiesvy 228
koedoebessie 163
koedoeklapper 281
kokerboom 96
koorsboom 218
kremetart 102
laeveldsterkastaiing 294
laventelboom 172
laventelkoorsbessie 154
Lebombowattel 166
lekkerbreek 237
lekkerruikpeul 212
lemoenhout 220
lepelhout 132
makwassieboom 154
mankettiboom 162
mapipi 128
Maputalandoordeelboom 120
maroela 82
matoppie 126
meerstamvalsdoring 191
melkbessie 290
mingerhout 278
mitserie 254
moepel 288
mopanie 118
mopiepie 128
msasa 114
nieshout 264
njalaboom 251
noeniebos 128
noorsdoring 158
olienhout 241
opregte geelhout 262
oudoring 213
outeniekwageelhout 259
paddaboom 90
papierbasdoring 214

papierbaskanniedood 107
papierbasvalsdoring 192
peulmahonie 112
platkroon 186
platorandboekenhout 267
poeierstamkanniedood 110
poerabessie 177
raasblaar 147
riviervaderlandswilg 142
rondeblaarkiaat 250
rooiblaarrotsvy 226
rooiboekenhout 266
rooiboekenhout 267
rooiboswilg 139
rooiessenhout 183
rooi-ivoor 275
rooisering 113
rooistinkhout 276
sambokpeul 116
sandgeelhout 149
sandkanniedood 106
sandkroonbessie 280
sebrabaskanniedood 111
sekelbos 196
sesambos 253
shakamapruim 87
silwersuikerbos 270
snuifpeul 212
soetdoring 210
spikkelneut 162
stamvrug 287
sterkastaiing 296
sterkbos 148
stinkbessie 177
stinkboom 176
stinkhout 178
stinkwitgat 128
suurpruim 238
swartapiesdoring 200
swarthaak 206
swartstinkhout 178
swartysterhout 240
tambotie 164
tontelhout 176
vaalboom 149
valskatjiepiering 282

valsmaroela 81
valsmufuti 115
valstambotie 256
Vanwykshout 244
vlerkboon 252
wag-'n-bietjiedoring 201
waterbessie 234
waterboekenhout 278

waterpeer 236
wilde okkerneut 162
wilde-amandel 274
wildekastaiing 297
wildekatjiepiering 282
wildekweper 250
wildemango 245
wildemispel 283

wildeperske 76
wildepruim 78
wildesering 113
wildevlier 298
witels 150
witgat 126
witklokke 282
witmelkhout 290

witsering 174
witstamkanniedood 110
witstinkhout 134
wonderboomvy 229
worsboom 100
wurgvy 224
wurmbasvalsdoring 188
ysterhout 240

## HERERO COMMON NAMES (H)

omumborombonga 144

omungete 162

## isiNDEBELE COMMON NAMES (ND_

inkiwane 225
inkiwane 229
intenjane 222
isidwadwa 266
singa 216

umdoni 236
umdubu 142
umfola 208
umgoma 162
umhlati 251

umkhiwa 230
umkululu 233
umnaga 275
umnonjwana 194
umonyeli 266

umqobampunzi 163
umthofu 283
umzinzila 274

## SEPEDI (NORTHERN SOTHO) COMMON NAMES (NS)

kgalagangwe 258
kgomo-nahlabana 244
lešitšane 197
mamba 183
mmaba 182
mmetlakgamêlô 108
mmidibidi 180
mmilo 283
mmola 136
mmopu 81
mmupudu 288
moduba-noka 142
moduba-tšhipi 147
modubu 140
modukguhlu 100
modumela 175
mofehlo 122
mogôbagôba 259, 262
mogobôya 230
mogohlo 198, 208, 212
mogohloro 276
mogokgomo 274

mogo-tshetlo 232
mohlakô 266, 267
mohlalabata 194
mohlalakgakga 190
mohlanare 118
mohlatša 229
mohlatswa 287
mohlohlo 158
mohlohlo-kgomo 160
mohlokohloko 176
mohlomê 278
mohlôpi 126
mohlware 241
mohwahlapa 250
mohwelere 139
mohwelere-tšhipi 144
mokabi 143
mokgalwa 272
mokgoba 292
mokgwakgwatha 296
mokgwethe 146
mokongono 138

molalakgwedi 297
mologa 154
molope 124
monamane 237
monatô 113
mongangatau 206
monkgobo 282
monokane 221
monokane 226
monoko 83
montlho 234
mooka 203, 210, 213
mooka-leselo 204
mophala 168
mopipi 128
mopsinyugane 284
morašane 239
morekuri 164
morêtšê 196
moritidi 207
morôtô 248
morula 82

morula-môpšane 80
mošalakgwale 189
mosehla 218
mosehla 122
mošu 216
motha-thaa 84
mothêkêlê 78
motholo 201
motlhabare 300
motsêrê 254
motšhakhutšhakhu 86
motshekga 220
motšhetšhe 94
motšhidi 238
motsibi 156
moumo 222
moumo 224
mphahlašilo 76
mphata 246
mphaya 225
mphoka 214
segwapi 268, 270

## SHONA COMMON NAMES (SH)

mukashu 90
mungongoma 162

mupangara 196
mutowa 88

mutsonzowa 163

## SESOTHO (SOUTHERN SOTHO) COMMON NAMES (SS)

lekgatsi 100

lekhatsi 76

mohlware 241

mosilabele 86

## siSWATI COMMON NAMES (SW)

imbondvo lemhlophe 140
imbondvo lemnyama 139,
  146
inkhokhokho 228

inkokhokho 225
inkunzana 170
inkunzi 172
inshakwe 212

lidlebe-lendlovu 250
ligowane 186
liletsa 284
lusekwane 196

sinhletje 239
siphiso 126
sisefo 267
sivangatane 194

thunzikhulu 245
umbhaba 294
umenwayo 129
umhlala-magcwababa 254
umhobohobo 168
umhomuhomu 246
umkhambane 214

umkhanku 120
umkhaya 200
umkhiwane 229
umkholikholi 112
umkhuhlu 183
umlahlabantfu 272
umnquma 241

umntulwa 283
umnumbela 287
umnunu 98
umnyamatsi 180
umphehlavatsi 176
umsasane 216
umsenge 94

umsonti 259
umtfombotsi 164
umtsatse 264
umvangatana 194
umvusamvu 258
vovovo 124, 245

## XITSONGA COMMON NAMES (TG)

chochelamandleni 124
geludzu 168
himbi 138
mbava 294
mbhandzu 246
mbhesu 194
mbulwa 136
mbvhinya-xihloka 201
molela 190
mondzo 144
mpatakhamelo 258
mpfilwa 283
mphasamhala 272

mpulu 113
mugavi 139
muthwa 234
muyataha 250
mvumayila 174
mvumbangwenya 213
ndzari 264
ndzedze 122
ndzenga 196
ndzerhe 254
ndzopfori 164
nhlantswa 288
nhlarhu 251

nhlulawumbe 224
nkanyi 82
nkaya 207
nkelenga 218
nkombekwa 280
nkowankowa 214
nkuhlu 183
nkuwamaribye 221
ntoma 152
ntsalala 281
ntsowa 88
nulu 98
nxiri 256

nyamarhu 180
nzololo 237
sasani 216
swatima 255
thathasani 172
tzonzo 115
xaxandawu 148
xikukutsi 146
xikwakwaxu 284
xiluvarhi 292
ximapana 132
xinhun'welambeva 176
xivuvule 245

## SETSWANA COMMON NAMES (TS)

mfafu 203
mhota 251
mmilo 283
mmola 188, 189, 190, 194
moboana 253
mobola 136
modubana 147
modubatshipi 146
moduba-tshipi 147
modumêla 174
modutu 134
mofalatsane 286
mofudiri 139
mogôkatau 198
mohata 246
mokakata 296
mokgalo 272
mokgofa 292

mokgwa 200
mokha 214
mokhu 213
mokoba 207
mokokonala 255
mokômoto 108
mokongwa 162
mokwa 248
molalakgaka 189
molepelepe 116
moleye 88
moloto 202
momelantsweng 221
monamane 132
monatô 113
monêpênêpê 116
mongana 206
monghônghô 162

monoga 188
monyêlênyêlê 237
monyena 266
mophane 118
mophaphame 107
mophoka 203
mophumêna 184
mopipi 128
morala 281
morôka 106
morukuru 164
morutlhare 201
mošabêlê 86
mosêlêsêlê 196
mosêtlha 122
mosidi 197
mositsane 197
mosu 216

motlhatsa 226, 229
motlhatswa 287
motlhôpi 126
motlhware 241
motšha 212
motšhaba 230
motsintsila 274
motsiyara 148
motswiri 144
moumo 222
mowana 102
munga 210
nkondze 160
thate 264
umutwa 124

## TSHIVENDA COMMON NAMES (V)

muaṱaha 250
mubandulakhali 83
mubululu 288
mubvumela 174
mudedede 172
mudzungu 252
mudzwiri 144
muelela 186
mueneene 168
mufhanda 246
mufhanza 259
mufhaṱa-vhufa 76
mufhaṱela-ṱhunḓu 147

mufhorola 154
mufhulu 113
mufula 82
mugavhi 143
mugwiti 146
muhoto 198
muhovho-hovho 262
muhuhuma 87
muhuyu-lukuse 230
mukarakara 107
mukhobigwa 280
mukonde-ngala 158
mukumba-kumbane 255

mukuvhavhadinda 188
mulala-maanga 276
muḽa-ṋotshi 300
mulelu 192
mulondo 202
mulondwane 258
mulubi 124
mumvumvu 134
munanga 207
muṋari 264
munembedzi 206
muṋie 274
munombelo 287

munukha-tshilongwe 176
munzere 254
munzhounzhou 184
muonze 164
muphatavhafu 100
mupone 235
muratha-mapfeṋe 282
murenzhe 196
muruthu 156
musaunga 214
musese 122
mushakaladza 86
musingidzi 139

musiri 239, 240
musivhiṱha 208
musuma 152
mususu 149
muṱahadzi 110
muṱamba-na-mme 129
muṱamba-pfunda 194
muṱamvu 228
muṱango 266, 267
muṱhobi 126
muṱhowa 88
mutlhwari 241

muṱonḓowa 163
mutonyombiḓi 111
mutshato 251
mutshetshete 272
mutshikili 183
mutsilari 189
mutsiwa 114
muṱu 234
muṱuhu 182
mutulume 278
muṱwari 148
muukhuthu 108

muumo 222, 224, 229
muunga 210
muunga-gwena 218
muunga-khanga 216
muvhaḓelaphanga 84
muvhaha 297
muvhola 190
muvhonela-ṱhangu 116
muvhula 136
muvhumbu 80
muvhuyu 102
muvumba-ngweṋa 213

muvuvhu 142
muvuvhu-thavha 140
muzwilu 283
tshibibi 128
tshiḓiḓiri 270
tshiḓzungu 268
tshihaka-phele 202
tshikululu 221, 225, 226, 233
tshiṋonzhe 253
tshipengo 220
tshisese-thavha 197
tshiṱhoṱhonya 237

## isiXHOSA COMMON NAMES (X)

igqwaka 130
ilitye 284
ingobamakhosi 242
inqudu 242
inunkisiqaqa 177
isadlunge 268
isikhali 300
isiqalaba 270
ulandile 140
umbhaba 297
umcheya 262
umdubo 142

umgxam 124
umhlahla-makhwaba 254
umhlakothi 84
umhlakotshane 86
umhlandlothi 186
umhlebe 240
umjelo 92
umkhakhase 276
umkhiwane 232
umkhoba 259
umkhobeza 298
umkhokhokho 76

umkhuhlu 182
umkhwenkwe 258
umkokoko 100
umngenalahla 242
umnini 275
umnonono 242
umnquma 241
umnukane 178
umphafa 272
umsenge 94
umswi 234
umthathi 264

umthombe 222, 224, 225, 226
umthundisa 92
umvilo 283
umvumvu 134
umzukuza 282
uqangazane 176
uqangazani 176
uvethe 220
ximafana 290

## isiZULU COMMON NAMES (Z)

amabulwa 136
ifamu 176
igowane-lehlati 245
impayi 221
impondondlovu 144
indlandlovu 250
ingwavuma 132
inkehli 112
inkhuzwa 172
inkokhokho 225
isefu 266
isifico 83
isihomohomo 246
isiklalu 76
isiqalaba 268, 270
isiqathankobe 282
isisantu 229
nmumu 274
udongolokamadilika 166
ugagane 196
ugobandlovu 98
umahlabekufeni 154
umakhwelafingqane 290
umathunzini 182

umbhaba 297
umbondwe omhlope 146
umbondwe omnyama 139
umbondwe wasembudwini
  147
umdoni 234
umdubu wehlanze 142
umdubu wehlathi 140
umdumezulu 276
umenwayo 129
umfomothi 166
umfula 278
umfusamvu 258
umganunkomo 81
umgonswane 226
umgqogqo 284
umgwenya 78
umgxamu 124
umhlalamgwababa 254
umhlalankwazi 198
umhlalavane 143
umhlambamanzi 92
umhlambandlazi 300
umhlonhlo 158

umhlosinga 218
umhlwazi 130
umhlwehlwe 220
umhohlo 244
umkhahlu 90
umkhamba 214
umkhaya 207
umkhaya wehlalahlathi 200
umkhiwane 232
umkhoba 262
umkhobeza 298
umkhuhlu 182, 183
umkhwangu 120
umnala 188, 191
umnalaqho 191
umncaka 275
umncongo 230
umngamanzi 213
umnqawe 212
umnquma 241
umnukane 178
umnumbela 287
umphafa 272
umphimbi 138

umphushane 288
umsasane 216
umsehle 122
umsenge 94
umsishane 239
umsonti 259
umthathe 264
umtholo 201
umthombe 222, 224
umthombothi 164
umthunduluka-obomvu 238
umunga 210
umvangazi 248
umvithi 128
umviyo 283
umvongothi 100
umvumvu 134
umzimane 240
umzithi 256
unhliziyonkulu 292
usolu 186